Advances in African Economic, Social and Political Development

Series Editors

Diery Seck, CREPOL—Center for Research on Political Economy, Dakar, Senegal
Juliet U. Elu, Morehouse College, Atlanta, GA, USA
Yaw Nyarko, New York University, New York, NY, USA

Africa is emerging as a rapidly growing region, still facing major challenges, but with a potential for significant progress—a transformation that necessitates vigorous efforts in research and policy thinking. This book series focuses on three intricately related key aspects of modern-day Africa: economic, social and political development. Making use of recent theoretical and empirical advances, the series aims to provide fresh answers to Africa's development challenges. All the socio-political dimensions of today's Africa are incorporated as they unfold and new policy options are presented. The series aims to provide a broad and interactive forum of science at work for policymaking and to bring together African and international researchers and experts. The series welcomes monographs and contributed volumes for an academic and professional audience, as well as tightly edited conference proceedings. Relevant topics include, but are not limited to, economic policy and trade, regional integration, labor market policies, demographic development, social issues, political economy and political systems, and environmental and energy issues.

More information about this series at http://www.springer.com/series/11885

Wolfgang Stuppert

Political Mobilizations and Democratization in Sub-Saharan Africa

 Springer

Wolfgang Stuppert
Berlin Graduate School of Social Sciences
Humboldt University of Berlin
Berlin, Germany

ISSN 2198-7262 ISSN 2198-7270 (electronic)
Advances in African Economic, Social and Political Development
ISBN 978-3-030-22791-3 ISBN 978-3-030-22792-0 (eBook)
https://doi.org/10.1007/978-3-030-22792-0

This Springer imprint is published by the registered company Springer Nature Switzerland AG
The registered company address is: Gewerbestrasse 11, 6330 Cham, Switzerland

Acknowledgements

This book marks the end of a long journey. On the way, many people have carried me forward with their advice, encouragement, and practical support. First of all, I would like to express my gratitude to Prof. Dr. Wolfgang Merkel and Prof. Dr. Dieter Rucht. Both took the time to read through sketches and proposals of the dissertation project this book is based on at critical points in its development and gave me invaluable feedback. Without their critical questions and insightful advice, the theoretical framework would be much less coherently argued, and my empirical research much less stringently designed. While the data that I use in this book is mainly derived from secondary sources, I did not conduct my research on protests and elections in Sub-Saharan Africa exclusively from afar. Between October 2012 and April 2013, I spent three months in Zambia and three months in Uganda. In both countries, I conducted all together more than 80 interviews with party politicians, NGO leaders, and civil society experts, and participated in two local election observation missions for parliamentary by-elections. These insights and experiences have proven invaluable for the development of the book's theoretical framework. Besides these interview partners, I want to express my gratitude to McDonald Chipenzi and his research team at the Foundation for Democratic Process in Zambia, to Crispy Kaheru from the Citizens' Coalition for Electoral Democracy in Uganda, and to the research division at the Foundation for Human Rights Initiatives in Uganda. Their generous sharing of office space, knowledge on civil society and politics, and contacts to interview partners made my research a most rewarding experience, both personally and academically. I also want to thank Meghan for her unwavering support during the writing of this book. Had it not been for the prospect of spending more time with her once it was done, I would not have been motivated enough to spend those days and nights writing. I know that she now knows more about protests and elections in Sub-Saharan Africa than she ever wished to. I thank her for her patience, and for the time she took to read through my texts. I am dedicating this book to my parents, for all the obvious reasons, and this particular one: I am grateful that they continued to ask me throughout all these years how my work was progressing, and never frowned at my answers.

Contents

Chapter 1
Introduction

Despite a history of multi-party electoral politics in Sub-Saharan Africa that spanned more than 20 years, by 2012 only a few countries had made a successful transition to democracy. This is despite the fact that 30 of the 48 countries on the subcontinent have been holding direct national multi-party elections in an uninterrupted series since multi-party elections were (re-)introduced in their respective polities. Moreover, most elections in that time were relatively free and fair, participatory and consequential for the selection of executive leaders. Yet, in 2012, democratic governance was still an exception in Sub-Saharan Africa. In that year only five of the 48 countries could be considered liberal democracies. Five more had crossed the threshold of electoral democracies. The bulk of African regimes, i.e., 32 countries, remained electoral authoritarian (see Table 2.2 for a classification of political regimes in Sub-Saharan Africa in 2012). Why did the democratization processes of electoral authoritarian regimes in Sub-Saharan Africa make so little progress? This book seeks to answer that question.

Several explanations for the lack of democratization of electoral authoritarian regimes have been ventured in comparative politics. Applied to Sub-Saharan Africa, more recent analyses would point to, for example, the lack of a sustained, effective revolutionary threat in African societies (Acemoglu and Robinson 2005), the lack of experience of African political elites with regular multi-party elections (Lindberg 2006), the strength of party-based ruling elite coalitions (Brownlee 2007), the weak diffusion of values of self-expression in African societies (Welzel and Inglehart 2008), or the organizational strength of the ruling party combined with African countries' lack of international links to the West (Levitsky and Way 2010).

This book takes a different approach. It employs collective action theory to investigate the effects of societal mobilizations on democratization processes in Sub-Saharan Africa. It focuses on electoral competitiveness as a central aspect of democratic practice. It shows that meaningful competition in multi-party elections is strongly associated with the protection of political rights and civil liberties by political regimes across Sub-Saharan Africa. That is, it shows that a lack of electoral

© Springer Nature Switzerland AG 2020   1
W. Stuppert, *Political Mobilizations and Democratization in Sub-Saharan Africa*,
Advances in African Economic, Social and Political Development,
https://doi.org/10.1007/978-3-030-22792-0_1

competitiveness means that elections do not produce the "institutionalized uncertainty" for political elites (Przeworski 1986, p. 58) that is necessary for the regime to provide vertical accountability for citizens. Based on analysis of all authoritarian direct national multi-party elections between 1990 and 2012 in Sub-Saharan Africa, the book demonstrates that a credible mobilization threat by societal groups in the pre-election period leads to stronger electoral competition among political elites, and thus promotes democratization. By voicing grievances against ruling elites in political mobilizations such as protests, riots and strikes, societal groups increase the political power of oppositional political elites, thereby increasing electoral competitiveness. Considering the limited progress of democratization processes on the subcontinent, the book thus suggests that the weak mobilization threat of societal groups is a major explanatory factor for the lack of progress in democratization processes in Sub-Saharan Africa.

The remainder of the introductory chapter clarifies the empirical scope of the study, explains how collective action theory is applied to democratization processes, and shows how this theoretical approach leads to a new appreciation of the role of civil society in the struggle for democracy. The final section will present an overview of the structure of the book.

1.1 Democratization Processes in Electoral Authoritarian Regimes

This book will focus on the democratization of electoral authoritarian regimes. Electoral authoritarian regimes are a type of "hybrid" regime which combines elements of democracy with elements of autocracy (Diamond 2002, p. 23). Like democracies, electoral authoritarian regimes hold regular national multi-party elections for executive recruitment. Yet, ruling elites maintain a style of governance, including arbitrary rule and state repression, which is similar to that of autocracies.

In the literature on political transitions, various terminologies have been proposed for regimes of this kind. Levitsky and Way (2002), for example, speak of "hegemonic" and "competitive" authoritarian regimes, and Schedler (2002) generally of "electoral authoritarianism". Approaching the study of hybrid regimes from the democratic end of the spectrum, O'Donnell and Schmitter (1986) define them as "democradura," while Merkel et al. (2003) call them "exclusive" or "illiberal" democracies. For the purpose of this study, all regimes in which regular national multi-party elections are held to recruit executive leadership, but in which the political rights and civil liberties of citizens are only partially protected or not at all, will be defined as "electoral authoritarian". According to this definition, an electoral authoritarian regime comes about when an authoritarian regime turns "electoral," i.e., when authoritarian ruling elites hold the first de jure direct national multi-party election, or when a democratic electoral regime turns "authoritarian," i.e., when ruling elites significantly limit the political rights and civil liberties of citizens. In turn, an electoral authoritarian regime ceases to be authoritarian when a relatively free and fair multi-party election is prepared and carried out under democratic conditions.

In contrast to other types of non-democratic regimes, electoral authoritarian regimes allow for regime change by "constitutional evolution" over the course of many election cycles. As electoral authoritarian regimes represent a mixture of quasi-democratic institutions and authoritarian governance, democratization processes can take place without breaking with the current constitution. Instead, a gradual process takes place, in which collective actors who organize as participants of authoritarian multi-party elections propel or hinder increasing respect for the constitutional framework through their actions and counter-actions.

This book will focus on this specific democratization path of this type of regime. It is therefore not about "regime breakdowns" (Geddes 1999; Bermeo 2003), "electoral revolutions" (Bunce and Wolchik 2006; Kuntz and Thompson 2009), or "eventful democratization" (Della Porta 2014). It is likely that the factors which determine the likelihood that military coups, for example, interrupt democratization processes, are different from those that explain the stalling or progress of gradual democratization processes over the course of election cycles. Revolutions, coups, and counter-coups may represent the beginnings or the ends of the episodes of democratization that this book attempts to shed light on, but they will not feature in the theoretical framework as an explanation of the successes and failures achieved during such episodes.

Studying singular events that lead to highly contingent outcomes favors studying the irregular over the regular, and the unpredictable over the predictable. As O'Donnell and Schmitter (1986, p. 4) admit at the beginning of their seminal treatise on transitions: "'Normal science methodology' is inappropriate in rapidly changing situations". The present study takes this precept to heart and rather seeks the merit in studying the regular instead of the irregular, both because it can be better explained and explains more of what unfolds around us. With respect to research on democratic transitions, this means prioritizing the "longue durée" of repeated interactions in slowly evolving democratization processes over the apparent momentous impacts of singular democratization events.

Although elections feature prominently in the definition of the beginning and the end of the kind of transitions to democracy that this study focuses on, they are not necessarily a causal factor for the success of these transitions. Put differently, "democratization while holding elections" does not imply "democratization by elections". Most prominently, Lindberg (2006, p. 17) posited a virtuous circle in which elections beget democrats and democrats beget more democratic elections, thereby transforming de jure participatory, contested, and legitimate periodic elections into de facto democratic multi-party elections over time. Thus, cycle by cycle, Lindberg argued, authoritarian electoral regimes slowly become electoral democracies and—through the improvement of civil liberties as a corollary to the exercise of political rights—liberal democracies (Lindberg 2006, p. 3). As will be shown in the analyses in this book, empirical evidence points to the importance of *competitive* elections for the democratization of electoral authoritarian regimes. The success of democratization processes is not certain just because elections are introduced. It is necessary to explain how and when elections become more competitive, and governance more democratic.

Table 1.1 Stability of electoral regimes in Sub-Saharan Africa

Year	Number of elections	Average length of election series (number of election cycles)	Elections followed by breakdown (%)
1990–1994	47	1.46	12.8
1995–1999	61	1.93	11.5
2000–2004	55	2.86	7.3
2005–2009	63	3.45	6.3
2010–2012	41	3.93	2.4
Total	267	2.70	8.2

Notes General elections are counted as one election. A regime breakdown is a breakdown of the constitutional order through, e.g., a revolution or a military coup. An insurrection or coup attempt was only counted as a breakdown of the electoral authoritarian regime when elected powerholders were successfully ousted. Temporary suspensions of the constitutional order that ended in a reinstatement of the previously elected representatives were not counted as regime breakdowns

At the same time, since 1989 regularly holding multi-party elections has become so widespread a practice in authoritarian regimes around the world that it seems safe to say that "democratization while holding elections" will be the main avenue by which future gains in democratization are achieved. Today, therefore, democratization is likely to occur as the democratization of electoral authoritarian regimes. In 2012 in Sub-Saharan Africa, for example, the only non-electoral authoritarian regimes were Eritrea, Somalia, and South Sudan. Moreover, data from Sub-Saharan Africa shows that terminations of electoral series in authoritarian regimes has become less and less frequent. Since the widespread introduction of national multi-party elections across the continent in 1989, the average length of electoral series has increased steadily over time, while the percentage of elections that were followed by a breakdown through, e.g., coups or foreign interventions, has become smaller and smaller (see Table 1.1).

Moreover, international pressure to resume holding national multi-party elections is high for any putschists. For example, at the end of 2012, when data collection for this study concluded, electoral regimes were temporarily abolished in Guinea-Bissau, Madagascar, and Mali. By 2014, all of these countries were again under the rule of elected leaders. Hence, the likelihood is high that if liberal democracy takes hold in a country in Sub-Saharan Africa, it will do so while national multi-party elections are regularly held. The present study's limitation of scope to processes of "constitutional evolution" in electoral authoritarian regimes is important as a theoretical specification, but empirically only excludes the fringes of current democratization processes.

1.2 Collective Action as a Theoretical Approach to Democratization

The interactions between mobilized non-elites and ruling elites in the democratization process can be conceptualized as a struggle over solutions to the collective action problem (Lichbach 1995). This understanding of the democratization process starts from the premise that only a group which is able to reliably overcome its collective action problem can participate in a political struggle, and gain the political power to realize its interests.

The book argues that democratization takes place when political power becomes more evenly distributed between political elites, oppositional political elites, and societal groups. Societal groups contribute to the balance of power through socio-economic and pro-democratic mobilizations or a credible threat thereof. Socio-economic mobilizations provide opposition parties with a political platform, whereas pro-democratic mobilizations assert the constitutional framework and the regulatory responsibility of the state. Through these collective actions, societal groups increase the power of oppositional political elites—which translates into increased electoral competitiveness—and propel the democratization process forward.

Thus, democratization appears as a conflict where the balance of power among collective actors determines outcomes on the macro level. Given the weak institutional framework of electoral authoritarian regimes in Sub-Saharan Africa, the book claims that only when both institutional positions and the neo-patrimonial power networks of collective actors are analyzed as sources of political power can the trajectories of political struggles in electoral authoritarian regimes be understood. Collective action theory provides an understanding of political power that appreciates both sources of political power. From this perspective, power is ultimately derived from a collective actor's capacity to mobilize adherents in the face of adversity. More precisely, control over solutions to the collective action problem, such as selective incentives, organizational structures, or shared information and values (Lichbach 1994), determines the mobilization capacity of ruling elites and their opposition. This, in turn, does not fully determine mobilization success. Between mobilization capacity and successful mobilization lies the "fortuna" and "virtu" (O'Donnell and Schmitter 1986, pp. 4–5) of collective action entrepreneurs in choosing the right mobilization tactic at the right moment in time. Both the assumed capacities for and actual past mobilizations build up the credible mobilization threat of the respective groups over time. This threat translates into political power.

The book uses political mobilizations as an indicator for a collective actor's mobilization threat. Political mobilizations are direct public engagements of ruling elites, oppositional political elites, and societal groups with their opponents. Data on such public collective actions is used to investigate trajectories of political mobilizations by these actors in Sub-Saharan Africa. In the empirical test of the effects of collective actions by societal groups on democratization processes, political mobilizations in the pre-election period are employed as predictors of electoral competitiveness.

Thus, collective action theory provides an analytical perspective on democratization that takes the role of mobilized societal groups seriously. In consequence, it takes the interests and strategies of societal groups in a direct conflict with ruling elites seriously as well, as it is these interests and strategies that determine the mobilization capacity of both regime challengers and regime defenders.

1.3   A New Look at Civil Society in Democratization Processes

This book argues that if societal groups engage in collective action, they can drive the democratization process of electoral authoritarian regimes in Sub-Saharan Africa. As actors who do not attempt to hold public office themselves, their influence on the democratization process is indirect. First, they provide oppositional political elites with protected spaces to promote their skills and networks, and with political platforms based both on government-critical information and an increased understanding on the part of citizens that their capacity for collective action is important. Second, by mobilizing against violations of political rights and civil liberties by authoritarian ruling elites, societal groups safeguard the rules of the democratic political game, including the political space to act, for themselves and the political opposition. Through both these mechanisms, societal groups increase the competitiveness of elections which increases uncertainty for political elites, and improves vertical accountability for citizens.

This means that the explanation for the widespread phenomenon of "elections without democracy" in Sub-Saharan Africa lies first and foremost in the limited mobilization threat of societal groups. It is argued that this limited mobilization threat is the main reason for limited electoral competitiveness in Sub-Saharan Africa. This book's main hypothesis is therefore that the more societal groups are able to engage in socio-economic and pro-democratic mobilization in the struggle with ruling elites, the more competitive authoritarian elections will become. Since societal groups in most countries in Sub-Saharan Africa cannot effectively raise the costs of their suppression, their political space is limited, and their ability to increase the extra-institutional mobilization power of oppositional elite factions or safeguard the democratic rules of the political contest is limited, too. Put differently, "a lack of institutionalization of the political opposition, as well as weak support from civil society groups, make it difficult for the opposition to be effective and to win electoral support" (Uddhammar et al. 2011, p. 1062). Thus, ruling elites in electoral authoritarian regimes will continue to dominate the political arena, keep uncertainty out of the electoral process, and deny vertical accountability to their citizens.

To be sure, the weakness of civil society has been ventured by other political scientists as the main reason for the non-democratization of electoral authoritarian regimes before (see, e.g., Rueschemeyer et al. 1992, p. 6; Linz and Stepan 1996b, p. 18; Bunce and Wolchik 2011, p. 33). For Sub-Saharan Africa, Bayart (1986,

p. 119) noted well before the onset of the "third wave of democratization" that "the concept of civil society seems best able to explain—by its absence—the continued existence of African autocracy". Moreover, neo-patrimonialism as the backbone of African autocracy has often been linked to the weakness of civil society. As Ihonvbere (1996, p. 9) explains: "Elites loot the treasuries because they can get away with it. The dominant classes privatize the state and its resources because civil society is deformed, weak and highly fractionalized".

This book's perspective on the role of societal groups in the democratization process is, however, different from common conceptualizations of civil society. Its approach to "democratization from below" significantly broadens the role of civil society in democratization processes in at least two ways. First, it provides a broader perspective on who is important in civil society. The book's view of people power does not focus on elitist civil society organizations in Sub-Saharan Africa. Instead, it includes the urban underclass and other non-formalized actors with their mostly spontaneous public mobilizations that have often played an important role in protest movements on the subcontinent (Branch and Mampilly 2015). Whereas explicitly or implicitly the focus of conventional research on civil society in non-democracies is often on the "NGO scene," the centrality of the concept of mobilization capacity for the present study makes it clear that one should expect trade unions, student unions, and informal groups, such as urban youth or marketers, to often play more important roles in their countries' democratization processes. Second, the focus on mobilization threat as the basis for the involvement of civil society in the democratization processes highlights the importance of the ability of societal groups to intensify political conflict and directly engage ruling elites in achieving democratic progress. Civil society's conventional human rights and democracy programs come only second to that.

The claim that the disruptive force of societal groups increases electoral competitiveness, and thereby facilitates democratization is more controversial than it may at first seem. Some scholars of political transitions have argued that successful democratization requires the control of societal groups by political elites (Karl 1990, p. 8), so that they remain "docile and patient" (Przeworski 1986, p. 63) while transitional pacts are negotiated. As the argument goes, if societal groups keep mobilizing, the regulatory capacities of the fledgling democratic political system may be overwhelmed, and the system can collapse into renewed authoritarian rule. In part, this controversy can be explained by the lack of differentiation between social unrest and political mobilization. As the quantitative analyses of the effects of societal mobilization on electoral competitiveness in Sub-Saharan Africa show, public direct engagements of one societal group with another are indeed detrimental for democratization. Yet, the more societal groups address the state with their grievances through public protest, the more the political system democratizes.

Thus, this book shows that "ordinary citizens" have an important role to play in the democratization processes of electoral authoritarian regimes. By mobilizing in protests, riots, and strikes that are critical of the government, societal groups provide a basis for increasing competition between factions of political elites. In conclusion, the study indicates that democracy is not a product of elite learning and institution building alone, but a struggle for power that requires societal groups to mobilize and engage with political elites.

1.4   Structure of the Book

The second chapter takes a look at the widespread phenomenon of "elections without democratization" in Sub-Saharan Africa. It presents data on all direct national multi-party elections on the subcontinent that were held between 1990 and 2012. It shows that these elections fulfilled democratic standards in many respects. Yet, authoritarian ruling elites deprived them of a core functional principle: Meaningful competition between powerholders and the political opposition. It is shown that, contrary to previous research, electoral practice of de jure participatory, competitive, and legitimate elections does not contribute to democratization. Instead, only competitive elections are associated with substantial improvements in democratic governance.

The third chapter analyzes political power in electoral authoritarian regimes in Sub-Saharan Africa from a collective action perspective. From this perspective, it argues that political power can be understood as the ability to project a credible mobilization threat into the political arena. The analysis shows that authoritarian ruling elites in Sub-Saharan Africa have strong advantages over oppositional elites in both building up and maintaining such a threat. Societal groups therefore represent the most important alternative source of political power in these regimes. Data on social conflicts is used to trace the trajectories of political mobilizations of ruling elites, oppositional political elites, and societal groups in Sub-Saharan Africa across countries and over time.

The fourth chapter focuses on the role of societal mobilizations for the democratization of electoral authoritarian regimes in Sub-Saharan Africa. It argues that collective actions by societal groups increase the power of oppositional political elites in two ways: By providing opposition parties with a political platform, and by asserting the constitutional framework and the regulatory responsibility of the state. Thus, societal groups increase electoral competitiveness and propel the democratization process. The effects of societal mobilizations on electoral competitiveness are demonstrated in case studies and tested in multiple linear regression analyses of data on all authoritarian multi-party elections in Sub-Saharan Africa between 1990 and 2012.

The fifth chapter concludes the book with a summary of the theoretical framework and the empirical findings, and provides a discussion of the implications of these findings for democracy promotion by international actors in Sub-Saharan Africa. It argues that international democracy assistance should shift its focus with regard to the civil society organizations it supports. Instead of channeling the bulk of support through professional advocacy organizations, international donors should broaden the scope of organizations they collaborate with and provide assistance to organizations that represent their members in the political process through public demonstrations and strikes, such as trade unions and student associations. The chapter closes with suggestions for further research.

References

Acemoglu D, Robinson JA (2005) Economic origins of dictatorship and democracy. Cambridge University Press, New York

Bayart JF (1986) Civil society in Africa. In: Chabal P (ed) Political domination in Africa: reflections on the limits of power, Annual meeting of the African Studies Association, vol 26. Cambridge University Press, Cambridge, pp 109–125

Bermeo NG (2003) Ordinary people in extraordinary times: the citizenry and the breakdown of democracy. Princeton University Press, Princeton, NJ

Branch A, Mampilly ZC (2015) Africa uprising: popular protest and political change (African arguments). Zed Books, in association with International African Institute, Royal African Society, World Peace Foundation, London

Brownlee J (2007) Authoritarianism in an age of democratization. Cambridge University Press, Cambridge

Bunce VJ, Wolchik SL (2006) Favorable conditions and electoral revolutions. J Democracy 17(4):5–18

Bunce VJ, Wolchik SL (2011) Defeating authoritarian leaders in postcommunist countries. Cambridge University Press, Cambridge

Della Porta D (2014) Mobilizing for democracy: comparing 1989 and 2011, Oxford University Press, Oxford

Diamond LJ (2002) Thinking about hybrid regimes. J Democracy 13(2):21–35

Geddes B (1999) What do we know about democratization after 20 years?: annual review of political science. Annu Rev Polit Sc 2(1):115–144

Ihonvbere JO (1996) Economic crisis, civil society, and democratization: The case of Zambia. Africa World Press, Trenton, N.J

Karl TL (1990) Dilemmas of democratization in Latin America. Comp Politics 23(1):1–21

Kuntz P, Thompson MR (2009) more than just the final straw: stolen elections as revolutionary triggers. Comp Politics 41:253–272

Levitsky S, Way L (2002) The rise of competitive authoritarianism. J Democracy 13(2):51–65

Levitsky S, Way L (2010) Competitive authoritarianism: hybrid regimes in the post-Cold War era. Cambridge University Press, Cambridge

Lichbach MI (1994) Rethinking rationality and rebellion: theories of collective action and problems of collective dissent. Rationality Soc 6:8–39

Lichbach MI (1995) The rebel's dilemma (Economics, cognition, and society). University of Michigan Press, Ann Arbor

Lindberg SI (2006) Democracy and elections in Africa. Johns Hopkins University Press, Baltimore

Linz JJ, Stepan A (1996) Toward consolidated democracies. J Democracy 7(2):14–33

Merkel W, Puhle HJ, Croissant A, Eicher C, Thiery P (2003) Defekte Demokratie: Band 1: Theorie. Leske + Budrich, Opladen

O'Donnell GA, Schmitter PC (1986) Transitions from authoritarian rule: tentative conclusions about uncertain democracies. The Johns Hopkins University Press, Baltimore

Przeworski A (1986) Some problems in the study of the transition to democracy. In: O'Donnell GA, Schmitter PC, Whitehead L (eds) Transitions from authoritarian rule: comparative perspectives. The Johns Hopkins University Press, Baltimore, pp 47–63

Rueschemeyer D, Huber E, Stephens JD (1992) Capitalist development and democracy. University of Chicago Press, Chicago

Schedler A (2002) The Menu of Manipulation. J Democracy 13(2):36–50

Uddhammar E, Green E, Söderström J (2011) Political opposition and democracy in sub-Saharan Africa. Democratization 18:1057–1066. https://doi.org/10.1080/13510347.2011.603466

Welzel C, Inglehart R (2008) The role of ordinary people in democratization. J Democracy 19(1):126–140

Chapter 2
Elections Without Democratization: How African Electoral Authoritarianism Survived

By the late 1980s, only a minority of countries in Sub-Saharan Africa allowed their citizens to choose from more than one candidate in national contests for legislative and executive power, and, if they did, in most cases the electorate's choice was restricted to candidates of the ruling party (see Table 2.1). This system of governance was often backed by a view that formal opposition groups are "unnecessary in developing politics with primary goals of nation building and economic development" (Decalo 1992, p. 132). In the late 1980s on the subcontinent, choosing among contenders from different political parties in national elections with universal suffrage was an experience only shared by Gambians, Batswana, Mauritians, and Senegalese.

This changed dramatically in the first half of the 1990s. In that time, 31 of the then 48 internationally recognized countries in Sub-Saharan Africa introduced direct national multi-party elections, most of them for the first time in their history. These political reforms were carried forward by a wave of mass protests across Africa in the wake of the collapse of the Soviet Union (Bratton and van de Walle 1992). Hopes were high that African civil society had not only awoken from its slumber since the days of independence movements to assert its role as a "catalyst for the advent

Table 2.1 Political regimes in Sub-Saharan Africa in 1989

Regime type	Type of elections	n
Military Oligarchies	No regular elections	11
Plebiscitary One-Party Systems	Regular single-candidate one-party elections	16
Competitive One-Party Systems	Regular competitive one-party elections	13
Settler Oligarchies	Regular multi-party elections, restricted suffrage	2
Multi-Party Systems	Regular multi-party elections, universal suffrage	5

Notes Adapted from Bratton and van de Walle (1997, p. 79)

© Springer Nature Switzerland AG 2020
W. Stuppert, *Political Mobilizations and Democratization in Sub-Saharan Africa*,
Advances in African Economic, Social and Political Development,
https://doi.org/10.1007/978-3-030-22792-0_2

Table 2.2 Types of political regimes in Sub-Saharan Africa in 2012

Political regime	n	Example cases
Closed Authoritarian	2	Eritrea, Somalia
Hegemonic Authoritarian	15	Cameroon, Ethiopia, Rwanda
Competitive Authoritarian	17	Kenya, Nigeria, Zambia
Electoral Democracy	5	Comoros, Niger, Tanzania
Liberal Democracy	5	Cape Verde, Ghana, South Africa

Note Classification based on Howard and Roessler (2006), adapted to accommodate criticism by Bogaards (2007, pp. 1231–1232). Guinea-Bissau, Madagascar, Mali, and South Sudan were excluded from the list, as they all were in a situation of interregnum at the end of 2012

of democracy" (Lewis 1992), but also that—embedded in such a newly invigorated civil society—multi-party democracy would finally take hold in Africa.

Indeed, since multi-party elections were (re-)introduced in their respective polities, 30 of the 48 countries on the subcontinent have been holding direct national multi-party elections in an uninterrupted series. Moreover, as the data presented on the following pages will show, most such elections in Sub-Saharan Africa between 1990 and 2012 were relatively free and fair, participatory and consequential for the selection of executive leaders. In his book "Democracy and Elections in Africa" Lindberg (2006a, p. 51) asserts that "the mere repetition of de jure participatory, competitive, and legitimate elections—regardless of their qualities—contributes to democratization". Based on this dictum and given the rich experience in holding at least formally democratic elections in Sub-Saharan Africa, we would expect that, over time, electoral practice would have led to substantial improvements in political freedoms and civil liberties.

Yet, in 2012, democratic governance was still an exception in Sub-Saharan Africa. In that year, only five of the 48 countries could be considered liberal democracies. Five more had crossed the threshold of electoral democracies. The bulk of African regimes, 32 countries, remained electoral authoritarian (see Table 2.2). As the following detailed analysis will show, Freedom House data tells a similar story of stagnation, rather than progress, when it comes to improvements in democratic governance over time.

How did African authoritarianism survive continuous electoral practice? This chapter will not only show that empirically de jure participatory, competitive, and legitimate elections do not propel democratization forward, but that theoretically we should not expect them to do so. Instead, only truly competitive elections make a difference for both citizens and political elites. At the same time, it will be argued that such elections must be seen as indicators and not as causes of democratization. The evident suppression of electoral competition has meant that African authoritarianism has survived continuous electoral practice because that practice is deprived of the core functional principle of a democratic regime. This also means that a theoretically coherent and empirically sound explanation for the lack of democratization in Sub-Saharan Africa must be sought elsewhere. The present chapter will provide a theoretical and empirical basis for such an investigation.

First, the chapter will argue that in a procedural-minimum conception of democracy, electoral competitiveness is a central aspect of democratic practice. Only when elections offer a meaningful choice to the electorate does regularly holding elections introduce uncertainty among political elites, and provide vertical accountability to citizens. While the analysis will therefore affirm the centrality of regular multi-party elections for democratic regimes, it concludes that such elections must be competitive to represent meaningful democratic practice. In addition, they must be treated as *indicators for* rather than *causes of* progress in democratization.

Second, the chapter will provide a detailed look at trends in democratic governance in Sub-Saharan Africa for the period under study. It will show that regime changes that introduced multi-party politics are not only linked to important improvements in African citizens' ability to exercise political rights, but also in the degree to which they are able to enjoy civil liberties. At the same time, the evidence suggests that the introduction of regular multi-party elections did not guarantee a steady improvement of democratic governance over time, at least not for all countries in Sub-Saharan Africa.

Third, we will take a look at the continent's experience with multi-party elections as a partial regime of democracy. In this context, Lindberg's (2006a, p. 51) assertion that "the mere repetition of de jure participatory, competitive, and legitimate elections—regardless of their qualities—contributes to democratization" will be discussed. Contrary to his claim, the analysis will show that continuous electoral practice in Sub-Saharan Africa is not associated with substantial improvements in democratic governance. This is despite the fact that the large majority of elections on the subcontinent were meaningful in that they fulfilled important procedural aspects of democratic elections. They were consequential regarding the selection of political leadership, they took place without gross interference by the ruling elite in the electoral process, they were contested by the main political parties, and the majority of the electorate cast their votes in them. Electoral practice alone is not associated with progress in the democratization process, even if that electoral practice is in line with important aspects of democratic procedure.

This will lead us, fourth, to electoral competitiveness as an important feature of the electoral experience of countries in Sub-Saharan Africa. The data shows that not only do opposition parties seldom make a strong showing in direct national multi-party elections across Sub-Saharan Africa, but also that electoral turnovers are exceedingly rare. If the extent of electoral competitiveness is taken into account, however, our picture of the democratization process in Sub-Saharan Africa becomes much more coherent. The holding of competitive multi-party elections as the most central aspect of partial regimes of democracy is strongly associated with variations in democratic governance. If a regime regularly holds de jure national multi-party elections that are marked by low competitiveness, democratic governance is not a necessary corollary to this practice. If, however, such elections are characterized by strong competitiveness, the protection of political rights and civil liberties strongly improves over time. African authoritarianism survived continuous electoral practice because that practice lacked electoral competitiveness. It is the absence of this central feature of elections that explains why we have witnessed a lot of electoral practice in Sub-Saharan Africa, but so little substantial democratization.

2.1 Electoral Competitiveness as a Central Regime of Democracy

The book will follow a "procedural-minimum conception" (Levitsky and Way 2010, pp. 5–6) of democracy. The following analysis will show that if this conception of democracy is approached from a collective action perspective, vertical accountability and institutional uncertainty emerge as important functional principles of a democratic regime. Electoral competitiveness, in turn, emerges as the central aspect of democratic practice that provides vertical accountability to the masses and institutional uncertainty to political elites.

As summarized by Levitsky and Way (2010, pp. 5–6), a procedural-minimum conception of democracy includes four key attributes: "(1) Free, fair, and competitive elections; (2) full adult suffrage; (3) broad protection of civil liberties, including freedom of speech, press, and association; and (4) the absence of nonelected 'tutelary' authorities (e.g., militaries, monarchies, or religious bodies) that limit elected officials' power to govern". This definition centers on competitive elections. The other criteria can be seen as further "explicifications" of dimensions of the procedural definition of democracy "that are implicitly understood to be part of the overall meaning and which are viewed as necessary for competitive elections to take place" (Levitsky and Way 2010, p. 6).

Considering the broad range of definitions of democracy that have been brought forward in the political sciences, Levitsky and Way's conception falls into the tradition of procedural definitions that is said to have originated with Schumpeter (2006). Other prominent proponents of this type of democracy definitions are Przeworski (1991) and Schmitter and Karl (1991). Procedural definitions can be broadly distinguished from substantive conceptions of democracy that include outcomes of public decision-making in their definitions, such as the protection of civil liberties or social and economic rights.

Pure proceduralists often criticize these conceptions for the constraints they put on the democratic decision-making process. They argue that instead of leaving it to citizens themselves to decide which civil liberties to protect or which economic rights to grant, democratic theorists define the volonté générale in their place (Gutmann and Thompson 2011, p. 233). Another criticism that is important for the present research project is that most substantive conceptions of democracy are difficult to operationalize in such a way that democratic progress can be compared across countries.

Yet, as Whitehead (2004, p. 12) points out, a procedural definition cannot disregard policy outcomes entirely, lest it applies the label "democracy" to cases in which participation in the democratic process becomes affected by social exclusion and economic deprivation to such a degree that democratic procedure cannot provide for self-governance of the people. Seen in this light, however, Levitsky and Way's "procedural-minimum conception" is not that minimal, as their definition lists the broad protection of civil liberties among the key attributes of a democracy. Thus, they include prerequisites for participation in the democratic decision-making process into their definition of democracy without sacrificing the possibility of operationalizing their conception for comparative research.

As Levitsky and Way point out, their procedural definition is a widely-shared understanding of democracy among political scientists who research patterns in democratization on a regional or global scale. Given such a broad consensus, the present section will not provide an extensive discussion of the pros and cons of the aforementioned conceptions of democracy. Rather, it will point out the meaning of a democratic regime in their procedural conception from the viewpoint of the two main types of collective actors in the struggle for democracy: Political elites and societal groups. Here, political elites refers to political entrepreneurs that organize as participants in the political contests for public office. In the process, they can build their own organizational structures, such as parties, or they can rely on personal networks of organizations and individuals, or a mixture of both. Societal groups are all those groups that manage to organize collectively in the pursuit of their group-specific interests (Olson 2003, p. 8) without attempting to hold public office themselves. Examples of these are trade unions, member associations, or advocacy organizations, as well as groups with fluid boundaries, such as groups of protesters or non-formalized community-based organizations. As they do not organize as participants in the political contests for public office, they are outsiders to the political sphere in that narrow sense.

This approach to democracy from a collective action perspective will lead to additional "explicifications" of the procedural-minimum conception of democracy in the above sense. From the viewpoint of societal groups, vertical accountability emerges as a central implication of a democratic system of governance. For political elites, it is the institutionalized uncertainty of the democratic political process. It will be argued that both these features ultimately rely on electoral competitiveness to work.

2.1.1 Vertical Accountability for the Masses

From the perspective of outsiders to institutional politics, the responsiveness of the state to their demands is the most important feature of a democratic system of governance. Such a perspective makes the state-citizen struggle, or the struggle between political elites in control of the state and citizens, the center of the analysis. As Tilly (2007, p. 13) puts it, "judging the degree of democracy, we assess the extent to which the state behaves in conformity to the expressed demands of its citizens". State responsiveness, in turn, is provided by political, or vertical accountability which consists of the answerability of public officials to citizens and the capacity of citizens to impose sanctions on elites (Schedler 1999, p. 14). Vertical accountability is therefore an "explicification" of a procedural-minimum conception of democracy. Hereafter, it will be shown how this relates to the core democratic principal of electoral competitiveness.

Vertical accountability is an important aspect of today's democratic systems because these systems are almost always organized as systems of representation. Representation, in turn, involves a transfer of power from the people to their representatives. Thus, a principle-agent relationship is established where the central problem is control of the execution of power by the principles, i.e., the people. To achieve this control and hold agents accountable for their actions, principles must be able to sanction the execution of power by their agents. Vertical accountability is the main implication of a democratic political system from the perspective of non-elites. In turn, it crucially relies on the existence of regular competitive multi-party elections for public office.

Elections for public office give citizens an opportunity to act collectively in order to exercise control over political elites. Even though citizens are thereby only given a chance to sanction the actions of their representatives at these specific points in time, elections carry with them citizens' most powerful "weapon" against recalcitrant agents: The chance to strip political elites of their institutional political power. Thus, elections play an important role in establishing vertical accountability and hence for democracy from a non-elite perspective. Elections are designed to provide both aspects of vertical accountability: To make political elites answerable to citizens and give the latter the possibility of imposing sanctions on elites.

However, only if there are viable alternatives to political powerholders can elections work as sanctioning mechanisms. Vertical accountability needs electoral competitiveness to work. Whether alternatives are viable depends crucially on whether elections are truly competitive, so that different contenders for political office have a chance to replace those currently occupying public positions. Also, as mentioned previously, national elections only provide specific moments in time to "throw the rascals out," typically every four or five years. To establish vertical accountability between these electoral competitions, opposition factions that are powerful enough to provide checks and balances are needed to establish horizontal accountability throughout non-election years. Vertical accountability presupposes electoral competitiveness which provides horizontal accountability. With these reflections in mind, modern political democracy may also be defined as "a system of governance in which rulers are held accountable for their actions in the public realm by citizens, acting indirectly through the competition and cooperation of their elected representatives" (Schmitter and Karl 1991, p. 76).

2.1.2 Institutionalized Uncertainty for Elites

From the perspective of political elites, the main implication of a democratic political system is the "institutionalized uncertainty" of the political process (Przeworski 1986, p. 58). As Przeworski (1993, p. 62) explains, "In a democracy all forces must struggle repeatedly for the realization of their interests since no one is protected by virtue of their position. No one can wait to modify outcomes ex post; everyone must subject their interests to competition and uncertainty". Political elites thus "know what winning or losing can mean to them, and they know how likely they are to win or lose, but they do not know if they will lose or win" (Przeworski 1991, p. 13).

Democratic institutions organize the process by which the winners and losers of these intertemporal conflicts are determined in such a way that outcomes are neither predetermined by the participants' current position in the political system or the relations of production, nor completely indeterminate (Przeworski 1986, p. 58). In addition, they "render an intertemporal character to political conflicts. They offer a long-time horizon to political actors; they allow them to think about the future rather than being concerned exclusively with present outcomes" (Przeworski 1991, p. 18). A democracy works, because "no one can win once and for all" (Przeworski 1986, p. 57).

Because of the indeterminacy of the outcome of political conflict and the intertemporal character that periodical contests lend to winning and losing political conflicts, elites are drawn into democratic interplay. Put differently, elites are ready to accept the democratic institutional framework because a contest for executive recruitment is not a foregone conclusion, and every election provides them with a new chance to win the right to rule.

The uncertainty of political elites with regard to their electoral prospects is chiefly an outcome of the collective action problem. It can be argued that only because the collective action problem exists a democratic system is rendered stable. This argument goes beyond Przeworski's original conclusions regarding the definition and role of institutionalized uncertainty.

According to Przeworski (1991, p. 11), the outcomes of a democratic process are determined jointly by resources and institutions. This process "generates the appearance of uncertainty because it is a system of decentralized strategic action in which knowledge is inescapably local" (Przeworski 1991, p. 12). The institutional framework for the political conflict, as well as the positions in the political system occupied by all participants to the conflict are usually fully known. In a liberal democracy with its frequent opinion polls and elections on different levels of the political system, information about citizens' preferences is regularly available, too. If thus the material and human resources that participants can bring to the table are largely known as well, uncertainty would only consist of the strategic mistakes of leaders, as Przeworski seems to suggest.

If political entrepreneurs knew the size of their followership and the scope of the resources these followers were ready to contribute, mobilization itself would not need to occur. Stand-offs between groups of supporters of significantly different sizes and unequal possibilities of winning would be avoided. As Lichbach (1995, p. 88) notes: "One might even argue that if information were complete, there would be no need for conflict, no need for the parties to test one another; the winning side would present the losing side with its demands, and the conflict would be over". For institutionalized conflict in elections, this would mean that parties which knew they would be close losers would be reluctant to take part in the process in the first place, and seek other avenues to win. But it happens frequently that ruling parties lose electoral contests, trade unions register weak showings in industrial conflicts, and governmental information campaigns are drowned out by public protest. This happens not only in autocratic regimes, with their requirement of constant "preference falsification" by citizens, where the information about citizens' preferences is scarce, but in liberal democracies as well. If it did not, liberal democracies would indeed be volatile political constructs.

Democratic regimes are stable because uncertainty runs deeper than not knowing the next moves of other political contenders. Uncertainty prevails because of the collective action problem. Overcoming the collective action problem is important in a democratic political system because winning an election implies that the mobilization of citizens in political campaigns both as activists and voters has been achieved in sufficient numbers. Majorities in multi-party elections are not gained because citizens are polled and their answers counted as votes, or in some other way that would not require voluntary collective action by citizens. If, however, collective action is at the center of electoral wins, then the free rider problem is central to political contests. Because there is a mismatch between individual and collective rationality, the ability to realize group-specific interests is not a matter of a simple calculus for political elites. Political leaders cannot know with certainty whether they can capitalize on the preferences of potential voters, and to which degree followers are willing to chip in resources in the political struggle, which, in turn, influences their ability to garner enough votes to win. They cannot determine their political power by simply adding the material and political resources of those sharing in the same interest. Thus, neither they nor their opponents fully know what resources they can bring to the table, neither in terms of mobilized citizens (i.e., human resources), nor in terms of material resources.

This means that the collective action problem lies at the heart of the uncertainty of political elites when they estimate their prospects of winning an upcoming electoral contest. Because of the collective action problem, one's power to realize group-specific interests in the democratic process lies in one's ability to find solutions to the collective action problem and mobilize one's supporters to canvas, rally, and vote. As will be demonstrated in later chapters, such solutions do not concatenate to fully-specified causal chains. Instead of explanations, they provide mechanisms; instead of precise predictions, they merely allow us to identify highly contingent regularities. To an important degree, the amount of "resources in action" political entrepreneurs have command over only reveals itself once the "action" begins.

The inherent uncertainty in the collective action problem is crucial for drawing political elites into the democratic interplay. Because of the collective action problem, the electoral process as a mechanism of solving political conflicts can still be attractive to them while their institutional power, potential constituencies, and material resources differ considerably from each other. If it were not for the collective action problem, many electoral contests would not be carried out. Parties projected to lose closely would be reluctant to contest the vote, and democratic political systems would be less stable.

The core democratic institution that provides political elites with "institutionalized uncertainty" are regular *competitive* multi-party elections. Only if such elections produce losers that could win in the near future can political conflicts have an "intertemporal character" and their outcomes be acceptable to the losing side. These elections must be truly competitive. Moreover, if powerholders rule with large electoral majorities, they themselves will perceive a low risk of losing the necessary public support to continue their rule and vertical accountability will be weakened.

2.2 Trends in Democratic Governance

In the first half of the 1990s, a wave of regime changes swept across the African subcontinent. One authoritarian regime after another was forced to introduce multi-party politics. As one observer noted, in those years, "the third wave of global democratization finally reached the African continent" (Diamond 1999, ix). Table 2.3 indicates the pace of these momentous changes. In 1990, four countries in Sub-Saharan Africa held their first multi-party elections, in 1991 five, and in 1992 nine. By 1996, all but eleven countries on the subcontinent had transitioned to multi-party politics.

Most expert observers at that time were surprisingly skeptical regarding the extent and future of multi-party politics in Sub-Saharan Africa. As Gyimah-Boadi (1998, p. 18) laments in an early article, "much of the recent expert commentary on democratization in Africa is awash in dismissiveness and pessimism". This skepticism is especially striking if one contrasts reactions to African developments with expert assessments of the democratization processes which socialist countries of the former Warsaw Pact were embarking on at the same time. In spite of this pessimism, the data on breakdowns of the electoral regime per country in Table 2.3 indicates that in 30 African countries' regimes have remained electoral from the time of the introduction of multi-party politics until the end of 2012.

Along with the introduction of multi-party politics, governance in Sub-Saharan Africa became more democratic. Figure 2.1 depicts average Polity IV and Freedom House scores for the years 1990–2012 for all countries in Sub-Saharan Africa. The graphic is plotted in such a way that the scales for Polity IV and Freedom House on the y-axes are of equal length, with Polity IV's maximum combined autocracy-democracy score of $+10$ on the same level as Freedom House's maximum freedom score of 1.

Both indicators depict similar developments. From 1990 to the mid-2000s, democratic governance spread across the continent. From this moment onwards, by-and-large, stagnation set in. Polity IV, with its focus on the institutional set-up for the exercise of political rights, shows minimal fluctuation around the level reached at that

Table 2.3 Electoral experience across Sub-Saharan Africa, 1990–2012

Country	First election[a]	Legislative elections	Presidential elections	Breakdowns	Max. length of series[b]
Botswana	Before 90	5	0	0	9[c]
Gambia	Before 90	5	5	1	4[c]
Mauritius	Before 90	5	0	0	9[c]
Senegal	Before 90	5	4	0	8[c]
Namibia	07.11.1989[d]	5	4	0	5
Zimbabwe	23.03.1990	6	4	0	6
Comoros	04.03.1990	5	5	2	3
Gabon	04.11.1990	5	4	0	5
Ivory Coast	28.10.1990	4	4	2	2
Burkina Faso	01.12.1991	5	4	0	5
Cape Verde	13.01.1991	5	5	0	5
Sao Tomé & Principe	20.01.1991	6	5	0	6
Benin	17.02.1991	6	5	0	6
Zambia	31.10.1991	5	6	0	6
Cameroon	01.03.1992	4	4	0	4
Mauritania	24.01.1992	4	5	2	3
Ghana	03.11.1992	6	6	0	6
Republic of Congo	21.07.1992	5	3	1	3
Mali	08.03.1992	4	4	1	4
Angola	29.09.1992	3	1	1	2
Madagascar	25.11.1992	4	4	1	4
Djibouti	18.12.1992	4	4	0	4
Kenya	29.12.1992	4	4	0	4
Burundi	01.06.1993	3	2	1	2
Niger	14.02.1993	7	5	3	3
Lesotho	28.03.1993	5	0	0	5
Seychelles	20.07.1993	5	5	0	5
Central Afr. Republic	22.08.1993	4	4	1	2
Togo	25.08.1993	4	5	0	5
Equatorial Guinea	21.11.1993	4	3	0	4
Guinea	19.12.1993	2	4	1	3
Guinea-Bissau	03.07.1994	4	5	3	3
South Africa	26.04.1994	4	0	0	4

(continued)

Table 2.3 (continued)

Country	First election[a]	Legislative elections	Presidential elections	Breakdowns	Max. length of series[b]
Malawi	17.05.1994	4	4	0	4
Mozambique	27.10.1994	4	4	0	4
Ethiopia	07.05.1995	4	0	0	4
Tanzania	29.10.1995	4	4	0	4
Chad	02.06.1996	3	4	0	4
Sierra Leone	26.02.1996	4	4	0	4
Sudan	06.03.1996	2	3	1	2
Uganda	09.05.1996	2	4	0	4
Liberia	19.07.1997	3	3	1	2
Nigeria	20.02.1999	4	4	0	4
Rwanda	25.08.2003	2	2	0	2
D. R. Congo	30.07.2006	2	2	0	2

Note Eritrea, Somalia, South Sudan, and Swaziland do not feature in the table, as they did not hold a national multi-party election between 1990 and 2012. Numbers of legislative and executive elections include only elections held after 01.01.1990. Regime breakdowns are breakdowns of the constitutional order through, e.g., a revolution or a military coup. [a]Refers to the first direct national multi-party election after 1990. [b]Refers to series of elections uninterrupted by regime breakdowns. [c]Indicates series that contain elections which took place before 1990. [d]Categorizing Namibia as a country with its first multi-party election "before 1990," while technically correct, would give the wrong impression regarding its electoral experience

time, whereas Freedom House indicates a slight worsening of governance, which, however, does not undercut the average freedom scores that had been reached by 2000. Similarly, the percentages of countries in Sub-Saharan Africa rated "free" or "partly free" by Freedom House increase dramatically until the early 2000s, from 8.5 and 23.4% in 1990 to 22.9 and 43.8% in 2002, respectively. From that moment onwards, percentages have remained more or less stable. The reasons for these continent-wide trends are not the subject of the present study. It should be noted, however, that they coincide with trends in democratic governance in other world regions (Freedom House 2016).

The averages for the Freedom House Civil Liberties ratings show that the spread of multi-party politics in Sub-Saharan Africa not only improved the rights of African citizens in the sphere of institutionalized politics, but also in a wider societal realm. However, the smooth lines in Fig. 2.1 hide important variations in the trajectories of countries across the continent. The annual means of the Freedom House scores, for example, have a standard deviation between 1.30 and 1.69 (see Table A.1 in the appendix). Of the countries that introduced multi-party elections, some democratized over time, while others remained authoritarian, or slid back into authoritarianism.

These differences between countries can be traced to the very beginning of their experiences with democratic institutions. Not in all countries, for example, did the

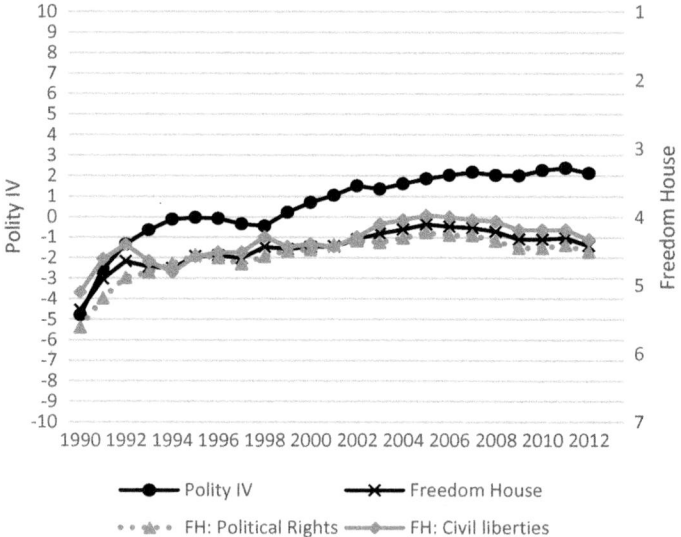

Fig. 2.1 Democratization in Sub-Saharan Africa, annual cross-country averages. *Notes* Means for all countries in Sub-Saharan Africa (N = 48). "FH" stands for Freedom House. Freedom House scores are on a scale of 7 to 1, where 7 indicates the worst and 1 the best freedom rating. The combined Polity IV autocracy-democracy score ranges from −10 to +10, with −10 indicating a strongly autocratic regime and +10 a strongly democratic one

introduction of multi-party politics signify a break with the authoritarian past. In 33 of the 60 democratization episodes in Sub-Saharan Africa that started after 1990, powerholders that oversaw the preparation of founding elections took part in them and won.

In 2012, the differences between countries in terms of the democratic qualities of their regimes remained significant. While at that time in most countries in Sub-Saharan Africa, democratic regime changes occurred more than 15 years in the past, 32 of their political regimes still have to be considered electoral authoritarian. At the same time, in only ten countries were free and fair elections held to select the current political leadership. This means that at that time only ten regimes could be classified as democratic. Five of these regimes were electoral, and five liberal democracies (see Table 2.2).

For the subsequent analysis, we should take note that the wave of regime changes in the first half of the 1990s made governance in Sub-Saharan Africa on average substantially more democratic. At the same time, the state of democracy on the subcontinent in 2012 indicates that the introduction of regular multi-party elections did not guarantee a steady improvement of democratic governance over time, at least not for all countries. The question of whether continuous electoral practice is linked to democratic progress, and if so in which ways, is not yet answered with the empirical evidence that has been provided so far. Per definition, holding regular direct national multi-party elections is a necessary component of a democratic regime. However, to determine whether this feature of a democracy is sufficient to produce democratic political systems by itself or whether it is a corollary of other democratizing forces, we must investigate the electoral practice of political regimes in Sub-Saharan Africa, and link variations in this practice to outcomes in democratic governance.

2.3 Electoral Practice

Between 1990 and 2012, 351 direct national multi-party elections were held in Sub-Saharan Africa. These comprised 64 election series with an average length of four elections. In most countries, these elections have been consequential for who is allowed to govern, and took place with strong participation by the electorate and the political opposition. This means that in 2012 for most citizens in Sub-Saharan Africa living under a government that came into power in an election they participated in was the norm and had been so since the early 1990s. In the following pages, this claim will be substantiated through a presentation of data on the sustainability of electoral regimes, the qualities of electoral processes, as well as the participation of voters and the political opposition. This electoral practice will then be related to progress in democratic governance.

As indicated in the previous section, electoral regimes in Sub-Saharan Africa have been relatively stable. A minority of founding elections were false starts of electoral regimes that ended quickly in coups and civil wars, such as in Ivory Coast (with founding elections in 1990, 2000, and 2010) or Niger (with first elections in 1993, 1996, 1999, and 2011). Most of the elections on the subcontinent were part of longer series of election cycles. Of all national multi-party elections held between 1990 and 2012 in Sub-Saharan Africa, 32.2% were first, 23.9% second, 17.4% third, and 14.8% fourth elections in uninterrupted series. The average length of electoral regimes in that time was four election cycles. Given that most election cycles are typically either four or five years long, and that between 1990 and 2012 lie only 22 years, most of the time, winners of elections in Sub-Saharan Africa were able to fulfill their terms in office.

In addition to this, the electoral process of most elections in Sub-Saharan Africa was meaningful in terms of its influence on the selection of political leadership. Table 2.4 shows the assessments of international observers with regard to the procedural quality of national multi-party elections in Sub-Saharan Africa. Overall, most elections on the subcontinent were judged "acceptable" by international observation missions (64.4% of those observed), and many were regarded as showing only minor or no violations of democratic norms (38.1%). The threshold "acceptable" implies that the overall result of the election reflected the will of the people. Hence, in these elections, by and large, ruling elites respected the cumulative voting decision by the electorate. In the language of international election observation missions, such elections were called, for example, "free and fair," "impartially carried out," or "legitimate" (Kelley 2010, pp. 12–13).

Table 2.4 Quality of elections in Sub-Saharan Africa

Overall quality (%)	Extent of problems	n	%
Unacceptable (26.3)	High	45	14.4
	Moderate	36	11.5
Ambiguous (9.3)	High	11	3.5
	Moderate	19	6.1
Acceptable (64.4)	Moderate	82	26.3
	Low	79	25.3
	None	40	12.8

Note Based on all direct national multi-party elections in Sub-Saharan Africa between 1990 and 2012 (N = 351). Data on elections before 2006 were taken from a database on election quality by Kelley (2010). Later elections were assessed by the author according to the same coding rules. 39 elections were either not internationally observed or documentation was not accessible

Yet, this does not mean that these elections were genuinely democratic in the sense that voters were offered "an effective choice of political authorities among a community of free and equal citizens" (Schedler 2002, p. 39). This becomes clear when the sample is reduced to elections that were held in regimes that at the time of the beginning of electoral campaigning were assessed as only partially respecting political rights and civil liberties. Among these authoritarian elections, we find that 54.7% were assessed as "acceptable" by international observers as well. While therefore an assessment as "free and fair" by international election observers does not necessarily mean that the respective elections were truly democratic, it does mean that votes, as they were cast by citizens, were made to count. This was the case in the large majority of elections in Sub-Saharan Africa.

It should be noted that 11.1% of the elections between 1990 and 2012 were either not observed by international delegations or the reports of their missions were not accessible. An empirical analysis of monitored versus non-monitored elections concludes that international observers do not choose elections to monitor based on their expected quality, but that their presence improves election quality (Kelley 2012). However, even if we were to assume that non-observed elections are invariably of lower democratic quality, the assessment of elections in Sub-Saharan Africa as predominantly consequential for the selection of the political leadership would still hold.

Finally, in most countries in Sub-Saharan Africa voters, as well as the political opposition, showed that they were taking elections in their countries seriously through their participation in the electoral process. For 80.8% of national multi-party elections between 1990 and 2012, reported turnout rates for eligible voters were over 50%, and in 30.0% of these elections more than three quarters of citizens turned out to vote. In many African countries, voters must register to be able to vote on election day. Poor infrastructure and low levels of formal education mean that sometimes a large share of the voting age population does not register. For this reason, comparing turnout rates on the basis of total voting age population is more meaningful. However, even

Table 2.5 Turnout rates in elections in Sub-Saharan Africa

Election cycle	Turnout (% registered voters)	Turnout (% VAP)
1st	65.19	57.78
2nd	66.59	57.04
3rd	63.65	57.63
4th	61.69	56.28
All (incl. later) elections	64.73	57.36

Note Based on all direct national multi-party elections in Sub-Saharan Africa between 1990 and 2012 (N = 351). VAP = voting age population. Data taken from the IDEA Voter Turnout Database (International Institute for Democracy and Electoral Assistance 2017)

Table 2.6 Participation of opposition actors in elections in Sub-Saharan Africa

Participation of the opposition	n	%
None of the major actors	30	8.5
Some, but not all major actors	45	12.8
All major opposition actors	276	78.6

Note Based on all direct national multi-party elections in Sub-Saharan Africa between 1990 and 2012 (N = 351). Data for elections before 2004 taken from Lindberg (2006b). Later elections were assessed by the author according to the same coding rules

if this stricter criterion is applied to elections in Sub-Saharan Africa, turnout rates indicate that a majority of potential voters in Africa participated in national elections throughout the period under investigation.

Besides the overall average turnout rates, Table 2.5 provides averages for the turnout in the first, second, third, and fourth elections in uninterrupted election series. It shows that there is only a slight decrease in voter turnout over the years. Even after the electorate in many countries in Sub-Saharan Africa had participated in several authoritarian elections, a majority of citizens were still willing to turn out and cast their votes.

Table 2.6 shows that the political opposition decided to participate in a large majority of elections in Sub-Saharan Africa, too. Based on Lindberg's (2006b) coding rules for his 2006 database on African elections, opposition participation was classified into three broad categories: Full participation, partial participation, and full non-participation. Note that only those parties and candidates are counted among the opposition that did not support the ruling party in previous years or publicly declared their opposition to incumbents during the election campaign. Based on this assessment, major political opposition candidates or parties participated in 91.5% of national multi-party elections in Sub-Saharan Africa. In 78.6% of elections, all major opposition parties and candidates participated.

While this evidence speaks to the meaningfulness of electoral practice in Sub-Saharan Africa at first glance, the regular holding of multi-party elections seems to be associated with only modest gains in democratic governance. In Fig. 2.2, time is

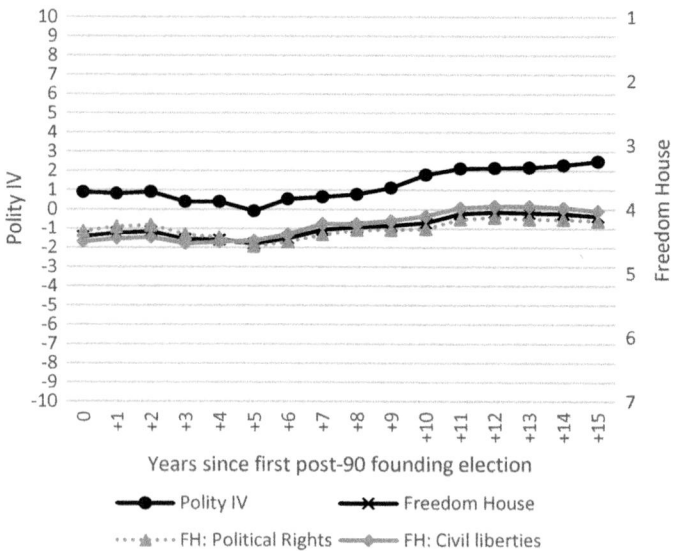

Fig. 2.2 Democratization in Sub-Saharan Africa, averages per year after founding elections. *Notes* Means for all countries in Sub-Saharan Africa that introduced multi-party elections between 1990 and 2012 (N = 41). On the horizontal axis, "0" marks the year of the first post-1990 founding election for each country. "FH" stands for Freedom House. Freedom House scores are on a scale of 7 to 1, where 7 indicates the worst and 1 the best freedom rating. The combined Polity IV autocracy-democracy score ranges from −10 to +10, with −10 indicating a strongly autocratic and +10 a strongly democratic regime

measured on the horizontal axis, in years, since the (re-)turn to multi-party politics in countries across Sub-Saharan Africa, starting with the year founding elections were held for the first time after 1990 in the respective country ("0"). Consequentially, "+1" provides the averages of indicators of democratic governance for the first year after the introduction of multi-party elections in each country.

As Table 2.3 indicates, most countries (re)turned to multi-party politics in the mid-1990s. However, some introduced de jure direct national multi-party elections for the first time since 1990 at a much later point in time, as for example Rwanda (2003) or the Democratic Republic of Congo (2006). In Fig. 2.2, breakdowns of the electoral regime are not accounted for. Rather than showing consecutive years of electoral practice, the graphic indicates the time that has passed since the first introduction of multi-party elections.

The graphic shows that on average after these (re-)turns to multi-party politics democratic governance only improved slightly over time. These improvements took place mainly in the first eleven years after multi-party elections had been (re-)introduced. Table A.2 in the appendix provides the exact means and standard deviations for each data point. The flat lines in Fig. 2.2 seem to suggest that the more dramatic improvements in democratic governance shown in Fig. 2.1 are mostly the result of the introduction of de jure direct national multi-party elections, and not of regular electoral practice. Given the fact that electoral practice has been continuous in most countries in Sub-Saharan Africa since the introduction of multi-party politics, average ratings of democratic governance of 2.50 (Polity IV) and 4.11 (Freedom House) in 2012 mean that across Sub-Saharan Africa "elections without democracy" was a common phenomenon.

Such an assessment stands in stark contrast to Lindberg's (2006a, p. 51) assertion that "the mere repetition of de jure participatory, competitive, and legitimate elections—regardless of their qualities—contributes to democratization". Note that Lindberg, in the empirical analysis leading to this statement, operationalized "competitive" as the participation of major opposition parties in the election, in line with the data provided in Table 2.6. His claim turns a necessary but insufficient part of the common understanding of a democratic political system into a cause for democratization itself. If his claim was true, the causal effect of the mere holding of multi-party elections would also cast doubt on the importance of electoral competitiveness as a marker for the progress of democratization processes in electoral authoritarian regimes. After all, electoral competitiveness would then only be a potential corollary to increasing electoral experience.

Lindberg's central finding that increasing electoral experience is associated with improved democratic governance is based on an ecological fallacy. As Figure 2.3 shows, when looking at country averages, later elections in an uninterrupted series seem, indeed, to be strongly associated with more democratic governance. As the graphic shows, founding elections are associated with lower average ratings of democratic governance than second, third, fourth, or fifth elections in an uninterrupted series. Table A.3 in the appendix provides the exact means and standard deviations for each data point. In addition, correlation analysis for the data on elections in Sub-Saharan Africa shows that the longer a country's longest or current series of uninterrupted elections is, the better its democratic governance ratings (see Table A.4 in the appendix). This seems to suggest that as long as countries keep holding elections, governance will become more democratic. However, what is true for countries on average is not necessarily true for the individual trajectories of countries.

A closer look at the dynamics of governance in African electoral regimes suggests a different explanation for the association of electoral experience with democratization. Upon closer inspection, Lindberg's data shows that positive changes in terms of election quality, political rights, and civil liberties mostly take place around first elections. Many of his indicators for democratization actually deteriorate with subsequent election cycles. In addition to this, authoritarian multi-party regimes are significantly more unstable than democratic multi-party regimes (Hadenius and Teorell 2007, p. 150). This means that on average we would expect democratic electoral regimes to last longer than authoritarian ones. This is indeed the case. Those electoral regimes in Sub-Saharan Africa that were judged as "free" by Freedom House in the year after their founding elections lasted for an average of five election cycles, whereas those that were judged as "partly free" or "not free" in the year after those first elections lasted for only 3.0 and 2.7 election cycles, respectively. That is, among later elections, those elections predominate that are held in regimes which have democratized quickly and then stayed democratic. In turn, those regimes that

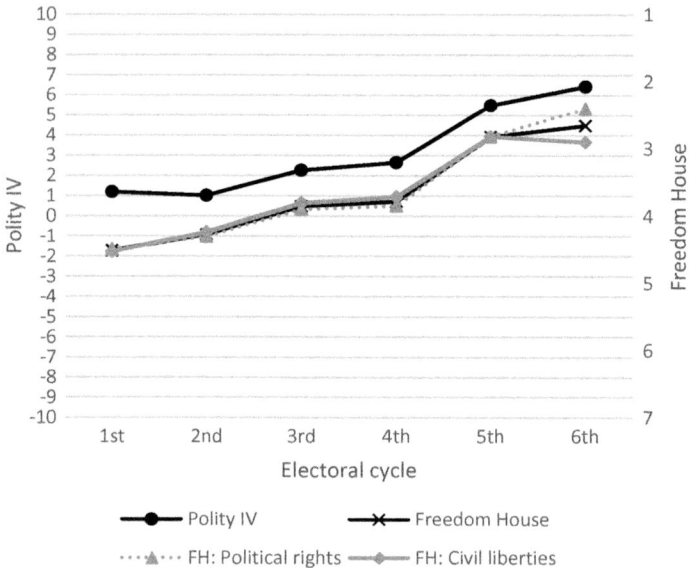

Fig. 2.3 Democratization in Sub-Saharan Africa, post-election averages per election cycle. *Notes* Means for all countries in Sub-Saharan Africa that held multi-party elections between 1990 and 2012 (N = 45). On the horizontal axis, the rank numbers of elections in an uninterrupted series are given. "FH" stands for Freedom House. Freedom House scores are on a scale of 7 to 1, where 7 indicates the worst and 1 the best freedom rating. The combined Polity IV autocracy-democracy score ranges from −10 to +10, with -10 indicating a strongly autocratic and +10 a strongly democratic regime

remained undemocratic after their first elections often did not last until the fourth or fifth election cycles. Hence, "rather than demonstrating the cumulative effect of consecutive elections," Lindberg's data "point to the importance of founding elections" (Bogaards 2014, pp. 26–27).

A more stringent test of Lindberg's claim that elections have a self-reinforcing power can be undertaken by narrowing the sample of electoral regimes down to those that have reached a certain length of electoral series. If among those regimes of equal "length," in terms of the number of election cycles in an uninterrupted series, later elections were associated with increased democratic governance, Lindberg's assertion that the mere repetition of elections, regardless of their democratic qualities, improves democratic practice would be supported by the data. If, however, we do not find such a relationship, this means that holding an election regardless of its quality is not consequential for the democratization of an electoral regime. The question would then be whether we can find an aspect of electoral practice that sets apart those elections that are associated with progress in democratization from those that are not.

The results of this analysis show that common indicators of democratic governance correlate not at all or very weakly with electoral experience. Measures for the democratic qualities of electoral practice, such as turnout, the quality of the

Table 2.7 Democratization and electoral experience in long democratization episodes

Indicator	1st	2nd	3rd	4th	Correlation
Polity IV (post-election)	0.84 (5.35)	0.90 (4.71)	2.46 (4.89)	2.73 (4.91)	0.172*
Freedom House (post-election)	4.15 (1.39)	3.95 (1.38)	3.79 (1.49)	3.79 (1.63)	−0.092
• Political Rights	4.06 (1.75)	3.96 (1.70)	3.83 (1.74)	3.88 (1.84)	−0.040
• Civil liberties	4.25 (1.16)	3.94 (1.17)	3.75 (1.31)	3.69 (1.50)	−0.173*
Turnout (%)	64.44 (18.8)	68.57 (18.0)	64.13 (14.6)	62.21 (18.2)	−0.086
Quality of electoral process (% acceptable)	59.18	47.92	55.56	66.67	0.046
Opposition participation (% full)	73.58	75.47	90.38	89.80	0.180**
Turnover (% yes)	22.73	3.77	21.15	4.08	−0.114
Electoral dominance	58.39 (25.6)	69.86 (20.8)	61.00 (20.4)	66.2 (15.5)	0.046

Note Based on all episodes of democratization that lasted four election cycles or longer (N = 28). Values are means, if not otherwise specified in the indicator column. Values in brackets are standard deviations. $*p \leq 0.05$, $**p \leq 0.01$, $***p \leq 0.001$. Spearman Correlations, significance tests two-tailed. Data on turnout taken from IDEA Voter Turnout Database (International Institute for Democracy and Electoral Assistance 2017). Data on the quality of elections before 2006 and on opposition participants for elections before 2004 was taken from (Kelley 2010), and Lindberg (2006b), respectively. Later elections coded by the author

electoral process, or opposition participation, likewise show no or very weak correlations with electoral experience. Holding regular elections does not alone have a substantial impact on democratization processes—had we been willing to interpret a correlation causally—or indicate progress in democratic governance. This is not surprising if we follow arguments for the centrality of electoral competitiveness as a key indicator for progress in democratization processes, as discussed in Sect. 2.1. As shown in Table 2.7, the share of seats or votes won by powerholders in elections does not correlate negatively with the rank number of the electoral cycle of the respective election, as should be expected if regimes did democratize with increasing electoral practice. Instead, except for a peak in second elections, electoral dominance of powerholders increases over time. All else being equal, in electoral authoritarian regimes, ruling elites consolidate their power with increasing electoral experience.

Table 2.8 Electoral competitiveness in Sub-Saharan Africa

Electoral support for powerholders	All elections		Authoritarian elections	
	Percent	N	Percent	N
Less than 50%	30.31	97	29.02	74
50–60%	15.94	51	14.51	37
60–70%	16.56	53	17.25	44
70–80%	14.06	45	12.94	33
80–90%	10.63	34	11.76	30
90–100%	12.50	40	14.51	37
Total	100.00	320	100.00	255

Notes Based on all direct national multi-party elections in Sub-Saharan Africa between 1990 and 2012 (N = 351). Electoral support for powerholders refers to the share of votes in first-round presidential elections and parliamentary seats in legislative elections, respectively, that were won by those holding power at the time of the elections and their coalition partners. Elections not contested by powerholders are excluded from this table. This happens, for example, when transitional governments oversee the preparation of elections. Authoritarian elections are those held in countries that did not received the status "free" by Freedom House in the year preceding electoral campaigning

2.4 Electoral Competitiveness and Democratic Governance

As discussed in Sect. 2.1, in a procedural-minimum conception of democracy, electoral competitiveness is a central aspect of democratic practice. Only when elections offer a meaningful choice to the electorate does regularly holding elections introduce uncertainty among political elites, and provide vertical accountability to citizens. If, in turn, electoral campaigns demonstrate that the mobilization power of opposition parties and candidates cannot call into question the ruling elites' claim to power, and official election results entrench this political dominance in the institutional system, elections do not contribute to the functioning of a democratic regime, whether they procedurally satisfy democratic standards or not.

It appears from this viewpoint that most elections in electoral authoritarian regimes in Sub-Saharan Africa are democratic in form, but not in substance. While most elections, as has been demonstrated in Sect. 2.3, attract the participation of the majority of the electorate and political opposition, and reflect the cumulative voting decision of voters, most of the time they also lead to overwhelming electoral majorities for powerholders, as Table 2.8 shows.

Among elections held in Sub-Saharan Africa, powerholders received less than 50% of the votes in only 30.31% of the cases. If at the time of the preparation of elections, the political system is classified as an electoral authoritarian regime, this percentage drops to 29.02%. In 37.19% of all elections, in turn, ruling elites received more than 70% of the seats or first-round votes in parliamentary and presidential elections, respectively. This share goes up to 39.21% among authoritarian elections. According to common classification schemes, in these cases, authoritarian electoral regimes would be categorized as hegemonic (see, e.g., Howard and Roessler 2006; Levitsky and Way 2002; Vanhanen 2003).

This goes hand in hand with low electoral turnover. Electoral turnovers do not directly result from the distributions of seats in the parliament or votes in first-round presidential elections between powerholders and the opposition. This is because receiving less than 50% of the seats or votes does not automatically mean that incumbents have lost power. Ruling elites often form post-electoral coalitions with selected opposition parties to maintain parliamentary majorities or win the presidency in run-off elections. Also, in the case of presidential elections, ruling elites sometimes increase the use of repression and manipulation in second round elections to stay in power. In fact, in only 52.58% of the cases where powerholders received less than 50% of the seats or votes could the opposition capitalize on their election wins and take over the government or presidency. In this respect, parliamentary and presidential elections do not differ much. Whereas among parliamentary elections in which powerholders received less than 50% of the seats 54.17% led to a transfer of power, among presidential elections in which the ruling party candidate received a minority of the popular vote in the first round, 51.02% were eventually won by the opposition.

In total, only 52 peaceful transfers of the presidency or the government took place in the 351 de jure direct national multi-party elections in Sub-Saharan Africa between 1990 and 2012. As 94 of these presidential and parliamentary elections were held in the framework of general elections, this corresponds to 36 points in time when a transfer of power through elections was achieved. Of these 36 electoral turnovers, 13 took place in founding elections, three in second elections, and six in third elections. These waves of electoral turnovers peak with fifth elections and abate throughout later election cycles, as Fig. 2.4 shows.

Electoral turnovers have been used to track democratic consolidation. An electoral turnover refers to a constitutional change in power, through an election, from those that held power at the time of the election to an opposition party or coalition. Such a turnover has taken place if the former opposition has taken over the presidency or is leading the government after the election. According to Huntington's two-turnover test, a democratic regime is consolidated if "the party or group that takes power in the initial election at the time of transition loses a subsequent election and turns over power to those election winners, and if those election winners then peacefully turn over power to the winners of a later election" (Huntington 1993, p. 267). If we follow this definition, only the 23 turnovers in later electoral cycles in Sub-Saharan Africa count towards the consolidation of democratic regimes. Furthermore, until 2012, electoral competitiveness would then have only led to consolidated democratic regimes in seven countries. These are Cape Verde, Ghana, Kenya, Madagascar, Mauritius, Sao Tomé and Principe, and Senegal.

It can be shown that electoral turnovers are the result of growing electoral competitiveness in the past. Developments in electoral competitiveness indicate changing prospects for democratization. Table 2.9 shows that this influence of electoral competitiveness can be traced back at least two electoral cycles. The extent of electoral dominance by powerholders in the current, previous, and penultimate election is

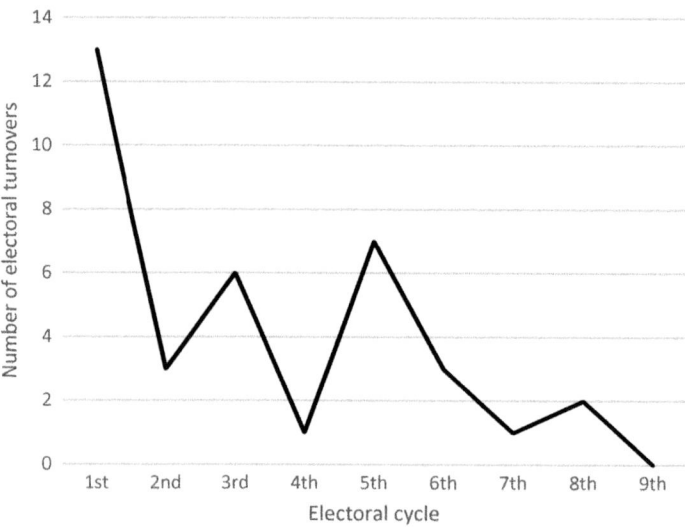

Fig. 2.4 Electoral turnovers across electoral cycles in Sub-Saharan Africa. *Notes* Based on all direct national multi-party elections in Sub-Saharan Africa between 1990 and 2012 (N = 351). On the vertical axis, the absolute numbers of electoral turnovers are given, while the horizontal axis shows the rank numbers of elections in an uninterrupted series. The figure shows, for example, that 13 electoral turnovers took place in founding elections in the period under investigation

Table 2.9 Electoral competitiveness and electoral turnovers in Sub-Saharan Africa

Electoral dominance	Corr.	n
Current election	−0.605***	246
One election earlier	−0.230**	167
Two elections earlier	−0.321***	104

Notes Based on all direct national multi-party elections in Sub-Saharan Africa between 1990 and 2012 (N = 351). Dependent variable is electoral turnover. Electoral competitiveness is measured as electoral dominance, i.e., the share of votes or seats won by powerholders in first-round presidential and parliamentary elections, respectively. Pearson correlations. Significance tests two-tailed. *$p \leq$ 0.05, **$p \leq 0.01$, ***$p \leq 0.001$

strongly and significantly negatively correlated with an electoral turnover in a given election.

Besides paving the way for eventual electoral turnovers, the data on elections in Sub-Saharan Africa suggest that changes in electoral competitiveness are an important indicator for the gradual progress of democratization processes in other respects as well. Table 2.10 shows that electoral dominance is strongly correlated with democratic governance, the quality of the electoral process, and opposition participation. It provides averages of these indicators for elections that exhibit different levels of electoral dominance by powerholders. From left to right, it provides data on elections where powerholders received less than 50% of the seats or votes in parliamentary and first-round presidential elections, respectively, to elections where they received between 90 and 100% of seats or votes, in increments of 10%. Polity IV and Freedom House scores are stated for the year after the elections, so that election outcomes do not directly influence the ratings.

The data show that democratic governance improves with every 10% decrease in electoral dominance by powerholders, suggesting that electoral competitiveness can serve as an indicator for the progress of democratization beyond, for example, a rough differentiation between hegemonic and competitive elections. It suggests that electoral dominance goes hand in hand with an increased responsiveness by powerholders to demands for participation in decision-making processes and the protection of individual freedoms.

The quality of the electoral process and opposition participation also strongly increase with growing electoral competitiveness. Among the most competitive elections, for example, 77.53% were deemed acceptable by international election observers, whereas among the least competitive elections, this was only the case for one in four. All correlations of electoral dominance with democratic governance, the quality of the electoral process, and opposition participation are substantially stronger than in the case of correlations of these aspects of democratic practice with electoral experience, as reported in Table 2.7. They even gain in strength when founding elections are excluded, as Table A.5 in the appendix shows.

Table 2.11 provides an additional perspective on the association between electoral competitiveness and democratization in the long term. It shows the results of a multiple linear regression analysis with countries as cases and Freedom House scores for 2012 as the dependent variable.

The table indicates that average electoral competitiveness across elections in the period 1990–2012 is strongly associated with democratic outcomes in 2012. In contrast, electoral experience, i.e., the mere holding of de jure direct national multi-party elections, is much more weakly and not significantly correlated with democratic governance.

2.5   Summary

This chapter argued that African electoral authoritarianism has survived because electoral practice, while fulfilling democratic standards in many respects, continuously fails to provide a core democratic function—namely, meaningful competition between powerholders and the political opposition.

Based on a procedural-minimum conception of democracy, the main implications of a democratic regime for both sides of the principal-agent relationship in representative democratic systems were laid out in Sect. 2.1. Whereas vertical accountability is the central implication of a democratic regime for societal groups, for political elites it is institutionalized uncertainty. Both these implications point to electoral competitiveness as the core principle of a democratic political system.

Table 2.10 Electoral dominance and democratic governance in Sub-Saharan Africa

Indicator	Electoral dominance						Corr.
	<50%	50–60%	60–70%	70–80%	80–90%	>90%	
Polity IV (post-election)	5.04 (3.48)	2.38 (5.10)	1.33 (4.91)	1.16 (4.98)	−1.38(4.56)	−2.26 (4.23)	−0.487**
Freedom House (post-election)	3.57 (1.48)	3.64 (1.59)	4.01 (1.45)	4.23 (1.53)	4.71 (1.35)	5.18 (1.27)	0.322**
• Political Rights	3.40 (1.69)	3.61 (1.88)	4.09 (1.73)	4.36 (1.75)	5.03 (1.50)	5.38 (1.43)	0.363**
• Civil liberties	3.73(1.36)	3.67 (1.40)	3.92 (1.24)	4.11 (1.40)	4.38 (1.33)	4.98 (1.21)	0.246**
Turnout (%)	64.72 (14.6)	71.31 (13.8)	63.56 (14.9)	64.03 (16.2)	63.47 (18.6)	65.37 (25.4)	−0.033
Quality of electoral process (% acceptable)	77.53	69.77	58.7	57.14	59.26	25.00	−0.338**
Opposition participation (% full)	90.72	96.08	88.68	77.78	55.88	27.5	−0.480**
n	97	51	53	45	34	40	

Notes Based on all direct national multi-party elections in Sub-Saharan Africa between 1990 and 2012 (N = 351). Values are means, if not specified otherwise. Population standard deviations in brackets. Pearson correlations with electoral dominance as dependent variable. Significance tests two-tailed. *$p \le 0.05$, **$p \le 0.01$, ***$p \le 0.001$. Electoral dominance is the share of votes or seats won by powerholders in presidential and parliamentary elections, respectively. For other indicators, see Table 2.7 notes

Table 2.11 Predictors of democratic governance

Variable	Indicator	
Electoral competitiveness	Average share of seats or votes won by powerholders in parliamentary and presidential elections between 1990 and 2012	0.436**
Economic development	GDP per capita/purchasing-power parity in 2012	−0.029
Electoral experience	Number of elections held between 1990 and 2012	−0.164
	Adjusted R^2	0.135
	Significance	0.039*
	N	40

Notes Multiple linear regression analysis with aggregate Freedom House scores for 2012 as the dependent variable. Aggregate Freedom House scores are the average of a country's Political Rights and Civil Liberties scores. Standardized beta coefficients. *$p \leq 0.05$, **$p \leq 0.01$, ***$p \leq 0.001$

Data on democratic governance and electoral competitiveness in Sub-Saharan Africa was analyzed to provide a wider context for investigation into the determinants of electoral competitiveness on the subcontinent. In Sect. 2.2, trends in democratic governance since the widespread introduction of multi-party elections in the early 1990s were investigated. It was demonstrated that the advent of multi-party politics is associated with significant improvements in political rights and civil liberties. However, these improvements were mostly concentrated around the introduction of multi-party elections. The regular holding of such elections seems not to be associated with further gains in democratic freedoms.

In Sect. 2.3, this finding was further substantiated with a detailed investigation of electoral practice across countries in Sub-Saharan Africa. It was shown that de jure direct national multi-party elections on the subcontinent attracted the participation of the majority of the electorate and the political opposition, and were assessed as in line with democratic standards in a large majority of the cases. Nevertheless, increased experience with such elections does either not at all or only weakly correlate with democratic governance. A test of Lindberg's (2006a, p. 51) widely cited assertion that "the mere repetition of de jure participatory, competitive, and legitimate elections—regardless of their qualities—contributes to democratization," with a set of electoral regimes of equal length revealed that his finding is based on an ecological fallacy. Instead, an analysis of the correlation of electoral competitiveness with electoral experience indicated that ruling elites in many electoral authoritarian regimes in Sub-Saharan Africa consolidate their power over the course of holding elections.

In Sect. 2.4, the association of electoral competitiveness with other aspects of democratization was further investigated. The analyses suggest that increasing electoral competitiveness paves the way for electoral turnovers, and is strongly associated with indicators of democratic governance, the quality of the electoral process, and the participation of major opposition parties and candidates in elections. A multiple linear regression analysis with Freedom House scores for 2012 as the dependent variable suggests that increased electoral competitiveness is a powerful predictor of democratic governance in the long term as well. This means that study of the determinants of electoral competitiveness not only provides an explanation for why democratic governance did not take hold in Sub-Saharan Africa despite continuous electoral practice, but also has the potential to provide important insights concerning the trajectories of progressing democratization processes in Sub-Saharan Africa.

References

Bogaards M (2007) Measuring democracy through election outcomes: a critique with African data. Comp Polit Stud 40:1211–1237. https://doi.org/10.1177/0010414006288968

Bogaards M (2014) Multiparty elections in Africa: for better or worse. In: Doorenspleet R, Nijzink L (eds) Party systems and democracy in Africa. Palgrave Macmillan, pp 22–44

Bratton M, van de Walle N (1992) Popular protest and political reform in Africa. Comp Polit 24(4):419–442

Bratton M, van de Walle N (1997) Democratic experiments in Africa: Regime transitions in comparative perspective (Cambridge studies in comparative politics). Cambridge University Press, Cambridge

Decalo S (1992) Democracy in Africa: toward the twenty-first century. In: Vanhanen T (ed) Strategies of democratization. Crane Russak, Washington, pp 131–142

Diamond LJ (1999) Introduction. In: Diamond LJ, Plattner MF (eds) Democratization in Africa: progress and retreat (pp. ix–xxviii, A Journal of democracy book). Md:Johns Hopkins University Press, Baltimore

Freedom House (2016) Freedom in the world 2017: populists and autocrats: the dual threat to global democracy. Freedom House. https://freedomhouse.org/sites/default/files/FH_FIW_2017_Report_Final.pdf. Accessed 29 Mar 2019

Gutmann A, Thompson D (2011) Deliberative democracy: beyond process. In: Farrelly C (ed) Contemporary political theory: a reader. Sage, Los Angeles, pp 232–241

Gyimah-Boadi E (1998) The rebirth of African liberalism. J Democracy 9(2):18–31

Hadenius A, Teorell J (2007) Pathways from authoritarianism. J Democracy 18(1):143–157

Howard MM, Roessler PG (2006) liberalizing electoral outcomes in competitive authoritarian regimes. Am J Polit Sci 50(2):365–381

Huntington SP (1993) The third wave: Democratization in the late twentieth century (1st ed., The Julian J. Rothbaum distinguished lecture series, Vol. 4). University of Oklahoma Press, Norman

International Institute for Democracy and Electoral Assistance (2017) Voter turnout database. http://www.idea.int/data-tools/data/voter-turnout. Accessed 29 Mar 2019

Kelley JG (2010) Data on international election monitoring: three global datasets on election quality, election events and international election observation: user guide. Inter-University Consortium for Political and Social Research, Michigan

Kelley JG (2012) Monitoring democracy: when international election observation works, and why it often fails. Princeton University Press, Princeton

Levitsky S, Way L (2002) The rise of competitive authoritarianism. J Democracy 13(2):51–65

Levitsky S, Way L (2010) Competitive authoritarianism: hybrid regimes in the post-cold War era. Cambridge University Press, Cambridge

Lewis PM (1992) Political transition and the dilemma of civil society in Africa. J Int Aff 46(1):31

Lichbach MI (1995) The rebel's dilemma (Economics, cognition, and society). University of Michigan Press, Ann Arbor

Lindberg SI (2006a) Democracy and elections in Africa. Johns Hopkins University Press, Baltimore

Lindberg SI (2006b) Elections and Democracy in Africa 1989-2003. SPSS portable data file. University of Florida. http://users.clas.ufl.edu/sil/downloads.html. Accessed 29 Mar 2019

Olson M (2003) The logic of collective action: public goods and the theory of groups (21st ed., Harvard economic studies, Vol. 124). Harvard University Press, Cambridge, Mass

Przeworski A (1986) Some problems in the study of the transition to democracy. In: O'Donnell GA, Schmitter PC, Whitehead L (eds) Transitions from authoritarian rule: comparative perspectives. The Johns Hopkins University Press, Baltimore, pp 47–63

Przeworski A (1991) Democracy and the market: political and economic reforms in Eastern Europe and Latin America (studies in rationality and social change). Cambridge University Press, Cambridge

Przeworski A (1993) Democracy as a contingent outcome of conflicts. In: Elster J, Slagstad R (eds) Constitutionalism and democracy (pp. 59–80, Studies in rationality and social change). Cambridge University Press, Cambridge

Schedler A (1999) Conceptualizing Accountability. In: Schedler A, Diamond LJ, Plattner MF (eds) The self-restraining state: power and accountability in new democracies. Lynne Rienner Publishers, Boulder, Colo, pp 13–28

Schedler A (2002) The menu of manipulation. J Democracy 13(2):36–50

Schmitter PC, Karl TL (1991) What democracy is… and is not. J Democracy 2(3):75–88

Schumpeter JA (2006) Capitalism, socialism and democracy (6th ed). Routledge; Taylor & Francis Group [distributor], New York, Florence

Tilly C (2007) Democracy. Cambridge University Press, Cambrigde

Vanhanen T (2003) Democratization: a comparative analysis of 170 countries (Routledge research in comparative politics, Vol. 7). Routledge, London, New York

Whitehead L (2004) Democratization: theory and experience (Oxford scholarship online). Oxford University Press, Oxford

Chapter 3
Mobilizing for Democracy? Collective Action and Political Power in Sub-Saharan Africa

Ruling elites of most electoral authoritarian regimes in Sub-Saharan Africa have been firmly dominating politics in their respective countries since the advent of multi-party politics. As election results indicate, few have experienced meaningful competition within the institutional framework of their rule. Even fewer have experienced defeat, at the ballot box or otherwise. Among the ruling elites is a group of autocratic leaders who have been ruling their countries since the 70s or 80s, such as José Eduardo dos Santos in Angola, Blaise Compaoré in Burkina Faso, Paul Biya in Cameroon, or Robert Mugabe in Zimbabwe. Not only have they overseen the introduction of direct national multi-party elections in their countries, they have also managed to stay in power despite regular electoral practice.

At the same time, some ruling elites in electoral authoritarian regimes in Sub-Saharan Africa seem to have strengthened their grip on power over many years, but then quickly disintegrated when challenged in an electoral contest. In 2011 in Zambia, for example, Michael Sata of the Patriotic Front took power from the Movement for Multi-Party Democracy that had ruled the country since 1991. More recently, in 2016, the long-standing autocratic leader of the Gambia, Yahya Jammeh, lost his re-election bid to a political newcomer after 20 years in power.

Given the weak institutional framework of electoral authoritarian regimes in Sub-Saharan Africa, in this chapter it will be argued that in the struggle for control over state and economy, the extra-institutional, patrimonial power of political actors trumps their institutional power. To adequately describe the power dynamics in electoral authoritarian regimes therefore requires an appreciation of the capacity of collective political actors to mobilize money, time, and material goods outside the channels of political institutions. From this perspective, the political power of three principal actors in African electoral authoritarian regimes will be analyzed: Ruling elites, oppositional political elites, and societal groups.

The analysis will show that ruling elites have strong advantages over oppositional political elites and societal groups in both maintaining and building up the capacity to mobilize time, money, and material goods in their struggle to maintain the status quo. This advantage lays mainly in their control over neo-patrimonial state structures and

© Springer Nature Switzerland AG 2020
W. Stuppert, *Political Mobilizations and Democratization in Sub-Saharan Africa*,
Advances in African Economic, Social and Political Development,
https://doi.org/10.1007/978-3-030-22792-0_3

the economy. This creates an environment for oppositional political elites that makes it seem unlikely that by their own effort they would be able to gain the capacity to balance out ruling elite power. A lack of public discourse around substantial political issues, the personalistic character of their political agendas, their lack of access to the domestic economy and international support, as well as the targeted repression they face at the hands of ruling elites all lead to a situation in which they have very limited opportunities to engage in public and intra-network communication, build organizational structures, and prepare for direct engagements with ruling elites.

It will be argued that despite the limitations of societal groups in fulfilling democratic functions, they represent the most important alternative source of political power in electoral authoritarian regimes in Sub-Saharan Africa. This hypothesis stands in contrast to many well-known accounts of politics on the African subcontinent, in which the capacities of local societies for collective action are depicted as subjugated by either colonial powers, international corporations, development organizations, local patrons, or all of the above (see, e.g., Bayart 1986; Chabal and Daloz 1999). Yet, historical accounts and quantitative data on protest events show that societal protests and uprisings have sometimes shaped the trajectories of political developments in Sub-Saharan Africa in important ways (Gyimah-Boadi 2004). Since the advent of the modern nation state, three major protest waves can be identified that washed across Sub-Saharan Africa: The first in the late colonial period, the second between the end of the 1980s and beginning of the 1990s, and the third gaining momentum around 2005 and culminating in the "Arab Spring" in 2011 (Branch and Mampilly 2015). Whereas the first wave brought about an end to colonial rule, the second wave is widely seen as instrumental for the onset of democratic regime changes across Sub-Saharan Africa in the first half of the 1990s (Bratton and van de Walle 1997). The third wave has yet to yield major lasting political consequences outside North Africa. Nonetheless, individual protest movements such as the "Walk to work protests" in Uganda in 2011 and Occupy Nigeria in 2012 shook up their respective polities temporarily (Branch and Mampilly 2015).

The present chapter will provide the theoretical background necessary to appreciate the role of extra-institutional collective action in democratization processes in Sub-Saharan Africa. It will thereby establish ordinary citizens as an important piece of the answer to the question of who could balance out the political power of ruling elites, and propel democratization forward on the subcontinent.

First, an important implication of electoral authoritarianism in Sub-Saharan Africa will be discussed. It will be argued that as this type of regime goes hand in hand with weak institutions, extra-institutional power trumps institutional power in the struggle for political dominance. For this reason, an appreciation of both sources of political power is necessary to understand the trajectories of political struggles in electoral authoritarian regimes.

Second, the chapter will argue that political power can be understood as the ability to realize one's group-specific interests in a political struggle. It will be shown that from the perspective of collective action theory, this ability is synonymous with the ability to project a credible mobilization threat into the political arena. This mobilization threat is rooted in a collective actor's ability to mobilize adherents in the face of adversity. Mobilizing adherents, in turn, requires the collective actor to overcome its collective action problem.

Third, the chapter will discuss solutions to the collective action problem, and their implications for the mobilization of adherents. It will be shown that inter alia both institutions and networks provide such solutions. Four mobilization tactics will be defined that actors can engage in to mobilize people and their resources: Intra-network communication, public communication, organization building, and direct engagements with neutral bystanders and one's opponents. It will be argued that among these tactics, direct engagement is the most complex to employ.

Fourth, based on the preceding discussion, the chapter will provide a fresh look at the political power of the principal collective actors in democratization processes in Sub-Saharan Africa: Ruling elites, oppositional political elites, and societal groups. In particular, collective action theory will provide a new perspective on the role of civil society in democratization processes in Sub-Saharan Africa. While the collective action approach affirms the importance of constructive, "civil" activism, such as development work, sensitization, get-out-the-vote-campaigns, or election monitoring, it will be argued that mobilization power and threat are important aspects of the role of societal groups in the democratization process as well.

Fifth, political mobilizations will be introduced as an indicator for a collective actor's mobilization threat. Political mobilizations are public direct engagements of a collective political actor with its opponents. As such they are both the most demanding and the most consequential form of mobilization with regard to the mobilization threat that a collective actor is able to project into the political arena. A high frequency of public direct engagements can therefore be expected to correlate with the extent the collective actor has been able to build up a mobilization threat through other mobilization tactics. The chapter will investigate trajectories of political mobilizations by societal groups, the political opposition, and ruling elites in Sub-Saharan Africa. While public collective actions by oppositional political elites are rare, the data suggests that societal groups continued to mobilize in public direct engagements with ruling elites despite harsh repressive countermeasures. Given the organizational weaknesses of civil society organizations in Sub-Saharan Africa, spontaneous, often violent protests by the urban underclass played an important role in government-critical political mobilizations. Evidence on national protest movements in several countries on the subcontinent shows that such uprisings are not inimical to the political mobilizations of civil society organizations. To the contrary, it suggests that violent mass protests by the urban underclass often played an important role for the galvanizing of coalitions and the political success of national protest movements.

3.1 Electoral Authoritarianism and Political Power

Different kinds of authoritarianism "differ from each other as much as they differ from democracy" (Geddes 1999, p. 121). It will be argued that the democratic-authoritarian amalgam that electoral authoritarian regimes represent are associated with lowered state capacity. In consequence, the extra-institutional power of political actors trumps institutional power. This means that an understanding of the dynamics of democratization processes of electoral authoritarian regimes requires an appreciation of the extra-institutional power of collective political actors.

State capacity is "the degree of control state agents exercise over persons, activities, and resources within their government's territorial jurisdiction" (McAdam et al. 2001, p. 78). If it is low, state institutions are weak, and given weak state institutions, rule tends to be indirect, geographic peripheries often not penetrated, state practices and identities not standardized, and the means of carrying out intended policies limited (McAdam et al. 2001, p. 78). Electoral authoritarianism goes hand in hand with low state capacity, because situations of transition imply a weakening of the institutional framework, and in electoral authoritarian regimes, authoritarian governance constantly undermines the strength of state institutions. This weakening of state institutions by authoritarian elites is intentional. As Chabal and Daloz (1999, p. 14) explain for the African case: "The very weakness and inefficiency of the state has been profitable to the African political elites. [...] It has allowed them to respond to the demands for protection, assistance and aid made by the members of their constituency communities in exchange for the recognition of the political prominence and social status which, as patrons, they crave". This leads to a situation where extra-institutional power is crucial for political survival. That is, the power granted by positions in the institutional network is not enough to pursue one's political agenda.

That institutions are rather weak at the beginning of the democratization process, when electoral authoritarian regimes come into being, is most evidently the case when genuine regime change has taken place, i.e., when an authoritarian regime ended with the overthrow of the incumbent authoritarian government, be it as a result of foreign intervention, mass mobilization, or elite splits. Such regime transitions themselves imply a weakening of the institutional framework, because they represent a phase of pronounced "dedifferentiation" or "dissolution" of the institutions of the old regime (Merkel 2010, p. 94) that goes along with the rulers' loss of power. As such, regime transitions are "an interval of intense political uncertainty during which the shape of the new institutional dispensation is up for grabs by incumbent and opposition contenders" (Bratton and van de Walle 1997, p. 10).

However, even if the introduction of national multi-party elections preempted a violent overthrow and authoritarian ruling elites managed to survive the first elections in office, the institutional framework of the electoral authoritarian regime will be weak and continue to be weakened. Strong institutions are anathema to autocratic incumbents who require the ability to bend the rules to survive elections in office, be it through outright repression or—more subtly—by favoritism and manipulation. The widespread and permanent undermining of democratic institutions by neo-patrimonial power networks and brute violence creates the "uneven playing field" (Bunce and Wolchik 2011, p. 10) on which authoritarian elites manage to win national elections by landslides.

Moreover, since the post-communist regime changes in the early 1990s, the time of democratic transitions occurring in countries with relatively strong institutions is finally over. Most of today's authoritarian ruling elites preside over post-colonial states that never had strong institutions or whose institutional framework never recovered from being dismantled by colonial powers or the subsequent onslaught by neo-liberal development programs.

Be it because of tumultuous transitions, the constant meddling of incumbents, or the structural consequences of underdevelopment, having their beginnings in such weak institutional frameworks means that today's democratization processes take place in an environment where extra-institutional, patrimonial power trumps institutional power. The differentiation of extra-institutional, patrimonial power and institutional power encapsulates Przeworski's idea that the probability that a group "will realize its interests to a specific degree and in a particular manner" in a political process is "determined jointly by resources and institutions" (1991, p. 11).

Institutional power is the realization of a collective actor's group-specific interests through the exercise of functions invested in it by its position in the institutional system. The exercise of institutional power relies therefore on other individuals and institutions who are incentivized to contribute to the realization of an actor's group-specific interests by the existing rules and regulations of the institutional system—and the mechanisms of reward and punishment they trigger. As long as it is exercised in accordance with the existing rules and regulations of the institutional system, this form of a collective actor's political power is reliable in the sense that both the collective actor and its opponents have a high expectation that the collective actor will be able to exercise that power tomorrow.

Extra-institutional power, in turn, is the realization of a collective actor's group-specific interests through the mobilization of money, time, and material goods outside the channels of political institutions. Here, power relies on a collective actor's link to communities, command over organizational structures, access to means of mass communication, and relationships to resource-rich individuals and organizations. In other words, extra-institutional power is based on a network of individuals and organizations formed around common interests. Such a network underlies what others have defined as a social movement (Rucht and Neidhardt 2007, p. 634; della Porta and Diani 2006, p. 20). As such, it is much more volatile in shape than the channels of mobilization provided by political institutions. In the absence of permanent, pervasive, hierarchical structures, the collective action problem that a collective actor needs to overcome to exercise extra-institutional power remains acute. Hence, the reliability of extra-institutional political power is considerably lower than in the case of institutional power: The probability that a collective actor will be able to exercise extra-institutional power tomorrow to the same degree as yesterday is perceived as lower, both by the actor itself and by its opponents.

In electoral authoritarian regimes, extra-institutional power trumps institutional power because, first, the line between the political parties of ruling elites and state institutions is blurry when institutions are weak. State resources are then used by incumbents in the political struggle. Second, especially in post-colonial states, extra-institutional power trumps institutional power because the post-colonial state is only institutionally present in the urban space. In rural areas in Sub-Saharan Africa, it is often reduced to administrative outposts with a meager police force. Thus, "weak institutions" indicate a situation where the state's reach into the "rag rug" of the fiefdoms of chiefs and warlords is limited. Hence, being at the top of the state apparatus and using official chains of command is not sufficient to control them; winning political struggles in electoral authoritarian regimes requires extra-institutional, patrimonial means as well.

Patrimonial power trumping institutional power means that patrimonial power undermines the principals of legal-rational bureaucracy. This creates neo-patrimonial power networks that span relationships between patron and client in the public and private realm. Hence, both the control over the client's personal assets and the client's position in the institutional framework will be employed to further the patron's interest (Erdmann and Engel 2007).

3.2   Mobilization Threat as Political Power

Collective action theory provides a unifying perspective on the sources of power in a political struggle. From this perspective, political power can be defined as the capacity of a group to realize their group-specific interests (Przeworski 1986, p. 57). In the struggle for political dominance, political power is then, more specifically, the power to realize a group's interest in the face of adversity. To participate in this struggle, political entrepreneurs must form a collective actor; to succeed, they must mobilize people and their resources. From a collective action perspective, political power translates into solving one's own collective action problem, while exacerbating the collective action problem of one's opponents (Lichbach 1995). As Lichbach (1994, p. 21) puts it: "Oppositions know that they are kept from power because of their collective action problem; regimes know that they stay in power because of their opponents' collective action problem".

Collective action theory tells us that not every group that has a common interest will act jointly to realize this interest (Olson 2003). In fact, as Olson shows, it is always individually rational to free-ride on other members of the same group working to realize a common interest. This common interest is understood to be a "public good" to the group in question. The definition of a public good implies that everybody, or every member of a given group, will profit from it once it is produced, regardless of whether he or she has contributed to it. Furthermore, it is assumed that every individual contribution is unnecessary for its production. If these circumstances are given, it is individually rational for every member of the group to leave it to the other members of the group to contribute to the production of the public good. If one assumes, however, that this thought-process applies to all members of the group, the public good will not be produced. This shows that the best course of action for each individual member of the group does not lead to the best outcome for the group as a whole, which in turn means that every member of the group is left off worse than they would be if they had not tried to maximize their utility in the first place.

In game theory, this situation is known as the Prisoner's Dilemma (Axelrod 2006, p. 7; Rapoport and Chammah 1970). In this game, there are two players who have no means of communicating with each other. They are both given two choices: To cooperate with each other, or to defect. In the original formulation, to "cooperate" means that the prisoner remains silent with regard to the crime that he or she committed together with his or her partner. If both keep silent, the prosecution will not have enough evidence to convict either of them as the principal offender, and both will get off with a light sentence as accessories to the crime. To defect would mean that the prisoner talks to the prosecution. It is understood that in this case he or she would blame the crime on their partner. To induce both prisoners to talk, the prosecution offers a deal to each of them: Whoever talks will have their sentence (as an accessory to the crime) considerably reduced. If both talk, they will be convicted as co-perpetrators. As both prisoners face the risk of their partner defecting, and hence being sentenced for the crime as the principal offender if they themselves keep silent, they will both defect, blame their partner, and be sentenced as co-perpetrators.

Whether formulated as a public good problem or the Prisoner's Dilemma, the theoretical examples show that groups only gain the capacity to act if they overcome this fundamental collective action problem. Realizing their group-specific interests in the face of competition, in turn, requires them to wield sufficient mobilization capacity to push their own agenda and weaken the mobilization capacity of others. According to collective action theory, neither the former nor the latter is likely to come about.

Based on Olson's initial formulation, Lichbach (1995, pp. 16–17) points out four ways in which extensive collective action of opponents to a political regime is improbable:

> First, in spite of the common interests of its potential members, a dissident group does not readily, naturally, and automatically coalesce. Many potential dissident groups never form; potentially common resources remain unpooled. Second, even if a dissident group does form, many potential supporters do not join. With self-exclusion from politics, or political apathy, passivity, and inertia the norm, most dissident groups fail to move beyond a narrow core of supporters. Their major problem is that dissidents try to free ride and let others do the dirty work of rebelling. Third, even if a dissident group does form, those who join participate in few activities. Most neither attend the group's meetings, nor join its marches, nor pay their membership dues. Finally, even if a dissident group does form, even if potential dissidents do join, and even if members do participate in the group's activities, low-cost and short-lived activities predominate.

For the same reasons, cooperation among dissident organizations is, in principle, unlikely (Lichbach 1995, p. 19).

Ruling elites face the same core problem in mobilizing supporters for collective action: The status quo is a public good and those who would have an interest in upholding this status quo are unlikely to act jointly to realize this interest. Joining pro-government rallies in the streets, manipulating elections, dispersing protesting crowds, or shooting rioters comes with personal costs to regime supporters, and free-riding is always an option—its own cost depending, inter alia, on the quality of the elites' system for monitoring defections.

Mobilization in support of ruling elites is less improbable than in the case of challengers to the regime because ruling elites control the state and its resources, and with that often the national economy, too. This control translates into powerful solutions to the collective action problem. As Slater (2009, p. 208) puts it: "Authoritarian regimes tend to hold huge advantages over their opponents in coercive and remunerative power because they command the state apparatus, with its army, police, and treasury". Ruling elites can use their positions in the institutional framework to nurture their neo-patrimonial power networks. Nonetheless, splits can exacerbate coordination problems among ruling elites and a shortage of financial means as selective incentives can, for example, convince the army to stay in the barracks instead of defending the regime. The disastrous implications of the collective action problem are not unknown to authoritarian ruling elites.

Even though extensive collective action for a public good, such as regime change, is improbable and rarely happens, challengers to the existing social order do quite regularly form groups and build up a limited mobilization capacity even under the adverse conditions posed by authoritarian regimes. For example, in the year before the onset of political campaigning for the 238 authoritarian elections that were held in Sub-Saharan Africa between 1989 and 2012, societal groups on average staged four highly-visible protests, with the majority planned by civil society organizations and opposition parties, against the government and its policies. During election campaigns, an additional three such protests took place on average. This shows that a theory of collective action must explain why most people do not collectively act to produce a public good while some people regularly do, even under adverse circumstances. As we will see in the following sections, this task is addressed by identifying various solutions to the collective action problem.

As stated previously, political power is realizing one's interests, and hence solving one's collective action problem. In short, political power is the ability to mobilize. However, collective action theory also tells us that mobilization is not permanent. The gathering of protesters is as temporary as the mobilization of voters or the deployment of troops. Political entrepreneurs must therefore overcome the collective action problem not once, but over and over. This means that political actors never simply "possess" mobilization power. This means also that at no point in time will the opponents in a political struggle be able to say for certain how many people and resources the other side will be able to mobilize in its support.

From this it follows that, more exactly, political power is the mobilization threat as it is perceived by one's opponents. Like not every instance of collective bargaining between employers and trade unions leads to a general strike, not every episode of confrontation between the opposition and the state must lead to large-scale protest and the massive deployment of security forces, respectively. Actors try to gauge and anticipate each other's mobilizable force to avoid unnecessary costs in the political struggle. In the case of ruling elites, for example, we should assume that they attempt to estimate the likelihood of societal mobilization and the ensuing "costs of suppression" (Bermeo 1997) and based on these estimates decide on a preemptive mixture of repression and concessions. For the context of authoritarian elections, their guiding questions could sound something like: How much mobilization capacity is there among societal groups? How much will it translate to support for opposition parties? How much will we have to tilt the playing field to win? How much support for opposition parties do we have to publicly admit? In short, it is the perceived threat of counter-mobilization that makes actors act and react the way they do.

Past episodes of highly-visible collective action provide cues for the assessment of the mobilization threat. Lichbach (1995, p. 57), for example, states: "Collective violence at time t […] always carries an implicit threat of collective violence at time t +1". If a regime has proven that it can deploy the army to repress protests thoroughly and violently, opposition parties will change their tactics to avoid such open defeat the next time around. If the opposition has proven that it can mobilize thousands of supporters in the streets in the wake of the jailing of their leaders, the regime will update its cost-benefit calculations regarding concessions and repression, and may choose to negotiate with leading opposition politicians in the future instead of imprisoning them. A proof of its mobilization threat is especially important if an opposition group is new to the political scene and has been previously excluded from institutional politics. As Lichbach (1995, p. 57) explains: "If a group does not have access to conventional political channels, its viewpoint will be dismissed unless it can somehow signal its strength. Only strong dissidents are credible threats to regimes".

It seems plausible that the threat emanating from past mobilizations has different "half-life periods" for the regime and its opponents. As the collective action problem poses itself every time a collective actor wants to mobilize, to remain credible the threat must be periodically renewed. Whereas societal groups and oppositional political elites rely on extra-institutional power networks, ruling elites can use the state's elaborate organizational structures. Hence, ruling elites' mobilization capacity is much more "permanent" in nature and their mobilization threat more credible for a much longer time. However, even ruling elites face situations where it is an open question whether they can order the army and police to mobilize and follow their commands again the next day, and where the opposition knows, too, that this mobilization may be unlikely to repeat itself. The dynamics of the overthrow of Slobodan Milošević in the Federal Republic of Yugoslavia in October 2000 are a case in point (Collin 2001, pp. 232–233; Thompson and Kuntz 2004, p. 168). Nonetheless, past mobilizations, if relatively recent, provide important cues for the likelihood of their timely repetition, more so in the case of ruling elites than in the case of the political opposition or societal groups.

Of course, actors in the political struggle could form the most accurate picture of their opponents' mobilization threat if the availability of solutions to the collective action problem for these opponents was known to them. First, future mobilizations will be the direct result of the availability of such solutions for their opponents, much as past mobilizations were. Second, even if the absolute "stock" of solutions of a particular actor is not known, information on changes in the availability of solutions to the collective action problem for collective actors, relative to their previous capacities, provide important updates to opponents' estimates of the mobilization threat that they pose. To illustrate this point, suppose organizational structures were preconditions for a number of solutions to the collective action problem, as they indeed are (Lichbach 1995). Now suppose further that after a mass protest of opposition parties, ruling elites have successfully identified and imprisoned opposition leaders, as well as confiscated their organizations' assets and membership lists. Ruling elites will update their estimates of the mobilization threat opposition parties currently pose accordingly, and not as readily assume that a mass protest of this scale is likely to soon repeat itself, as it might have had they not successfully implemented these repressive measures. Hence, a collective actor's mobilization threat as perceived by its opponents in a conflict is based on past mobilizations as well as estimates of current mobilization capacity.

To sum up, from a collective action perspective political power translates into solving one's own collective action problem, while exacerbating the collective action problem of one's opponents. Both institutional and extra-institutional power stem from solutions to the collective action problem that are provided to collective actors by their positions in the institutional framework and their command over extra-institutional organizational structures and resources, respectively.

At the same time, mobilization capacity may exert power even when it is not employed. This is because actors try to anticipate each other's mobilizable force to avoid unnecessary costs in the political struggle. Hence, one's political power is more accurately one's mobilization threat as perceived by one's opponents. This threat, in turn, is based on one's command of solutions to the collective action problem past and present, or more precisely, on one's past mobilization successes and failures as well as other's information on more recent changes in one's mobilization capacity.

3.3   From Collective Action Solutions to Mobilization Tactics

If one's political power ultimately depends on the availability of solutions to one's collective action problem, what do these solutions constitute and how can a collective action entrepreneur improve their own access to these solutions?

This section will proceed with a discussion of the solutions to the collective action problem that have been identified in collective action literature. The concept of mobilization capacity will be used to refer to the availability of solutions to the collective action problem for a group. To interpret the summative availability of solutions to the collective action problem as an actor's mobilization capacity, the underlying assumption is that the more a collective actor is able to trigger any of the underlying solutions, the more likely it is that some of them will be successful in mobilizing adherents. This is an assumption that is widely shared in social movement literature, and a conclusion of pertinent research studies repeatedly drawn throughout the years (see, e.g., Gurr 1974, p. 305; Freeman 1979, p. 183; Lichbach 1995, p. 54). Based on the discussion of solutions to the collective action problem, four mobilization tactics will be defined that actors can engage in to mobilize people and their resources: Intra-network communication, public communication, organization building, and direct engagements with one's opponents and neutral bystanders. At the end of the section, presuppositions for the employment of these tactics will be discussed.

Lichbach (1994, 1995) identifies 22 solutions to the collective action problem from the extensive literature on collective action and groups these into four sets: Market-based solutions, community solutions, contract-based solutions, and hierarchy solutions. The solutions of a given set make different assumptions about the possibility of deliberation and the existence of institutions between individuals who try to cooperate. Are individuals assumed to be able to reflect on their situation and discuss a common approach to it? Are there structures assumed to be in place within which individuals decide whether to act collectively? There are four possible combinations of answers in response to these two questions.

The first combination constitutes the negation of both questions. Solutions in this set assume that individuals are neither able to deliberate and forge a resolution, nor are they embedded in an institutional context that could help them solve their collective action problem. Put differently, individuals are assumed to make their decisions about whether to contribute to the production of a public good in mutual ignorance. They are "isolated atoms" (Lichbach 1995, p. 111). Solutions that start from this premise are called "market solutions" by Lichbach.

The second combination negates the first, and affirms the second question. Solutions in this set assume that "institutions exist, and that they are so effective as to render social planning unnecessary" (Lichbach 1995, p. 20). Here, institutions are not intentionally designed or employed by individuals to solve their collective action problem. The idea is rather that a "Gemeinschaft" (Lichbach 1995, p. 20) provides a conducive background for solutions to the collective action problem. Embedded in a network of relationships, individuals develop a common belief system. Solutions that assume such common beliefs to be in place among individuals who try to collaborate are called "community solutions" by Lichbach.

The third combination affirms the first and negates the second question. Solutions in this set assume individuals are able to deliberate as independent agents without mutually binding structures on the type of institutions they want to create in order to solve their collective action problem. The resulting agreements forge a "Gesellschaft" (Lichbach 1995, p. 20). Solutions that allow for such planned order to emerge among individuals are called "contract solutions" by Lichbach.

Finally, in the last combination both questions are answered in the affirmative. Solutions in this set assume not only that individuals are embedded in an institutional framework, but also that they employ this institutional framework deliberately to solve their collective action problem. This includes preexisting organizations that are utilized to engage in mobilization tactics. Solutions that start from the premise that such structures exist and are intentionally used are called "hierarchy solutions" by Lichbach.

All four of Lichbach's sets of solutions to the collective action problem provide different types of answers to the question of what aspects of social reality collective actors should pay attention to in order to build up their mobilization capacity and thereby increase their political power. Market solutions draw our attention to the immediate decision-making process of the individual. Lichbach identified twelve solutions that focus on different parameters of this process: The information available to the individual, the benefits, the costs, and the probabilities attached to the successful production of the public good. Even more so than those of the other sets, market solutions point out what happens when these parameters have different values for specific groups of people, or when these parameters are changed, rather than what could be done to change them.

The first market solution discussed by Lichbach is "Use incomplete information". Starting from the premise that individuals do not have access to all relevant information, or cannot process it in due time, this solution discusses the ample field of publicity and propaganda, or information and framing, for the success of mobilization. The next solution, "Increase team competition between enemies," points to the importance of collective framing for an individual's decision to join the political struggle. If intergroup antagonism is rhetorically heightened, collective action becomes more likely. As Lichbach (Lichbach 1995, p. 102) writes: "Intergroup conflict between regime and opposition begets intragroup cooperation".

Under the market solution "Increase benefits" Lichbach discusses the importance of "zealots," people who attach a very high value to a public good (1995, p. 36). In the case of collective action for a change of government, zealots could be found, for example, among those who have personally suffered under extreme forms of state repression. Among fervent regime supporters, zealots may be those who, in the case of a regime change, anticipate punishment for human rights violations they committed in the name of the current government. Zealots are important to a collective action endeavor because they are the crucial first movers that start protests or build organizations. Other market solutions that deal with increasing the benefits attached to the public good by potential collaborators are "Reduce supply of the PG," "Increase the probability to make a difference," "Restrict exit," and "Change type of public good".

The market solution "Lower costs" deals inter alia with the consequences of tactical decisions: Does a group chose violent or non-violent forms of collective action? Violent forms of protest, for example, create more costs for protest participants. Hence, organizers can expect less people to turn up when they do not expressly commit to non-violence. Also, structural factors such as the economic dependency of citizens on the state are discussed as potential costs of would-be protesters. Lichbach (1995, p. 43) states, for example, that "the greater the economic pressure that can be brought to bear on dissidents, the greater their opportunity costs and, hence, the less their dissent". Another solution that deals with the lowering of the (relative) costs of collective action is "Increase risk taking". Increased risk taking is more likely among the wealthy, the independent, and the unsuccessful, for example, because they can easily pay the costs of collective action (e.g., middle-class citizens) or the opportunity costs of collective action are lower for them (e.g., free professionals cannot be fired, the poor have nothing to lose).

"Increase probability of winning" deals with individuals' estimates of the probability that a public good will be successfully produced in a situation of adversity. Here, Lichbach discusses the importance of appearances. For example, playing up one's strength in numbers or determination increases the probability would-be supporters attach to winning in the political struggle, and hence makes their participation in collective action more likely. Modern dissident movements make use of this insight when they spray stencils of their movement all over a nation's capital, so that they appear more numerous than they actually are (Bunce and Wolchik 2006, p. 60; Kandelaki 2006, p. 7). Other solutions that aim to influence the probability of winning for a group in a political struggle, or the estimates thereof by would-be participants, are "Increase resources" and "Improve productivity of tactics".

Lichbach's set of community solutions assumes a network of social relationships is in place. The more extensive, dense, enduring, exclusive, and mutually reinforcing the interactions of the members of such a community are, the more conducive their network is for collective action. Here, "extensive" refers to the number of different concerns people communicate about, "dense" means the frequency of their contact, "enduring" indicates the temporal aspect of these relationships, and "mutually reinforcing" refers to the overlapping nature of the relationships (Lichbach 1995, pp. 141–142). Through their interaction in a community, people have some information about each other and develop a common belief system. They can make their decision to contribute to a public good in light of the information they have about the likelihood that others contribute as well, and tap into sources of motivation to rally around a common cause other than immediate self-interest. Thus, communities are bedrocks of collective action. In a political struggle, "regimes and oppositions thus compete for the loyalty of preexisting social networks; they are, in essence, struggling over control of the social infrastructure of society" (Lichbach 1995, p. 154).

The first community solution that Lichbach discusses is "Overcome mutual ignorance". The overcoming of mutual ignorance refers to the development of common knowledge among the members of a group with regard to each other's perceived costs and benefits. Based on that common knowledge, a small number of first movers may be sufficient to create a bandwagon effect among individuals to act jointly for the realization of a common interest (Kuran 1991). Assuming that there is "safety in numbers," individual risk assessments may lead to a cascade of collective action. First movers that are less risk-averse or have a strong motivation to contribute to the collective good help more risk-averse persons cross over their participation threshold (Petersen 2001, pp. 22–24). Also, if first and later joiners are part of the same community, pioneers can acquire knowledge about the levels of risk aversion of other community members and thus have more confidence that others will join their efforts later on. They may thus be more likely to make the first steps. Such mutual expectations of individual contributions to collective action can be fostered by the existence of "focal points" (Schelling 1980, p. 57) for collective actions, i.e., signals as well as "natural" places and times for collective action (Lichbach 1995, p. 112). Commonly understood signals that can serve as cues for simultaneous collective action are, e.g., incidents of repression or dissident activities of public figures. Such events can also be consciously created by activists (Francisco 2010, pp. 17–18).

Critical mass theory further qualifies the expectation of bandwagoning in a community. According to critical mass theory, bandwagoning does not always result from common knowledge about participation thresholds in a community. Instead, it maintains that whether bandwagoning takes place depends on the nature of the public good the group seeks to produce. The interdependencies of individual contributions to collective action are discussed as "production functions" of a public good (Oliver et al. 1985; Oliver and Marwell 1988; Marwell et al. 1988; Oliver and Marwell 2001). Ideal-type production functions of public goods are either "accelerating" or "decelerating" (Marwell and Oliver 1993). In both cases, each additional contribution adds to the likelihood of the production of the public good. However, in the case of a decelerating production function, the size of the addition declines with every additional contribution made, whereas in the accelerating production function the size increases. An example for the former type of public good is the founding of an organization, or more generally all cases where a few people can provide a good for all. An example for the latter type of public good would be mass actions, such as strikes and boycotts, the effect of which increases with the number of participants (Marwell and Oliver 1993, p. 63). They conclude that a bandwagon effect is only likely to take place if the production function of the public good is rather of an accelerating nature (Oliver et al. 1985), as in the case of protests.

Through their repeated interactions, community members are believed to develop common beliefs and norms. Based on this premise, Lichbach discusses the second community solution, "Overcome pecuniary self-interest". Here, the solution to the collective action problem is based on other sources of motivation to contribute to a public good other than self-interest in the strict sense. This can be first a "process orientation" (Lichbach 1995, p. 121), where participation in collective action is itself the benefit contributors seek. Second, such alternative sources of motivation can be communal norms, like altruism or fairness. Third, social incentives can be motivating factors when communities, for example, bestow prestige on those who "sacrifice themselves" for the common good. Common to all three ways of solving the collective action problem that Lichbach discusses for the solution, "Overcome pecuniary self-interest," is that it seems unlikely that they can be meaningfully influenced by collective action entrepreneurs in a way other than by strengthening community ties and hoping for the best.

Contract solutions are based on social mechanisms that work under the condition that no community ties yet exist among potential contributors to a public good. They assume that individuals, as "free agents," may "devise their own rules, institutions, and processes to avoid free riding, shirking, and opportunistic behavior" (Lichbach 1994, p. 16). The tit-for-tat strategy (Axelrod 2006) represents such a "contract": People will contribute to a collective activity if their contribution is followed by the participation of specific others. They will stop doing so if their contribution is not met by contributions of others to the collective good. This assumes that contributors are engaged in repeated interactions, as is the case, for example, when a protest campaign is carried out. The idea of forging contracts can also be extended to mutual exchange agreements that involve goods other than contributions to the collective good in question.

Finally, hierarchy solutions assume that there are pre-existing organizations that facilitate collective action. Lichbach identifies five solutions that build on this premise. The first solution consists of the imposition, monitoring, and enforcement of agreements by such organizations (Lichbach 1995, pp. 210–244). They can monitor individual behavior, and punish non-participation (or reward participation) in collective activities. The solution to the collective action problem that Olson (2003) most prominently referred to in his writing—selective incentives—is based on this principle. Selective incentives are "'selective' so that those who do not join the organization working for the group's interest, or in other ways contribute to the attainment of the group's interest, can be treated differently from those who do" (Olson 2003, p. 51). However, organizations can use the basic mechanism of monitoring and sanctioning behavior to implement all market and contract solutions that were previously discussed. Second, organizations can mobilize members to engage in activities that increase the organization's resources ("Locate principles or patrons"), or its reach into society and the community to promote framings conducive to its cause ("Increase team competition among allies"), or form groups that can engage more efficiently in collective action ("Reorganize"). Thus, organizations and their leaders can plan collective actions, sustain communication networks, pool the necessary resources, and provide strategies and tactics (Lichbach 1995, p. 261). Put differently, such organizations are like storage places for solutions to the collective action problem. In social movement studies, the importance of organizations has been discussed in similar ways by proponents of the resource mobilization approach (McCarthy and Zald 1977).

Despite the language of tactics used by Lichbach, the solutions to the collective action problem he discusses do not lend themselves easily to the identification of activities that increase chances for successful collective action. To be sure, Lichbach formulates his solutions as instructions for action, e.g., "Use incomplete information" or "Increase risk taking" (Lichbach 1995). However, at second glance, what he explains under these headers is best described as social mechanisms for the emergence of collective action (Gross 2009, p. 364). Most of these social mechanisms cannot be directly employed as tactics by collective action entrepreneurs in a political struggle. Moreover, only some of the explanatory factors he enlists on the macro- and meso-level represent factors that can be influenced by actors in the framework of a strategy which is critically limited in time.

Because of Lichbach's decision to focus on social mechanisms, the same activities for the improvement of the availability of solutions to one's collective action problem may be scattered across a multitude of his solutions. The same activity that is described as increasing the likelihood that mobilization occurs may pop up in the description of several solutions. In turn, activities can be identified that trigger several mechanisms that increase the likelihood of collective action taking place. In the following paragraphs, such types of activities will be referred to as mobilization tactics.

The first mobilization tactic that can be derived from Lichbach's discussion of solutions is to communicate widely to potential supporters and opponents alike. Communication can include the benefits of the collective endeavor to various groups of people, the involvement of other people already contributing or planning to contribute to the public good and how to join them, and the political power of the group undertaking the endeavor. Solutions that can be triggered by disseminating such information broadly are "Use incomplete information," "Reorganize," "Overcome mutual ignorance," "Increase resources," and "Increase probability of winning". The number of solutions triggered shows how important public communication is for the success of collective action in a political struggle. This is widely recognized by actors themselves. Ruling elites and regime challengers engage in propaganda and counter-propaganda, and battle over communication networks to control the flow of information. An information war is always fought alongside a struggle for physical control.

First, spreading information about the public good sought by a collective actor and how different societal groups will profit from it increases the chances that people will perceive the group's collective endeavor as a solution to their perceived grievances. As Lichbach (1995, p. 200) puts it, "one of the tasks of entrepreneurship [for collective action] is to show how this is possible—that a single public good can actually provide different types of individual benefits". Successfully reaching out to the public in this way includes convincing potential contributors of the link between their personal grievances and the concrete political solutions set forth by collective action entrepreneurs, and the legitimacy and feasibility of the chosen strategies (Klandermans 1993, p. 386; Schock 2005, p. 13). Promoting specific interpretations of the social situation in general and the group's sought-after public good is, in Lichbach's (1995, pp. 86–96) words, "Using incomplete information".

When communicating publicly, collective action entrepreneurs can purposefully develop interpretations of the political struggle that facilitate the linking of personal grievances to the group's political goals. Then, they can redefine those goals in light of which additional groups of supporters could be gained by alterations. In Lichbach's (1995, p. 198) understanding, collective action entrepreneurs can "manufacture grievances to maximize their following," and thereby reshape the group seeking to produce the public good. This is referred to as "Shaping an efficacious group" under the solution "Reorganize" (Lichbach 1995, p. 197). The framing literature in social movement studies highlights a similar phenomenon when it discusses activities carried out by social movements to frame the social situation in ways that allow them to link their endeavor with personal grievances of potential adherents. The options for achieving such an alignment are referred to as "frame amplification," "frame extension," and "frame transformation" (Snow et al. 1986). Generally, a group thus communicates more inclusively by taking into consideration the grievances of a wider range of potential supporters. By increasing the pool of potential supporters, the likelihood increases that a collective action entrepreneur will find people willing to contribute to the public good.

Second, potential supporters' mutual expectation of joint contribution to the public good can be fostered through public communication in order to improve the "conversion rate" of potential supporters into actual supporters. Thus, adherents can overcome the trap of mutual distrust in the original Prisoner's Dilemma game. As Lichbach (1995, p. 112) writes: "Anything that increases the perception that others will protest is […] likely to bring about protest". As argued earlier, this can include mutually understood signals, places, and times. Along with the individuals themselves, the resources possessed by individuals are also mobilized. Resources are understood here as things that can be consumed: "principally time, money, and material goods" (Marwell and Oliver 1984, p. 15). Hence, communicating about the intentions of people to contribute to the public good, and providing concrete information on when and how they are able to contribute triggers the "Overcome mutual ignorance" and "Increase resources" solutions to the collective action problem (Lichbach 1995, pp. 111–120).

Third, establishing regular communication with a wide audience can contribute to building up mobilization capacity when it projects an image of the collective actor as politically powerful, and those opposing the production of its sought-after public good as weak. The more convincing this image is, the more likely it is that potential supporters will adjust their estimate of the chances that the public good will be produced, which is a major variable in the individual decision-making process (regarding whether to contribute to a collective undertaking). Portraying oneself as powerful and one's opponents as weak triggers the solution "Increase probability of winning" (Lichbach 1995, pp. 62–82).

Besides communicating to a wider audience, communicating inside one's network of contributors is also important. This is the second mobilization tactic that can be identified in Lichbach's discussion of solutions to the collective action problem. Generally, past contributors are more likely to contribute again than non-contributors are to start contributing. Nonetheless, potential "repeat contributors" must overcome their collective action problem every time they are called to action as well. When talking about the link between intra-network communication and mobilization, it is assumed that contributors are also recipients of the communication directed to larger audiences. It is further assumed that communication inside one's network is more personal and frequent. This form of communication can therefore pursue additional goals. To do this, different factors are important. Solutions that are triggered by engaging in intra-network communication are "Increase benefits," "Increase resources," "Increase the probability to make a difference," "Increase team competition between enemies," "Overcome pecuniary self-interest," and, in a more privileged way than public communication, "Overcome mutual ignorance".

First, intra-network communication can be used to "promote an ethos, a vision of the future, or a moral code" (Lichbach 1995, p. 37) and increase the perceived benefits of the public good's production ("Increase benefits"). Thus, "zealots" may emerge among active supporters who, as previously discussed, play important roles in the (re-)mobilization and organization building of groups. This will also increase the amount of time, money, and material goods that individuals on average are ready to contribute ("Increase resources"). Moreover, common values can be promoted that may provide other sources of motivation to contribute to a public good than pure self-interest, as previously discussed ("Overcome pecuniary self-interest," see page 53).

Second, intra-network communication may promote the group identity of contributors, that is, stress the importance of each individual contribution, and the intensity of the conflict with opponents. By stressing the importance of individual contributions, intra-network communication increases the sense of efficacy among followers, which, in turn, makes them less likely to free-ride ("Increase the probability to make a difference"). By rhetorically intensifying the conflict with opponents, fraternization with the enemy becomes less likely. Thus, intra-network communication promotes inter-group conflict which in turn promotes intra-group cooperation ("Increase team competition between enemies"). Third, intra-network communication can take place person-to-person, and convince, instead of merely inform, potential "repeat contributors" to join the collective action. It thus represents a privileged way of spreading information about intentions to contribute to a public good ("Overcome mutual ignorance").

A third mobilization tactic is to employ organizational structures. As discussed earlier (see page 54), organizations can be understood as storage places for solutions to the collective action problem. They provide mechanisms for implementing contract solutions, and accumulate resources to incentivize additional contributions to the public good. They may also foster communities of activists around them by providing the basis for repeat interactions between contributors. In short, as Lichbach (1995, p. 261) describes regarding the collective action of anti-regime activists, "To sustain participation, the movement needs organization to supply leadership, financing, ideology, communication, strategies, and tactics. In short, enduring dissident action requires dissident organization".

By virtue of their permanence, organizational structures can serve the production of a public good in two additional ways. They can serve as insurance providers to contributors ("Increase risk taking"), and employ organizational resources to subsidize individual contributions ("Lower costs"). First, by guaranteeing potential contributors that they will be supported by the organization in the event that their individual contributions lead to excessive personal costs, organizations help more risk-averse individuals cross over their participation threshold. Such guarantees can come in the form of actual insurance policies, such as when personal liability insurance is taken out for regular contributors, or consist of legal and logistical help if activists are persecuted by one's opponents. Second, organizational resources can be used to subsidize individual contributions. This can take the form of individual transfers of organizational resources to current contributors, as when trade unions hand out strike pay to those who man the picket lines. Subsidizing individual contributions with organizational resources can also mean that organizational resources, such as real estate or means of transport, are placed at the disposal of those who intend to contribute to the realization of group-specific interests. Thus, the individual costs to contribute are lower than they would be without the organizational resources, which in turn increases the likelihood that people will chose to participate in the production of a public good. As Lichbach (1995, p. 50) puts it, "Group resources […] qualify individual resources. As a dissident group's resources increase, a dissident's personal resources may have less of an impact on his or her participation in collective dissent".

By establishing permanent mobilization structures, a group gains the ability to purposefully shape its form through the requirements it sets for potential contributors. Here, two ideal types of group forms can be identified, which have far-reaching consequences for the mobilization capacity of an actor. First, groups can opt for an exclusive design by communicating their radicalism and implementing strict membership regulations. Second, groups can attempt to maximize their reach in society by doing the opposite—By communicating their moderation and applying low membership requirements. In the first case, groups will be small, therefore relatively easy to mobilize ("Increase the probability to make a difference"), and likely to implement demanding forms of collective action to offset their weakness in numbers. In the second case, groups will be larger, and therefore relatively hard to monitor and mobilize, and likely to organize in ways that allow a large group of people to contribute little in order to maximize their strength in numbers.

The fourth and final mobilization tactic that can be identified in Lichbach's discussion of solutions to the collective action problem is directly engaging those who oppose or do not yet support one's attempt at realizing one's group-specific interests. This tactic is similar to what is often referred to as the "action repertoire" of a movement: Outward-directed activities that are addressed to an opponent or a third party (Rucht 1990, p. 164). However, the term "action repertoire" makes it sound as if this is all that collective actors do in a political struggle. Yet, "a great deal of every movement's energy is not directly devoted to public actions" (Rucht 1990, p. 164). Hence, discussing direct engagements as one of four tactics of social movements to build up mobilization capacity is not only in line with the findings of collective action theory, but is likely to more adequately reflect the mix of activities of collective actors in political struggles, too.

Direct engagements include confrontative and cooperative, clandestine and public, non-violent and violent, as well as spontaneous and planned activities. Depending on the form of engagement chosen by the group, such activities can trigger one or several of the following solutions to the collective action problem: "Lower costs," "Increase resources," "Increase probability of winning," "Locate principles or patrons," "Reduce supply of public good," and "Increase team competition among allies".

Any form of direct engagement chosen by a collective actor will lay at an intersection of the definitional spaces of the four pairwise differentiations mentioned. However, with the help of these binary differentiations, the functions that different forms of direct engagements are said to have in building up mobilization capacity can be disentangled. For example, Amenta et al. (2010, p. 297) state that "protest for threat is characterized by withholding compliance with political and other institutions, whereas protest for persuasion is meant to influence politicians by winning over bystanders through large-scale demonstrations of support, such as peaceful marches". With the following analytical distinctions, we can translate this into a discussion of the consequences of the confrontative and the public aspect of non-violent direct engagements.

Confrontative activities increase the costs of collective action for one's opponent. Strikes, for example, directly hurt the budgets of employers, or—if public enterprises are hit—the state budget. Riots cause destruction of state and private property, mass demonstrations increase the costs of maintaining public order. For anti-government activists, on the other hand, state repression increases the organizational and personal costs of collective action. In addition, confrontative activities can also serve to increase one's resources, e.g., when guerilla groups raid police stations or protesters loot state deposits for food ("Increase resources").

Cooperative activities imply a wager. A group will provide some form of support to its opponent now in the hope that this will reduce the mobilization capacity of that group or its ability to produce the public good it desires in the long run. Well played, these moves can increase one's access to one's opponent's resources ("Locate principles and patrons") or fractionalize one's opponent's group ("Reduce supply of public good" and "Increase team competition among allies"). To achieve the former, opposition movements can, for example, seek patronage by the state to increase their resources and build organizational structures that will help them effect regime change in the future. Ruling elites, in turn, may make symbolic political concessions in order to give the impression that the supply of the public good anti-regime activists seek is increased. If the supply of a good is increased, demand is reduced. Less people will mobilize against a regime that gives the impression it can be reasoned with. Moreover, ruling elites may try to split an anti-government coalition by accommodating the demands of a more moderate faction of the opposition. By doing this, they increase "team competition among allies" and thus exacerbate the coordination problem of their opponents (Lichbach 1995, p. 203). The demands of opposition factions that ruling elites fulfill can be personal, through co-optation, or political, through reform. Opposition activists can use the same strategy to split ruling elites. When posing a credible mobilization threat to the government, their cooperation with moderate ruling elites can induce reformists to turn against hardliners.

Both confrontative and cooperative activities can be public or clandestine. As clandestine activities, thefts or secret pacts can serve to diminish the mobilization capacity of an opposing group or its ability to produce the public good it desires. Public confrontations always have a dual function. Attacks, protests, and strikes are, like thefts, directed against one's opponent, but in contrast to the latter they are also always a form of communication with the public (Rucht 2008). If opposition groups, for example, temporarily seize control of public space through protest, they signal to the public that support for the ruling elite is not universal and that the power of the state has limits. In very repressive regimes, these signals can lead to dramatic changes in the estimate of the probability that potential opposition activists attach to collective action achieving regime change ("Increase probability of winning") which, in turn, may decisively lower the participation threshold of potential contributors in collective action directed against the government.

Another important distinction between different forms of engagement with one's opponent is whether they are non-violent or violent. Non-violent engagements are less costly to participants than violent ones. Violent encounters carry, for example, a higher risk of personal injury and legal persecution. Choosing non-violent over violent activities lowers the costs for potential contributors. Therefore, "nonviolent collective action seems more likely to attract new participants than violent collective action, if for no reason other than the concerns of potential participants about their personal safety" (Ulfelder 2005, p. 317). Thus, "dissident groups are in the paradoxical position of being able to mobilize more legal (i.e., regime-accepted) than illegal (i.e., regime-denied) forms of participation. They can put together more collective participation than collective dissent, and more collective dissent than collective violence" (Lichbach 1995, p. 42).

If the chosen non-violent activities are confrontative and public, they create a dilemma for an opponent who is strong at playing the game of violence, but weak in numbers. For example, if authoritarian ruling elites do not react decidedly and effectively to non-violent public protests by employing the security apparatus, they will appear weak before the public, and more contributions to anti-government activities may ensue ("Increase probability of winning"). If they do use violence against non-violent protesters, the personal networks of participants will update the utility they attach to regime change ("Increase benefits") and, all else being equal, become more likely to join the ranks of anti-government activists. The effects of a violent reaction to non-violent protest may cause even further reaching ripples. As Sharp (2003, pp. 32–33) maintains, "The stark brutality of the regime against the clearly nonviolent actionists politically rebounds against the dictators' position, causing dissention in their own ranks as well as fomenting support for the resisters among the general population, the regime's usual supporters, and third parties". However, such broad positive effects of the violent suppression of non-violent activities for one's mobilization capacity depend on the availability of information on the non-violence of one's protest and the violence of the opponent's reaction to the general population. As Rucht (1990, p. 160) explains, "Civil disobedience can only flourish when there is a large public which is not a priori partisan to the conflict and whose opinions cannot be directly controlled or easily manipulated by power-holders. Obviously, the presence of modern mass media enhances the efficacy of civil disobedience". Hence, the oft-discussed benefits of non-violent activism in causing large-scale mobilization by creating public outrage over the perceived injustice of violent repression by ruling elites depend, at least partially, on the availability of independent means of mass communication.

Violent activities, on the other hand, present—ceteris paribus—a higher direct threat to one's opponent. They cause more organizational and personal costs to one's adversaries than non-violent activities ("Lower costs"). Also, violent activities send a clear message to the state and the public alike. As Gurr (1974, p. 212) explains, "A common indirect use of violence is to demonstrate symbolically the demands of those who use it and their capacity to disrupt society if their demands are not satisfied". Violent activities affect the estimated probability of winning for ruling elites and the public alike ("Increase probability of winning"). Moreover, violence may improve one's bargaining position in a political struggle. By demonstrating one's determination (or "irrationality"), one may increase one's mobilization capacity as perceived by one's opponent's side and thereby gain more concessions than otherwise possible (Lichbach 1995, p. 58).

A final characteristic of direct engagements that has consequences with regard to one's mobilization capacity is whether collective activities are planned or (appear to the potential contributors as) spontaneous. In a political struggle with authoritarian ruling elites, public gatherings in the wake of government crackdowns or street riots in reaction to food shortages may be perceived less risky to participate in than otherwise comparable, but planned activities ("Lower costs"). This is because announced public acts of protest, whether legal or not, give the government time to prepare, and make it more likely that police surveillance will be comprehensive and state repression effective. Planned activities have the obvious advantage that an organizing group can inform more potential contributors and put risk-mitigating measures in place.

This account shows that depending on whether they are confrontative or cooperative, public or clandestine, violent or non-violent, spontaneous or planned, engagements with one's opponent can trigger different solutions to one's collective action problem and thus help to build up one's mobilization capacity and threat. In part, their effect depends on structural conditions, such as the repressiveness of the political regime. In other words, in a given environment, certain types of direct engagements will represent a consistently inferior choice for a given collective actor. At the same time, environmental factors do not limit choice in the sense that one form of engagement would emerge as the single best type of activity with which to engage one's opponent. Instead, most forms of engagement appear complimentary.

Violent activities, for example, may provide the background for non-violent forms of engagement to be successful. This is sometimes called the radical flank effect. Such an effect occurs when "the leverage of moderates is strengthened by the presence of a so-called radical wing that has more extreme goals and incorporates violent strategies. The presence of a radical wing makes moderate strategies and demands appear more reasonable, and radicals may create crises that are resolved to the moderates' advantage" (Schock 2005, p. 47). Lichbach (1995, p. 57) maintains that this effect may be especially important for a group which does not have access to conventional political channels, since "its viewpoint will be dismissed unless it can somehow signal its strength" through violent activities. Schock (2005, p. 47) warns that a "negative" radical flank effect could also occur "when the activities of a radical wing undermine the leverage of moderates" by "discredit[ing] the entire movement's activities and goals and threaten[ing] the ability of moderates to invoke third-party support". In a similar vein, Sharp (2003, p. 32) argues that

> even limited resistance violence during a political defiance campaign will be counterproductive, for it will shift the struggle to one in which the dictators have an overwhelming advantage (military warfare). Nonviolent discipline is a key to success and must be maintained despite provocations and brutalities by the dictators and their agents.

However, for such a negative radical flank effect to occur, the organizers of both violent and non-violent activities must be identified by both opponents and bystanders as one collective actor. If this is not the case, a negative radical flank effect cannot occur, but a positive radical flank effect can.

In sum, we have identified four mobilization tactics: Intra-network communication, public communication, organization building, and direct engagements. All trigger several solutions to the collective action problem. The summative availability of solutions can be understood as the mobilization capacity of a collective actor. The more a collective actor is able to trigger solutions to the collective action problem, the more likely it is that some of them will succeed in mobilizing adherents. A group that employs any of the mobilization tactics improves their mobilization capacity, or the likelihood that individuals contribute to its cause in the struggle with those opposing the production of the public good it desires.

The four mobilization tactics can be classified along two dimensions, complexity of required coordination and orientation of the action (see Table 3.1). Communication tactics, i.e., intra-network and public communication, can be differentiated from joint action tactics, i.e., organization building and direct engagements, in terms of the first dimension. The former only require loose coordination of contributions,

Table 3.1 Four mobilization tactics

Coordination	Inward-oriented	Outward-oriented
Loose	Intra-network communication	Public communication
Close	Organization building	Direct engagement

e.g., pamphlets are written by some persons and distributed by others. Organization building and direct engagements, on the other hand, typically require a close coordination: Contributors must be in the same place at the same time.

Intra-network communication and organization building can be differentiated from public communication and direct engagement according to the second dimension, orientation of action. Intra-network communication and organization are inward-oriented. Both represent work for and with those who have already proven that they are disposed to contribute to the realization of group-specific interests. On the other hand, public communication and direct engagements are outward-oriented. They imply the addressing of those who have not (yet) contributed to the group. These include bystanders and opponents.

Employing a mobilization tactic is in itself a public good. Engaging in public- and intra-network communication, or organization building and direct engagements requires a group to overcome its collective action problem. The classification of tactics along these two dimensions allows the relative complexity of their employment to be assessed. First, tactics that require loose coordination pose a collective action problem that is easier to overcome than tactics that require close coordination. Second, engaging in outward-oriented activities comes with higher individual costs than engaging in inward-oriented activities. For example, those that communicate publicly in the name of a group risk persecution and those that participate in direct engagements often face violent repression. As intra-network communication only requires loose coordination and is inward-oriented, it poses the least complicated collective action problem to overcome. In contrast, direct engagements with one's opponents is a mobilization tactic that requires a particularly well developed mobilization capacity.

In addition to the complexity of the collective action problem they pose to collective actors, the use of a tactic also requires certain environmental conditions. The employment and success of intra-network communication is aided when a community fosters adherents' repeat interaction and jointly held beliefs. Engaging in public communication requires access to means of mass communication, such as newspapers, radio, television, or the internet. This access is often tightly regulated by authoritarian ruling elites. For example, between 1989 and 2012 in electoral authoritarian regimes in Sub-Saharan Africa, Freedom House judged press freedom as "unfree" in 60.6% of the cases in the year before national multi-party elections. In all other cases, press freedom was assessed as "partly free". Group-owned alternative means of public communication, such as independent local radio stations or the distribution of leaflets, are less likely to be subject to censorship, but might have a comparatively limited reach.

Organization building comprises both the foundation of new organizational structures and the repurposing of existing organizations. The foundation of organizational structures entails large initial costs, such as the setup of rules and regulations and the acquisition of organizational assets. Therefore, engaging in this tactic exacerbates the "who moves first" problem of collective action. Also, the creation of a substantial bandwagon effect is unlikely during an organization's start-up phase, since this phase underlies a decelerating production function (Marwell and Oliver 1993). The foundation of organizational structures is greatly facilitated by the presence of highly-committed or resource-rich individuals or organizations. Highly-committed "zealots" are more easily located the stronger a community of activists is in terms of interactions and shared world views (Lichbach 1995, p. 22). To locate resource-rich "patrons" for the group, access to, e.g., the international community or domestic politico-economic elites is necessary.

However, establishing organizational structures for the production of a public good does not necessarily mean that collective action entrepreneurs have to purposefully build those structures. Organizations can be repurposed. For example, associations that served the narrow interests of their members can be used by the organization's leadership to pursue broader public goods, such as political change. This process is described by Hechter (1988, p. 123):

> In the first stage, individuals form groups to obtain joint private goods, like credit and insurance, but to do so they must also establish formal controls, which constitute a collective good. Once these controls are in place, a second stage becomes possible. The group's resources, now protected by the existence of formal controls, can be diverted […] to the production of further collective, or even public goods.

The organizational leadership thereby gains the discretion to pursue political goals and can enter negotiations with other societal actors.

This mobilization tactic can be utilized by ruling elites as well as oppositional political elites and societal groups. An abundance of historical examples of previously apolitical societal groups becoming spring-boards for anti-regime mobilizations exist, such as the national bar association in Zambia (Gould 2006), football hooligans in Milošević's Yugoslavia (Zelimir et al. 2015, p. 81), or Hip-Hop groups in Senegal (Gueye 2013). Cooperation among oppositional and societal groups for joint production of a public good is also possible, although it often requires complicated multi-level negotiations about the distribution of future benefits, since selective incentives are relatively scarce for such groups. On the other hand, ruling elites repurpose organizational structures to provide support for their claim to power. The state represents a formidable organizational structure for, e.g., the imposition and monitoring of contractual agreements, and the provision of selective incentives in their favor. By undermining the partisan neutrality of the state, ruling elites use their influence over formal state structures to nurture personal power networks. In Sub-Saharan Africa, this phenomenon is often referred to as "neo-patrimonialism" (Erdmann and Engel 2007), and can include rent extraction from businesses through taxes and regulations. In addition to this, ruling elites regularly use their administrative power to bring societal organizations with independent mobilization capacity under their control. The relations of ruling elites with trade unions in Zambia under Frederick Chiluba, the first president after the end of UNIP's one-party regime, provide a clear example of this. A former presidential aide explained the situation in an interview with the author:

> Chiluba was a president of the Zambia Congress of Trade Unions for 17 years before he became president. [You] wouldn't have wanted another person that uses the same ladder. To challenge him. [...] And consequently, he weakened it by ensuring that the person who succeeded him was one who was a stooge to him. [...] You find yourself to be tempering with the institutions that have existed even before you came to office. You buy their loyalty. And through buying their loyalty you weaken them (personal interview, 27 November 2012, Lusaka).

Still, rule of law and civil liberties set limits to the ambition of ruling elites in terms of repurposing existing state or civic organizational structures. Both of these aspects of a democratic governance system enhance the ability of oppositional elites and societal groups to engage in coalition building and improve their access to non-governmental organizational structures.

Direct engagement, as a consciously employed tactic of a group, requires organization. In principle, this can be provided by networks or communities, but hierarchical structures are better equipped to provide timely coordination. In addition, the ability to provide selective incentives as an organization allows more flexible distribution of tasks. In authoritarian regimes, the organizational requirements are especially high for non-violent, public forms of direct engagement, such as peaceful mass protest (Sharp 2003, p. 32). With repression, the individual costs of participation in public forms of direct engagement increase. As a result, mass participation in protests significantly increases if state repression is relatively low. If only zealots mobilize because repression and personal costs are high, violent protest is more likely. This likelihood further increases if mass means of communication are not accessible to the group. This in turn makes it unlikely that a protest could fulfill a public communication function and convince bystanders to contribute.

The relative complexity of the underlying collective action problem and the environmental conditions for their employment suggest a sequence for the employment of tactics by collective actors. In such a sequence, the first tactic employed can provide the structural preconditions necessary for the next, and so on. In a political struggle, this builds up a group's mobilization threat over time.

However, no empirical research in comparative politics starts with a political or societal vacuum. To the contrary, solutions to the collective action problem and preconditions for the employment of mobilization tactics are very specifically and unequally distributed among ruling elites, oppositional political elites, and societal groups. In addition, employing a mobilization tactic entails additional costs in terms of counter-activities by one's opponents. These must be taken into account. Only if we appreciate the implications of political and social conditions in electoral authoritarian regimes in Sub-Saharan Africa as they affect the mobilization capacity of principal actors in the democratization process can we understand why certain mobilization tactics are employed, and what the consequences of those tactics were. This step in the analysis of the role of collective action and political power in Sub-Saharan Africa will be provided in the next section.

3.4 Political Power of Collective Actors in Sub-Saharan Africa

In this section, the collective action perspective will be used to analyze the distribution of political power among ruling elites, oppositional political elites, and societal groups in electoral authoritarian regimes in Sub-Saharan Africa. Concepts of solutions to the collective action problem, mobilization tactics, mobilization capacity, and mobilization threat provide the theoretical angle from which previous research into the democratization processes of electoral authoritarianism can be evaluated and the dynamics of the political struggle better understood.

The overwhelming power of ruling elites in electoral authoritarian regimes in Sub-Saharan Africa is based on their ability to use institutional positions to increase their extra-institutional, neo-patrimonial mobilization capacity, while legitimacy is not a factor which meaningfully contributes to the stability of electoral authoritarian regimes. Neo-patrimonial authoritarian politics are extremely detrimental to the ability of opposition parties to develop constituency ties and organizational capacity. Given this, while societal groups themselves face mobilization problems because of repression, they nonetheless often represent the only alternative source of political power with national significance in electoral authoritarian regimes.

3.4.1 Ruling Elites and Political Power

Ruling elites make up the government and as such they are at the helm of state institutions. This position of leadership over vast organizational structures is the corner stone of their advantage over oppositional political elites and societal groups in mobilizing individuals in electoral authoritarian regimes. If democratic checks and balances were in place and the rule of law prevailed, the ruling elite's ability to use state leadership to foster their position of power would be severely limited. However, state institutions in electoral authoritarian regimes are continuously weakened in this regard. Personal power networks undermine the principles of legal-rational bureaucracy. This creates neo-patrimonial relationships between ruling elites and state employees that enable ruling elites to use their positions of leadership over state institutions to generate extra-institutional political power (Erdmann and Engel 2007).

In many electoral authoritarian regimes in Sub-Saharan Africa, ruling elites promoted state intervention in the economy as part of the buildup of a clientelistic system to support their claim to power. As Bratton and van de Walle (1997, p. 66) explain, "the fact that political authority rested on the selective allocation of state resources to individuals created a powerful incentive for extensive regulation of economic activity, through which the incumbent elite gained control over a wide range of monopolies and economic rents". This leads to a situation where not only is the state the "dominant economic agent," but "the success of businessmen in the private sector is highly dependent on the state because they need constantly to circumvent regulations to obtain official permits" (Bayart 1986, pp. 115–116).

The neo-patrimonial state is the institutional bedrock for the political survival of ruling elites. More precisely, "authoritarian regimes tend to hold huge advantages over their opponents in coercive and remunerative power because they command the state apparatus, with its army, police, and treasury" (Slater 2009, p. 208). The distinction between coercive and remunerative power goes back to Etzioni's (1975, p. 5) classic formulation, where coercive power "rests on the application, or the threat of application, of physical sanctions," whereas remunerative power "is based on control over material resources and rewards". In line with this distinction, the options ruling elites have to react to challenges to their authority are often discussed in literature on authoritarian regimes in terms of two types of countermeasures: "repression" and "concessions" (see, e.g., Goldstone and Tilly 2001). When authors ascribe far-sighted strategic thinking to elites' reactions to challengers, concessions are often interpreted as attempts at "co-optation": The exchange of some form of inclusion of the challenger for the establishment of some form of control over that challenger (Weipert-Fenner and Wolff 2015).

From a collective action perspective, the "raw" political power of carrot and stick, or co-optation and repression, finds its counterpart in solutions to the collective action problem that are made available to those controlling organizational structures. Through the army and the police, the state gives ruling elites the ability to monitor the behavior of adherents and opponents, and the possibility of raising the cost of collective activities for their opponents. Through rents and taxes, the state provides ruling elites with resources to distribute selective incentives among their supporters. Moreover, public office as well as preferential treatment—for example, privileged market access—can be used to "increase team competition among enemies" (Lichbach 1995, p. 102). In addition, regulation of the media through state institutions allows ruling elites to disseminate favorable information and suppress unfavorable information. The state thus provides the mobilizational capacity for elites to engage in public communication, build organizational structures, and mobilize for direct engagement with the public and their opponents.

Focusing on mobilization capacity as the central concept explaining ruling elites' power underlines the inherent gamble of using "co-optation" as a survival strategy. Whether it is changes in policy, legal recognition, or a public office, concessions have an immediate and substantial effect on the struggle over solutions to the collective action problem. They represent a shift of power to opponents in terms of relative mobilization capacities. For example, changes in policy increase the probability opponents attach to the success of government-critical action, and legal recognition and public office provide oppositional political elites with access to institutional structures and resources. However, the attempts of ruling elites to establish control over their opponents, whether directly by bringing selected opposition elites under their tutelage or indirectly by increasing intra-group conflict, is less immediate, both in terms of time and causality. It first requires that co-opted elites act in a ruling-elite friendly manner, as expected. Yet, co-opted opposition elites cannot themselves be the ultimate target of co-optation. For a co-optive measure to be successful, the supporters of co-opted elites must either continue to mobilize, this time in support of the regime, or at least demobilize, rather than, for example, throwing their weight behind other oppositional political elites.

To repression and co-optation, some scholars add a third "pillar" which is necessary for the survival of authoritarian regimes: Legitimacy, with legitimation as the corresponding activity of ruling elites (Kailitz and Tanneberg 2015). Legitimacy is treated as an additional source of power for authoritarian regimes, and a loss of legitimacy as an important reason for their downfall (Gerschewski 2013). Legitimation, the activity of rulers producing legitimacy, corresponds to Etzioni's (1975, p. 5) third type of power, normative power, which relies "on the allocation and manipulation of symbolic rewards and deprivations". Legitimation, understood as the application of normative power, has a theoretical anchor point in collective action theory (see discussion on intra-network communication on page 57). Legitimacy as a "pillar" on which the power of authoritarian ruling elites is imagined to rest does not. However, it does not take collective action theory to point out the elusiveness of legitimacy as a concept, both theoretically and in its measurement.

Theoretically, positing legitimacy as a "pillar" of the stability of authoritarian regimes is either prone to circular reasoning or untenable statements regarding the normativity of authoritarian rule. If legitimacy is defined as "acquiescence" of some sort, e.g., passive obedience, or toleration of the government by the population (Gerschewski 2013, p. 18), then legitimacy is control over agents. Yet, such control is not only the result of the application of normative power, but repressive and remunerative power as well (Etzioni 1975). Hence, legitimacy could not be a regime stabilizing factor in its own right. Among other factors, repression and concessions could be understood to produce it. Legitimacy would be a superfluous concept, and should, in the interest of parsimony, be dissolved into its component parts (Przeworski 1986).

The concept of legitimacy obtains an "irreducible essence" (Przeworski 1986, p. 51) only when its moral content is brought into play and taken seriously. From the perspective of an individual, legitimacy could then be defined as a motive for supporting the regime based on a "sense of righteousness" (Gerschewski 2013, p. 32), a belief in a "moral duty to obey" (Sharp 2003, p. 18), or some other purely normative reason, as collective action theory posits for tight-knit communities of activists (see discussion on page 53). Is it plausible, though, that electoral authoritarian governments rule over a population who by-and-large believes in the righteousness of their rule? If that were the case and given the strong international pressure on most countries that receive international aid to democratize, why would ruling elites then not conduct free and fair elections?

Even if, however, there were electoral authoritarian regimes to be found where a substantial share of the population believed in the righteousness of the authoritarian elites' claim to power, the collective action perspective would tell us to focus on more proximate reasons for regime stability and change. Outside free and fair elections, individuals who act in isolation do not shake the social order. Only organized political forces have the capacity to undermine a political system. Legitimacy does not by itself stabilize a regime "because the regime's supporters face Olson's Problem and need not come to the regime's defense" (Lichbach 1995, p. 259). For the same reason, not being legitimate is not a reason for a regime to collapse. As Olson (1990, p. 9) explains, "When there are no free elections and governments are able and willing to use force, political outcomes do not mainly depend on the hearts and minds of the people. Very often governments can be massively unpopular yet continue in power". In highly repressive settings, where the state is controlled by ruling elites, the collective action problem that proponents of democratic form have to overcome in order to pose a credible threat to ruling elites is enormous (Slater 2009, p. 215). In social movement studies, this observation has led to the well-known dictum "grievances are everywhere, movements [are] not" (Japp 1984, p. 316), which leads Przeworski (1991, p. 28) to state regarding authoritarian regimes "This is why 'legitimacy' understood in individual terms […] has little bearing on the issue of regime stability".

Irrespective of this, we would expect rational actors to verbalize acquiescence as belief in the legitimacy of a political regime, especially if the regime is authoritarian in nature (Kuran 1991). Citizens engage in such public "preference falsification" as a personal survival strategy and because it is advantageous to be seen on the winning side in political struggles (Lichbach 1995, p. 65). And they must not even be aware of this duplicity. As Coleman (2000, p. 498) explains, "The vesting of the right to control depends in part on the existence of control. If an actor holds effective power over others, the right to exercise that power is often forthcoming from them; if an actor is not able to exercise power, the right to do so is often withdrawn". If this is the case, then views and expressions of legitimacy would be merely a sign of acquiescence, of the acceptance of the inevitable, which we would expect individuals to hold only as long as the political regime appears as inevitable.

3.4.2 Oppositional Political Elites and Political Power

After 20 years of multi-party democracy in Sub-Saharan Africa, Rakner and van de Walle (2009, p. 109) stated that "the regularization of elections since 1989 has not in itself served to strengthen legislative oppositions, and the continuing weakness of opposition parties presents a serious and complex problem". Aspects of the nature of electoral authoritarianism foster the opposition's endemic weakness in mobilizing support. In Sub-Saharan Africa, these aspects are a lack of public discourse around substantial political issues, the personalistic character of opposition parties, and the reduced organizational capacity of these parties. This translates into very limited opportunities for oppositional political elites to engage in public and intra-network communication, build organizational structures, or mobilize for direct engagement with ruling elites and potential constituencies.

In electoral authoritarian regimes in Sub-Saharan Africa, opposition parties have little opportunity to tap into public discourse. First, ruling elites in electoral authoritarian regimes engage in patrimonial power politics. This leads to very personalistic rule where "institutions such as the ruling party, the electoral commission, the district governors, legislatures, and even formal opposition figures are heavily influenced or even governed by the president" (Uddhammar et al. 2011, p. 1059). The same could be said about ministers and their ministries, or local governors and their municipal administrations. This personalistic leadership style hinders decision-making in line with a political program. Instead, it turns all substantial political discussion into a discussion about loyalty. For these reasons, contemporary electoral politics in many authoritarian regimes in Sub-Saharan Africa lack discussion on substantive issues (Bleck and van de Walle 2011, p. 1126). Because of this lack of political discourse, "a key question in unstable or emerging democracies […] is what the opposition is opposed to" (Uddhammar et al. 2011, p. 1059), other than the personal leadership of the incumbents. Second, authoritarian politics is marked by repression, and repression leads to preference falsification. Hence, an open discussion about political preferences, whether in terms of parties or policies, is hardly possible. Under these conditions, it requires extraordinary political skill to organize "collective projects for an alternative future" (Przeworski 1992, p. 107).

For both of these reasons, opposition parties in electoral authoritarian regimes across Sub-Saharan Africa often "lack distinct constituencies of support, making it difficult for them to draw on reputational attachments to specific issues" (Bleck and van de Walle 2011, p. 1126). They cannot benefit from pre-existing framings of political issues in the public sphere in their attempt to mobilize citizens, and are hindered from engaging in creating and promoting such framings through public communication. In such a political environment void of substantial political issues, the electoral appeal of opposition parties is almost necessarily a narrow, personalistic one, leaving it to followers to guess what policy decisions their candidate would make once in power. This neither means that party names and occasionally programs of opposition parties would refrain from proclaiming grand political projects such as "development" or "democracy," nor that local oppositional groupings would not seek membership in ideologically matured international parties. But political claims remain lofty and ideological leanings flexible. What these parties rarely do is position themselves in ongoing reform projects with concrete political proposals. Political support by citizens is therefore often based on the expectation to benefit personally rather than through changes in the legal and institutional framework. However, for opposition politicians, the spoils of office are largely an uncertain thing in the distant future. One way to deal with this situation is for opposition politicians to appeal to kinship, tribe, or other such traditional institutions to create trust in their intention to deliver personal benefits to their followers. Even then, however, opposition parties are necessarily worse at the neo-patrimonial power game than those who already have state resources at their disposal with which to reward followers.

The personalistic nature of opposition parties is also one of the main reasons why popular dissatisfaction with the regime does not necessarily translate into support for the opposition. As political projects of individual collective action entrepreneurs, many opposition parties aim to facilitate the co-optation of their leadership by the ruling elite. In fact, the longer followers wait for selective incentives to materialize, the more pressure there is to get co-opted. As Eisenstadt (Eisenstadt 2000, p. 10) explains, "The scarcity of rewards available to opposition parties/movements in protracted transitions from authoritarianism force these regime opponents into the orbit of the authoritarian incumbents". For the same reason, it is complicated for opposition parties to cooperate with each other to bring down an authoritarian government.

Distrust in the public-mindedness of opposition leaders and personal bickering among oppositional splinter groups often prevents those disenchanted with the ruling elite from switching their support to the opposition (Bunce and Wolchik 2011, p. 96). Rather than having an advantage in normative or symbolic power, as, for example, Slater (2009, p. 208) claims, and being able to forge "collective identities and framing of causes through appeals to unconventional and extra-institutional collective action" (Eisenstadt 2000, p. 10), community solutions to the collective action problem are also unlikely to be available to opposition parties. Given the dearth of programmatic electoral appeal and recognizable normative stances, opposition parties have the same narrow patrimonial electoral appeal to voters as ruling parties. Thus, the instrumental side of voting comes to the foreground to the detriment of opposition party support. As Bunce and Wolchik (2011, p. 6) put bluntly: "Why bother to vote for the opposition if it cannot win power?"

Besides the lack of substantial political discourse and the often narrow personalistic appeal of opposition parties, another reason for the opposition's lack of mobilization capacity is weak organizational structures and limited access to resources. In many electoral authoritarian regimes in Sub-Saharan Africa, this is a consequence of several factors: an amalgam of the political and the economic; the doctrine of nonpartisanship that most international donors adhere to in the design of their democracy support programs, which results in a lack of support for opposition parties; and the targeted repression faced by opposition parties.

Economic success in most electoral authoritarian regimes in Sub-Saharan Africa is highly dependent on good relations with the ruling elite. Opposition parties are therefore largely excluded from access to domestic resources, be it in the form of donations, or the economic activities of their members. Given the scarcity of resources available to oppositional elites domestically, international support would be even more important for the organizational survival of opposition parties in electoral authoritarian regimes. However, for (non-political) development aid, "the incumbent and central government is often the preferred partner" (Uddhammar et al. 2011, p. 1064). Political aid programs, on the other hand, are often explicitly non-partisan. Instead of providing funds to opposition groups or other organizations that engage in contentious politics, political aid programs typically focus on NGOs that provide civic education or election monitoring, facilitate constitutional development, or report on human rights violations (Dicklitch and Lwanga 2003; Hearn 1999).

At the same time, the weak organizations of opposition parties and their members are easy targets for state repression. Opposition parties are necessarily public organizations that have to register and provide information about their membership, for example, when signatures are needed for candidatures. As parties, however, they lack the protective international linkages that come along with donor relations. Only opposition leaders can expect the international community to intervene on their behalf. Yet, such exceptional diplomatic action is only triggered in exceptional circumstances, for example, during election campaigning.

For these three reasons, opposition parties in electoral authoritarian regimes in Sub-Saharan Africa can be expected to have weak organizational structures with little access to resources. With the domestic economy inaccessible, and international donors preferring less controversial partners, access to organizational resources is very limited. Their organizational structures, on the other hand, are frequent and easy targets of state repression. Opposition groups have limited opportunities to build on hierarchy solutions to the collective action problem. Instead of selective incentives, their members likely face strong disincentives to mobilize.

All of the above means that opposition parties in electoral authoritarian regimes are unlikely to build up a mobilization capacity that would amount to a credible mobilization threat, which in turn might propel democratic reforms that would give them the opportunities and means to build a voter base, on their own. Instead, opposition parties in electoral authoritarian regimes should be expected to be weak in terms of mobilization capacity and continue to be so if left to their own devices. For them, regularly organizing as participants in the dodgy political game of authoritarian elections is the main challenge. Getting enough signatures to register candidates, organizing political rallies, and mobilizing party representatives for the monitoring of the election process regularly exhausts their mobilization capacity. Outside election times, the national headquarters of opposition parties often lay dormant; party organizations on the local level that could continue the organizational work are often non-existent (Erdmann 1999, p. 379). If, however, opposition parties gain an "electoral foothold" (Donno 2011, p. 28) by winning votes and seats in direct national multi-party elections, they are able to employ state structures and resources to strengthen their own mobilization capacity, and provide checks and balances in key committees and commissions to counter the influence of ruling elites over the public sphere and the electoral process.

3.4.3 Societal Groups and Political Power

The collective action approach significantly broadens the conceptualization of the role of civil society in democratization processes. First, this perspective does not focus on non-governmental organizations, trade unions, and other elitist civil society organizations in Sub-Saharan Africa. Instead, it includes the urban underclass and other non-formalized actors with their mostly spontaneous public mobilizations that have always played an important role in protest movements on the subcontinent (Branch and Mampilly 2015). Second, it does not limit the roles of organized and non-formal societal groups in democratization processes to their constructive, "civil" aspects, such as development work, sensitization, get-out-the-vote-campaigns, or election monitoring. While the collective action approach affirms the importance of such work in building mobilization capacity, it compels us to take into account mobilization power and threat as important aspects of the role of societal groups in the democratization process as well. In this section, the relationships of the terms "civil society" and "societal groups" will be discussed, as well as the role of organized and non-formal societal groups in the democratization processes of electoral authoritarian regimes in Sub-Saharan Africa in light of their capacity for collective action.

"Societal groups" refers to all those groups in society that manage to organize collectively in the pursuit of their group-specific interests, without attempting to hold public office themselves. These groups are "societal" in that they populate the realm between the family and the state. They can be short-lived or long-term, for-profit or non-profit, legally recognized by the state or not.

The entirety of these groups is not equivalent to what is most often understood by "civil society," but the two terms are intimately linked. In the literature on civil society, three different types of definitions along two definitional dimensions can be distinguished: Whether or not civil society is understood as a normative concept, and whether "society" refers to society as a whole (with "civil" expressing a quality of it), or only to a sub-system of it (Rucht 2009, p. 80). The two dimensions result in three, not four types of civil society definitions, because if a civil society concept referred to society as a whole and had no normative content, it would be just another word for "society".

Most common in the political sciences are civil society concepts that refer to a sub-system of society, which adheres to "civil" norms. Sometimes the normative content of these definitions is very explicit, as in Schmitter's (1997, p. 240) definition:

> Civil society can be defined as a set or system of self-organized intermediary groups that: (1) are relatively independent of both public authorities and private units of production and reproduction, that is, of firms and families; (2) are capable of deliberating about and taking collective actions in defense or promotion of their interests or passions; (3) do not seek to replace either state agents or private (re)producers or to accept responsibility for governing the polity as a whole; and (4) agree to act within pre-established rules of a "civil" nature, that is, conveying mutual respect.

Often, however, the normative content comes in a more hidden form. Linz and Stepan's (1996, p. 7) definition of civil society may serve as an example. They define civil society as the "arena of the polity where self-organizing groups, movements, and individuals, relatively autonomous from the state, attempt to articulate values, create associations and solidarities, and advance their interests" (Linz and Stepan 1996, p. 7). Only in the examples of civil society groups they give do the types of values they believe civil society to ordinarily express become clear. They name women's movements, trade unions, societal groups in opposition to authoritarian regimes, and groups in Eastern Europe that "served as vehicles for asserting the autonomy of those who wanted to act 'as if they were free'" (Linz and Stepan 1996, p. 7).

The normative content of these conventional definitions of civil society, hidden or not, has often been criticized, especially in transition studies. Such critical voices seek a value-neutral, spatial definition of civil society instead. As Diamond (1999, p. 227) explains, "If civil society is to be a theoretically useful construct for studying democratic development, it is important to avoid the tautology that equates it with everything that is democratic, noble, decent, and good". Thus, the definition should include an association that is "independent from the state, voluntary, self-generating, and respectful of the law and still […] undemocratic, paternalistic, and particularistic in its internal structure and norms," as well as "distrustful, unreliable, domineering, exploitative, and cynical in its dealings with other organizations, the state, and society" (Diamond 1999, p. 227).

Some argue that the normative content of conventional civil society definitions is not only logically problematic, but also tailored to the Western context to such an extent that it is not useful in comparative political research. For example, for the African context Kasfir (1998, p. 127) notes that "It is striking how little of African politics this concept of civil society captures. Much associational life and all unorganized protest or demands must occur outside civil society". Ethnic groups are excluded from standard normative definitions of civil society because they do not represent free associations of citizens. Many religious groups in Africa are excluded because they do not respect the religious rights of others. Movements of urban youth are excluded because they do not reject violence. Also, the African experience underlines the "importance of understanding civil society not simply as the arena of formal organizations" (von Lieres 2014, pp. 60–61). Instead, in Sub-Saharan Africa, "civil society's capacity to hold states accountable is shaped significantly by informal citizen action from below" (von Lieres 2014, p. 61). Boundaries between riots and organized demonstrations are fluid, and often, the success of coordinated protest movements in Sub-Saharan Africa builds on the leaderless mobilizations of the urban underclass (Branch and Mampilly 2015).

On the other hand, a value-free definition of civil society that would include all societal groups at all times runs the risk of calling a civil society vibrant that, for example, largely consists of exclusive religious sects and reclusive rural communes, or rebel groups and urban gangs. A potential way out of this definitional quagmire is to define civil society not as a realm, but as a way to engage with each other. This means that individual or collective actors do not belong to civil society regardless of what they do. Instead, they belong to civil society as long as they do "civil society things". This would, e.g., exclude an ethnic group from civil society some of the time, but not all the time, depending on the types of activities it engages in. A democratically organized reclusive commune could be excluded from this definition of civil society all the time.

Now, what are the things groups in civil society do? One answer would be to refer to a set of civil norms, and base belonging to civil society on the condition that actors act in accordance with these norms. This, however, would create a tautology with regard to the role of civil society organizations in democratization processes, similar to the one criticized above. Moreover, the problem with such a normative definition of "civil action" is that most activities of individual or collective societal actors may express one or several civil norms at a time, but rarely all of them at once. Many civil norms can be in conflict with each other when, for example, a societal minority group devises a strategy that involves violence to achieve equal rights in a highly repressive environment. What would be the threshold for the definition of an activity as "civil" and how would we account for tensions between opportunity structures and political goals?

Another answer for what type of activity is "civil" is buried in Hyden's (1997, p. 5) understanding of civil society. He writes that "civil society is more than just society. It is that part of society that connects individual citizens with the public realm and the state. Put in other words, civil society is the political side of society" (Hyden 1997, p. 5). This suggests an action-oriented definition of civil society in reference to the political character of the actions of societal actors. Every time citizens address the public and the state to realize their group-specific interests, they are part of civil society. They are part of it whether or not they do this violently, or in rejection of the rights of others.

This definition of civil society comes closest to the role of societal groups in democratization processes as it is understood in the context of the present study. When the role of societal groups in the democratization process will be discussed, the discussion will refer to the power they project in this process through activities which aim to influence society and the state. The only normative content one could read into this conception of societal groups is a sort of self-limitation in that they do not devise activities to hold public office themselves. If they did, their representatives would be part of the (oppositional) political elite. This broad definition of societal groups and their actions makes the actors that populate civil society in the sub-system conceptions of the term by and large a subset of the actors that the present study is concerned with. The only exception to this subset relation are civil society groups that do not engage in activities which aim to influence society and the state. Hence, when political scientists talk about the role of civil society in democratization processes, their theoretical assumptions and empirical findings should apply to a large part of societal groups and their activities as well.

The importance of civil society for the functioning of mature liberal democracies has been widely acknowledged. Merkel (2004, pp. 45–47), for example, names four main functions of civil society for a democratic system. First, as part of civil society, citizens organize collectively to protect themselves from arbitrary state rule. This is civil society's "protection function". Second, civil society organizations help the state to enforce the law while in exchange limiting state power. This is the mediation function of civil society. Third, societal groups are "schools of democracy" where citizens learn civic skills and democratic values. This is civil society's socialization function. Fourth, collectively organized citizens constitute the public sphere where they voice common interests that are fed into the political arena. With this, civil society fulfills its communication function. In fulfilling these functions, civil society acts at times autonomously and in opposition to and at times in collaboration with and in support of a democratic government.

This description of the role of societal groups in a liberal democracy envisages a civil society that not only has strong ties to communities, highly developed organizational structures, access to means of mass communication, and resource-rich patrons, it also presupposes a willingness of societal groups to put aside self-interest and engage in cooperation with each other when it seems necessary for the greater good. While such mobilization capacity and pervasiveness of cooperative norms among societal organizations seems a daunting task to achieve in a democratic setting, in the much more precarious situation of civil society in democratization processes they are especially unlikely to prevail.

At the time of the re-emergence of multi-party politics in Sub-Saharan Africa in the early 1990s, the situation of civil society on the subcontinent was bleak, as Bratton and van de Walle (1997, p. 72) explain, "As a result of state-directed repression and cooptation, civil society was generally weak and less developed in Africa than elsewhere in the developing world". In today's electoral authoritarian regimes in Sub-Saharan Africa, repression and the reliance on international donors contribute to the disengagement of many civil society organizations with national politics. Repression and reliance on external funding can also be seen as primary reasons for the lack of "rootedness" of civil society organizations, and especially development organizations, in many countries in Sub-Saharan Africa. Their connection with the constituencies they ostensibly represent is often wanting.

Repression forces leaders of societal groups to carefully weigh the costs and benefits of directly criticizing the government, whether through public communication or public direct engagements with ruling elites. The outcome of such a weighing of options is often a disengagement from politics. Such a disengagement from politics does not mean civil society organizations do not publicly voice their opinion on political issues at all. However, most organizations, even many human rights organizations, which due to their mission are arguably the most poised to criticize authoritarian state activity, carefully differentiate between those human rights topics that directly relate to the foundations of the ruling elite's political power, and other, less confrontational political issues. Engaging in the former is often labelled "partisan involvement" or simply "being political" by authoritarian ruling elites, which, it is understood, civil society should not engage in or be. As a representative of a national human rights network in Uganda explained to the author, such "political topics" are

> anything that belongs to governance, especially when it threatens the status quo. [...] Government does not want to hear you engage in really raising issues of corruption. [...] Issues of accountability, issues of the rule of law, issues of torture, issues of the security harassment of the people [...] those are some of the areas that the state does not want you to discuss. [On the other hand,] they say, okay, if you are able to talk about the rights of women, HIV/AIDS, water provision, service delivery—the government is very happy with that. But if you come and say, there is torture by security agencies, then you are becoming political" (personal interview, 12 March 2013, Kampala).

This means that civil society organizations have to maneuver carefully between the (partial) fulfillment of their mission to publicize governance deficits and raise human rights issues and "partisan politics".

Besides defining a no-go area for civil society organizations in terms of "political" topics, authoritarian ruling elites also use the accusation of "partisanship" or the "political" nature of civil society engagement to define periods in which criticism from civil society organizations in general, and public protests in particular, are unwelcome. This leads to a situation in many electoral authoritarian regimes in Sub-Saharan Africa where societal groups become the most silent around election times when their protests would arguably receive the most attention from political elites. As a representative of a Zambian community development organization explained to the author, when the time of elections approaches, "we have to be very careful when we go into work with communities. We do not want to be seen to be aligning to a particular party, ruling or not ruling" (personal interview, 21 November 2012, Zambia). A representative of the national human rights network in Uganda also explained that when elections are coming up all non-electoral activities are "put on hold" for fear of the organization being labeled partisan and, in consequence, becoming a target of state repression. As he explains, "the work continues but most of the organizations towards the last couple of months—there is a paralysis of their work" (personal interview, 12 March 2013, Kampala).

Repression also leads to a disconnection of civil society organizations from their constituencies. As discussed earlier, collective action other than that which is sanctioned by government is risky to ruling elites. To dominate in the struggle over solutions to the collective action problem, ruling elites have to establish control over public space. This means that even information campaigns on, e.g., constitutional amendments are sometimes deemed political gatherings and targeted by the security apparatus, and small protests are met with harsh repression. This leads to limited opportunities for civil society organizations to improve their ties with communities, especially in rural areas, where tight communal networks and a lack of closed meeting spaces mean that gatherings with the public almost always draw the attention of local officials.

Besides repression, a significant feature of civil society development in most electoral authoritarian regimes in Sub-Saharan Africa today is the strong role played by the international aid community, both in terms of the sheer volume of financial assistance provided by donors, especially when seen in the light of the weak economies of recipient countries, and in terms of its importance as a source of funding for domestic civil society organizations.

It is hard to put a number on this influence. Collaborations of civil society organizations in donor countries with civil society organizations in recipient countries represent an important share of international aid flows. These collaborations are based on private contracts, and are thus impossible to track by any one institution across countries. The figures on international aid provided by the Organisation for Economic Co-operation and Development (OECD), for example, exclude this type of aid flow. Nonetheless, in 2011, official development assistance (ODA) by OECD countries alone amounted to an unweighted average of 9.1% of the gross national income of countries in Sub-Saharan Africa, with numbers varying between 53.6% for Liberia and 0.2% for Angola. At the same time, an average of 14.4% of ODA disbursed globally by OECD member countries in this year was received by civil society organizations directly (OECD-DAC Secretariat 2013). In line with these numbers, in 2014, international donors were found to be the most important source of financial support for civil society organizations in all countries in Sub-Saharan Africa, with the exception of Angola (United States Agency for International Development 2015).

On the one hand, this foreign support makes local civil society an important force independent of ruling elites in the neo-patrimonial economy of authoritarian states in

Sub-Saharan Africa, and an employer favored by university graduates who are critical of the political regime. On the other hand, the international money comes with strings attached. Donors, whether bilateral or multilateral, public or private, have their own agendas. These agendas may align with or may be in conflict with the agendas of local civil society organizations. If they are in conflict, the international development market with its stiff competition among local providers of implementation capacity ensures that the donor's agenda prevails.

What is on the agendas of donors? When measured in terms of the volume of financial assistance, support for democratic governance figures rather low on most donors' development agendas. The United States Agency for International Development (USAID), for example, spent only 9% of the total aid it provided in 2003 on democratic governance assistance (Finkel et al. 2006, p. 26). A much larger share of development aid regularly goes into agricultural development, business development, education, or public health. The latter kind of development aid is welcomed by authoritarian rulers. It frees them of obligations to spend money on agricultural subsidies, public education, or health care. Where development aid takes over, the government typically retreats. This also means that local populations often depend on international assistance to secure their livelihoods, instead of on the state. This means that if international development organizations are forced to leave or forced to cease financial support to domestic service providers, local populations would suffer as a direct consequence.

In line with liberal ideology, donors commit to a "non-partisan" idea of civic engagement: Civil society is not to meddle with party politics. The development agenda depicted above helps explain why the donor mantra of "non-partisanship" often leads to exclusion (from donor support) of government-critical human rights work, which autocrats would define as undue "political involvement" of civil society organizations. Donors cannot risk being sent packing by authoritarian elites, lest they violate their obligations towards the local populations they support with, e.g. the service delivery programs they finance. As Dicklitch and Lwanga (2003, p. 507) explain,

> donors [...] fear annoying the government, so they choose not to fund overtly "political" or activist HROs [human rights organizations]. So, donors will fund activities like "civic education," election monitoring and constitutional development, but they will shy away from associating with NGOs or HROs which are deemed too critical of the regime or "too political".

It does therefore not require the assumption of a sinister conspiracy of public and private donor organizations around foreign national interests to understand why development aid can drive local activists away from pushing the government to fulfill its democratic obligations, rather than propelling democratization processes, even in the case of programs that explicitly aim at democracy-promotion.

The development of strong ties to local communities is also impeded by cooperation with the international aid community and in two ways. First, it promotes the professionalization of civil society organizations: Indirectly, through the knowledge and skills required to write successful funding applications, and directly, when international donor organizations provide capacity building to grantees. With this, a managerial stream-lining of organizations often takes place to the detriment of internal democracy and the involvement of constituencies. Tight deadlines favor hierarchical decisions over participatory processes in project implementation, and "development speak" impedes the participation of rank-and-file members in conversations about the design of programs. Financial regulations exclude non-formal economic activities and unregistered groups from receiving funding. Second, the development market requires flexibility regarding one's agenda, as trends in international development come and go, which means that organizations, rather than changing their goals in line with the needs of their constituencies, change the constituencies they serve in line with the funding opportunities they pursue. Moreover, the financial independence from local populations provided by international aid can be an additional stumbling block for civil society organizations in developing a genuine political agenda. As Jalali (2005, p. 6) explains, "By making constituency support irrelevant, internationalization through financial assistance has transformed conflict movements to consensus movements—a model that follows an institutional-resource-dependent, project based, non-conflictual strategy".

This means that on the one hand international cooperation sets limits for civil society organizations in mobilizing adherents, since the concerns of citizens do not necessarily inform the agenda of these organizations. On the other hand, international cooperation provides them with resources. As Lichbach (1995, p. 193) explains, patrons are a double-edged sword for societal groups:

> Dissidents reap decreasing marginal benefits and pay increasing marginal costs for external patronage. A little bit probably helps, a great deal probably hurts, so the tradeoffs between self-reliance and external support must be carefully weighed. A grass-roots strategy often begets a resource-poor dissident group, but one that is highly committed to the cause. A sugar-daddy strategy, by contrast, often begets a resource-rich dissident group, but the sponsors are often less committed to the dissidents' cause.

Whereas repression affects all types of civil society organizations in authoritarian regimes, development cooperation—with its positive and negative impacts—does not, simply because international donors concentrate their support on specific sectors of local civil societies. Member-driven organizations especially, such as trade unions or student unions, are usually excluded from international aid flows. National faith organizations, on the other hand, are supported in development work implemented by their specialized domestic agencies, but at the same time command a structure of local parishes that is organizationally independent from aid projects. However, since local development organizations are the most resource-rich societal groups in electoral authoritarian regimes in Sub-Saharan Africa, factors that affect them shape the capacity of civil society as a whole. Thus, the de-politicizing and de-rooting influences that stem from repression and international aid create a civil society in most non-democracies in Sub-Saharan Africa that can fulfill only some of the democratic functions discussed above, and only in limited ways.

First, donor-dependent civil society organizations are seldom participatory "schools of democracy". Internally, they are often hierarchically organized with ineffective channels of internal consultation with and control by the membership. As discussed, this is partly a result of donor criteria of professionalism, favoring organizations with no volunteer involvement and weak internal democratic structures that would otherwise complicate work relationships and make a partner organization less predictable in its behavior. However, such organizations still provide a professional environment in which employees can improve their leadership skills and make a name for themselves on the public stage. Moreover, local development professionals acquire subject knowledge on topics such as economics, education, or health care. Thus, these organizations can act as a reservoir of collective action entrepreneurs for the development of civil society. Opposition parties can profit from this, too. Many oppositional political elites in Sub-Saharan Africa have been or are intermittently working in international development. As Heilbrunn (1993, p. 277) notes, disaffected elites in authoritarian regimes often establish "independent bases of power in voluntary associations beyond the immediate reach of the state". A prominent example among many is the former leader of the Zimbabwean opposition party Movement for Democratic Change, Morgan Tsvangirai, who was the leader of the Zimbabwe Congress of Trade Unions for many years before joining the political opposition.

Second, the degree to which societal organizations in Sub-Saharan Africa can perform civil society's protection function is limited. Many of the human rights organizations on the subcontinent document human rights violations. Both repression and international aid, however, impede most organizations in building a large local following. Therefore, their ability to project a mobilization threat that could deter political elites from violating "the rules of the game" remains limited. When attempting to mobilize citizens for the protection of, e.g., constitutional rights, donor-dependent human rights organizations have to rely on more member-driven organizations, such as trade unions, that, in turn, often do not have the international linkage that would protect them from excessive repression. Only if these different types of organizations manage to work together, are they able to mount a credible mobilization threat to ruling elites. The Oasis Forum that successfully prevented the then Zambian president Frederick Chiluba from abolishing the constitutional two-turn limit for the presidency is a case in point. Only by combining the assets of such vastly different organizations as human rights organizations, the national bar association, and the churches could civil society create enough domestic and international clout to make Chiluba reconsider his plans to amend the constitution (Gould 2006, p. 933). As a governance advisor for a bilateral donor in Zambia told the author, "the church may have the masses but in terms of the technical brains the LAZ [Law Association of Zambia] holds it all. [...] They would be the ones to feed the churches with the kind of evidence that would make them stick or break in this kind of coalition" (personal interview, 14 November 2012, Lusaka).

Third, donor-dependent civil societies in repressive environments are limited in their ability to feed the grievances of local populations into the political process. On the one hand, this is because authoritarian political regimes often do not provide the channels for regular consultation with the public or its representatives. On the other hand, this is because civil society organizations themselves rarely have the internal structure or external relations to non-urban communities to capture and aggregate public opinion on a national scale. Member-driven organizations, such as trade unions and student unions, often have working internal democratic structures, but in Sub-Saharan Africa they are mostly concentrated in urban areas, with teachers' unions being a notable exception. Churches and other faith organizations, in turn, have a presence in rural areas, but rarely allow for democratic processes of opinion formation among their members.

However, even advocacy organizations without direct relations to their constituencies, through donor-sponsored research projects, are able to monitor the activities of the state and the ruling elites. Through so-called sensitization campaigns, they can disseminate information about government programs, political rights, and civil liberties to the public. Also, they thus promote "the gradual but increasing cultivation of a sense of ownership of the state by the non-elites which is required for changing the locus of accountability from external to internal constituents" (Osaghae 1999, p. 25).

Taken together, this gives them the ability to assess government performance, and develop alternative policy proposals that they can then publicly advocate for. Even without vocal constituencies, donor-dependent civil society organizations are able to fulfill a communication function in rural and urban spaces, albeit more as organizations that lobby both political elites and citizens than as "transmission belts" between citizens and political elites. By developing political platforms through their advocacy work, they provide oppositional political elites with an amplifier for their criticism of ruling elites if the political opposition takes up policy alternatives researched and developed by civil society organizations. As a representative of a Ugandan coalition of pro-democratic civil society organizations explained to the author, "the onus is on the civil society to generate popular issues that parties can draw on as campaign platforms. And that would take a bold civil society. A civil society that is not weary of associating with hardcore politics" (personal interview, 28 March 2013, Kampala).

The limitations in the ability of civil society in Sub-Saharan Africa to perform the above-mentioned functions point to the limitations societal groups face in overcoming the collective action problem and building up a credible mobilization threat. The professionalization of organizations contributes to a lack of ties to activist communities, while at the same time providing societal groups with the benefits of permanent mobilization structures. Constraints that civil society organizations face in the performance of their communication function are a product of their limited "rootedness" in local communities, which means that their ability to identify zealots and build a community of norms among a wider circle of activists are limited. At the same time, international donor cooperation gives civil society organizations the possibility to actively engage in reframing the grievances of citizens through programs and campaigns, in competition with ruling elites for hearts and minds. Thus, they are enabled to build mobilization capacity for situational activism, which does not require frequent interaction with adherents. Their restricted ability in fulfilling the protection function points to the limited following of established civil society organizations in Sub-Saharan Africa as well. As advocacy organizations with cursory relations to their constituencies, their capacities for action are often exhausted by monitoring the activities of ruling elites, and publishing violations of political rights and civil liberties to a wider audience.

With regard to the latter role in particular, the limited mobilization threat that civil society organizations in Sub-Saharan Africa often pose to ruling elites is brought to bear on their ability to influence the democratization process. Because only in rare circumstances can they raise the costs of their suppression so that they outweigh the costs of their toleration, their room for maneuvering is limited. This, in turn, directly impacts their ability to build up mobilization capacity, which limits the democratic functions they can perform. This represents a vicious circle that they can only escape if collective action entrepreneurs have the "fortuna" and "virtu" (O'Donnell and Schmitter 1986, pp. 4–5) to use their current mobilization capacity efficiently to engage in mobilization tactics that increase the mobilization threat of societal groups in the future.

Direct engagements are the most complex of the four mobilization tactics to employ. State repressiveness and donor-dependency create a civil society in Sub-Saharan Africa in which the commitment of adherents to a group's cause goes along with exposure to repression, and isolation from constituencies goes along with international protection. As we will later see, high-risk public protests are therefore rare in electoral authoritarian regimes in Sub-Saharan Africa, and among them, spontaneous demonstrations and riots play an important role. Nonetheless, whenever they take place, they renew the mobilization threat that societal groups pose to political elites, and thus provide the umbrella under which they can perform less antagonistic and more constructive roles in the democratization process.

3.5   Trajectories of Political Mobilizations in Sub-Saharan Africa

From a collective action perspective, the political power of ruling elites, oppositional political elites, and societal groups is synonymous with their ability to project a credible mobilization threat into the political arena. It was shown that this ability depends, in turn, on their mobilization capacity, or the sum total of solutions to the collective action problem that is available to them. An analysis of the political and social conditions in electoral authoritarian regimes in Sub-Saharan Africa demonstrated that such solutions are typically very unequally distributed among these collective actors. While ruling elites profit from their control over neo-patrimonial state structures and the economy in maintaining a formidable mobilization threat, this same situation creates a very unfavorable environment for oppositional political elites to develop their own mobilization capacity. The analysis concluded that despite the limitations of societal groups in fulfilling democratic functions, they represent the most important alternative source of political power in electoral authoritarian regimes in Sub-Saharan Africa. Through their collective actions, they can mount credible mobilization threats to ruling elites in electoral authoritarian regimes.

In the present section, an attempt will be made to trace the development of the mobilization threat of ruling elites, oppositional political elites, and societal groups in Sub-Saharan Africa across countries and over time. A mobilization threat is about the perception of the opponents of a collective actor regarding how likely it is that it will mobilize in order to safeguard its interests, and how large the pool of resources will be that it is able to mobilize. As discussed earlier, past public direct engagements of the collective actor with its opponents or neutral bystanders are likely to be the main source for opponents' estimates of its present mobilization threat. In addition to this, and relative to mobilization capacities indicated by previous public mobilizations, changes in the availability of solutions to the collective action problem for the group, such as changes in its ties to communities, organizational structures, access to means of mass communication, or relationships to resource-rich patrons, provide its opponents with clues with which to reassess their estimates of its mobilization threat. Moreover, a mobilization threat is a quantity relative to the opponents' perception of their own ability to (counter-)mobilize. Therefore, we cannot attempt to measure the mobilization threat posed by any one collective actor to its opponents in a political struggle without also considering the perceived abilities of these opponents to mobilize against that collective actor or each other.

In the following analysis, the public direct engagements of these actors with their opponents will be used as an indicator to trace the mobilization threat ruling elites, oppositional political elites, and societal groups pose to each other across countries and over time. Summarily, these types of direct engagements will be called "political mobilizations". It has been argued that a collective actor's engagement in public direct confrontations with its opponents is related to developments in its use of other mobilization tactics. This is because collective actors are expected to prepare for public direct engagements, which represent the most suppositional and the most consequential form of mobilization, with less resource-intensive and less risky activities as part of their overall strategy in a political struggle. A high frequency of public direct engagements can therefore be expected to correlate with the extent the collective actor has been able to build up mobilization capacity through mobilization tactics such as intra-network communication, organization building, and public communication. At the same time, public direct engagements are not equally strongly associated with all types of solutions to the collective action problem. Political mobilizations are most directly an expression of an actor's extra-institutional mobilization capacity. As actors draw their mobilization threat from a specific mix of solutions to the collective action problem, the construct validity of political mobilizations regarding their mobilization threat varies. Oppositional political elites and societal groups are collective actors who typically do not have control over vast organizational structures. Political mobilizations are therefore the basis for their involvement in the political struggle. In contrast, ruling elites may engage their opponents in every day acts of repression by exerting control over the security apparatus or the economy. Hence, while trajectories of political mobilizations may be employed to compare the mobilization threat of political challengers and societal groups over time and with each other, they represent a less adequate indicator for the threat ruling elites pose to their political and societal opposition.

Information on political mobilizations by ruling elites, oppositional political elites, and societal groups is taken from the Social Conflict in Africa Database

(Salehyan et al. 2012). The database follows a broad conception of "social conflict". It includes demonstrations, riots, strikes, and incidents of state-sponsored violence, as well as armed conflicts, mutinies, and coups. In total, ten different types of social conflicts are differentiated: Organized and spontaneous demonstrations, organized and spontaneous riots, general and limited strikes, pro-government violence, anti-government violence, extra-government violence, and intra-government violence. For each event, several pieces of information are provided. Among others, the database lists the actors involved in the conflict, the targets of the conflict, and the issues at stake in the conflict.

For the database, social conflict events were identified through keyword searches of international news wires. While this procedure does not capture "every conflict event on the continent" (Salehyan et al. 2012, p. 505), it "identifies the most politically significant conflict events; namely, large-scale events that draw many participants, significant acts of violence, and events that threaten political stability" (Salehyan et al. 2012, p. 506). The reliance on international news wires ensures "consistent reporting standards for all countries included" (Salehyan et al. 2012, p. 505), and with that provides the necessary basis for the comparability of the information contained in the database across countries. A social conflict event can be comprised of a series of actions if the issues, actors, and targets of these actions are the same. This means, for example, that work stoppages organized by one union in several factories count as one strike.

All demonstrations, riots, and strikes that did not express support of powerholders as one of the issues and targeted regional or central governments with their grievances were counted as public direct engagement of societal groups with ruling elites. Excluded from these social conflicts are those demonstrations, riots, and strikes in which opposition parties were listed among the actors. Among the public direct engagements of societal groups with ruling elites, "pro-democratic mobilizations" are differentiated from "socio-economic mobilizations". Demonstrations, riots, and strikes that addressed political and human rights were counted as pro-democratic mobilizations. This was determined based on the issues that were coded for the respective social conflict in the database. If "elections" or "human rights, democracy" were mentioned among the issues of the social conflict—while sufficing the other criteria for public direct engagements of societal groups with ruling elites—they were considered an instance of pro-democratic mobilization. All demonstrations, riots, and strikes that did not address political and human rights were counted as socio-economic mobilizations. Instead, such public direct engagements brought forward issues such as jobs and the economy, access to food and water, environmental degradation, ethnic or religious issues, education, or foreign affairs.

Similar to public direct engagements of societal groups with the ruling elite, the pre-electoral mobilizations of opposition parties were operationalized. All demonstrations, riots, and strikes that addressed regional or central governments with their grievances, did not express support of powerholders, and in which opposition parties were mentioned as a prominent actor were counted as oppositional mobilizations.

Furthermore, the database was used to operationalize public direct engagements of ruling elites with their opponents. These mobilizations comprise pro-government mobilizations of civilian supporters and proactive attacks of the security apparatus on government-critical individuals and organizations. All demonstrations, riots, and strikes which had "pro-government" among the issues coded for the respective social conflict were counted as mobilizations of civilian supporters of the ruling elite. Proactive attacks of the security apparatus were coded as a separate type of conflict in the database ("pro-government violence"). These were added to the count of pro-government mobilizations.

The Social Conflict in Africa Database also provides data on the repressive measures taken by the security apparatus in response to political mobilizations by societal groups and the political opposition. As discussed earlier, these direct counter-mobilizations provide a more accurate picture of the mobilization capacity of ruling elites over time. However, they cannot be used to compare the mobilization threat of ruling elites with that of their opponents because these repressive measures only enter the database as a corollary to political mobilizations by societal groups and oppositional political elites.

In Sub-Saharan Africa, political and societal opposition to modern authoritarian rule came to international attention primarily through three continent-wide waves of protest. The first of these washed across the subcontinent in the late colonial period and brought an end to colonial rule. The second took place between the end of the 1980s and beginning of the 1990s and is credited with the onset of democratic regime changes in Sub-Saharan Africa. The third one gained momentum around 2005 and culminated in the "Arab Spring" in 2011 (Branch and Mampilly 2015). Besides those moments of increased visibility and recognition, however, which trajectories did political mobilizations of oppositional political elites and societal groups follow? How did ruling elites react?

After the introduction of multi-party politics in most countries in Sub-Saharan Africa in the early 1990s, civil society is often thought to have considerably reduced its mobilization activities across the subcontinent. Two reasons for this are usually ventured. First, with pro-democracy movements winning power, collective action entrepreneurs were often drawn into official positions, thereby weakening the societal groups they were leading (Bratton and van de Walle 1997, p. 255). Second, having established feeble links to the masses during transitions in the spur of the revolutionary moment, many urban elites are said to have lost these ties quickly in the revolution's aftermath, when the mobilization of constituencies would have required regular information and consultation (Remi Aiyede 2003).

However, as Fig. 3.1 shows, despite such trends that may have exacerbated organizational weaknesses of civil society in the 1990s in Sub-Saharan Africa, the number of public direct engagements of societal groups with ruling elites on the subcontinent seems to have increased throughout that time. In 2000, it reached a first peak, only to surpass this level again in 2012. Moreover, national mobilizations on the subcontinent have also led to sustained movements and political consequences outside the heydays of the three protest waves. For example, during the 1990s and 2000s, broad-based civic movements stopped presidential third-term bids in Malawi and Zambia (Dulani 2011), while trade unions organized cross-sector strikes that emboldened opposition movements in Senegal (Bergen 2007) and Zimbabwe (Saunders 2007),

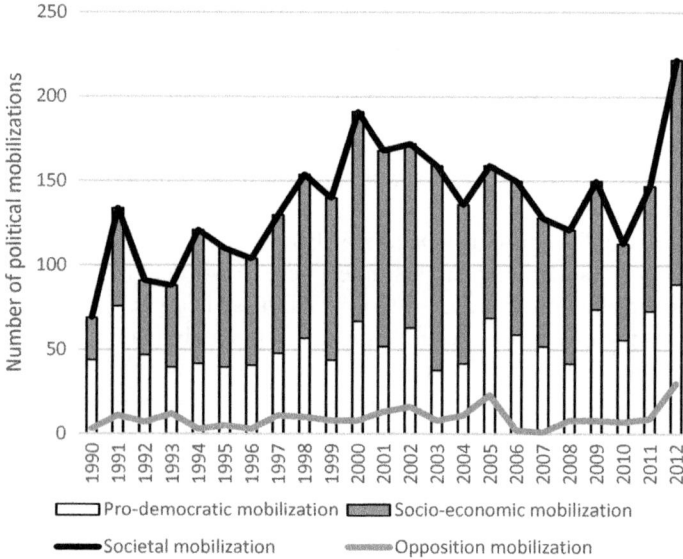

Fig. 3.1 Political mobilizations in Sub-Saharan Africa per year. *Notes* Numbers are absolute numbers of political mobilizations in countries in Sub-Saharan Africa with over one million inhabitants (N = 42). Societal mobilization refers to political mobilizations by societal groups, opposition mobilization to political mobilizations by oppositional political elites. Pro-democratic and socio-economic mobilizations are forms of political mobilizations by societal groups

and protest movements in response to rising food prices led to government interventions to improve food security in several countries in West Africa (Bush 2010, p. 122).

One explanation for this finding contrary to scholarly expectations may be that expert assessments are often focused on orderly mobilizations of organized civil society (Branch and Mampilly 2015, p. 7). Seemingly "spontaneous" and often violent demonstrations and riots, however, have always been and still are an important feature of societal mobilization across Sub-Saharan Africa. In this regard, national uprisings during the second protest wave show a pattern of mobilization that seems typical for Sub-Saharan Africa. At first, largely urban-based groups voiced public anger in spontaneous, often violent riots (Bratton and van de Walle 1997, p. 103). Then students and trade unions provided organizational capacities and political framings to these protests. Eventually, oppositional political elites, "drawn from churches, business, the professions" and the ranks of disgruntled former members of the ruling elite, claimed leadership of the emerging protest movements (Bratton and van de Walle 1997, p. 105). Thus, while the most important societal groups with formal organizations were students, unions of civil servants or workers, and churches (Bratton and van de Walle 1992, p. 423), "spontaneous" mobilizations of urban youth provided the basis for the success of these protest movements (Branch and Mampilly 2015).

In a similar fashion, later protest movements on the subcontinent show that unorganized, often violent urban uprisings cannot be separated from civil society organizations' public direct engagements with ruling elites in Sub-Saharan Africa. Instead, they often play an important role for the galvanizing of coalitions and the political success of protest movements. An example are the riots that took place in reaction to the global food crisis of 2007–2008 in at least 14 countries in Sub-Saharan Africa (Berazneva and Lee 2013). In several of these countries, riots led to the formation of broader protest movements that included opposition parties and formulated explicitly political goals (Bush 2010). Thus, while the organizational weaknesses of civil society certainly hamper the role that societal groups are able to play under multi-party politics in Sub-Saharan Africa, societal groups that belong to the urban underclass, while less strategically deployable than organizational constituencies would be, often provide crucial mobilization power to protest movements led by civil society organizations.

In line with the importance spontaneous mobilizations played in the examples discussed above, throughout the 1990s until 2012, an annual average of 47.49% of all political mobilizations by societal groups took place without clear organizational leadership. Over time, this share has fluctuated between 37.86% in 1999, and 64.63% of all political mobilizations by societal groups in 2011. Political mobilizations that are not led by civil society organizations are much more often violent than organized mobilizations are. Of all spontaneous political mobilizations registered in the Social Conflict in Africa Database for the period 1990 to 2012, 43.26% were violent, while among political mobilizations with an organizational leadership only 8.39% were violent. Tables A.6 and A.7 in the appendix provide the annual counts and percentages of organized versus spontaneous, as well as violent versus non-violent, political mobilizations in the period under investigation.

The three peaks of the graph for political mobilizations by societal groups in Fig. 3.1 have different explanations. Whereas the first peak corresponds to the second continent-wide protest wave in Sub-Saharan Africa, the second peak around 2000 seems to have resulted less from continent-wide trends than from coinciding national protest movements. In Burkina Faso, for example, the political assassination of the editor of an independent newspaper in December 1998 led to large anti-government demonstrations and riots across the country. These demonstrations and riots, in turn, gave birth to a coalition of human right groups, non-governmental organizations, trade unions, and opposition parties around the rallying cry "Trop c'est trop!" (Enough is enough). This coalition then organized largely urban protests for well over a year, that is, into the year 2000 (Harsch 2009, p. 274). At the same time in the Central African Republic, anger over unpaid wages led to general strikes by civil servants, which provided the grounds for rallies by opposition groups against mismanagement and corruption of the administration under then President Patassé. Meanwhile, Nigerian civil society experienced a thaw in societal relations in 2000 after the country's first multi-party elections took place in 1999, and a diverse set of societal groups took to the streets to voice their grievances. Overall, in 2000, 57.14% of the countries in Sub-Saharan Africa witnessed protest activity above their national average for the period 1990 to 2012. However, these national mobilizations occurred without an apparent overarching political framing that would unite them across countries.

Like the first peak around 1991, the crest of societal mobilization activity in 2012 resulted again from a continent-wide trend. It represents the subcontinental echo of the third protest wave that found its most visible expression in the "Arab Spring" in North Africa. As Branch and Mampilly (2015, p. 4) explain, "while in the West it may be conventional to imagine the Sahara as in impenetrable barrier dividing the Arab North from the rest of Africa […] we maintain that what has occurred across North Africa involves important similarities to and continuities with events unfolding elsewhere throughout the continent". In the slow build-up of the third continent-wide protest wave, the authors include protests around general elections in Ethiopia in 2005. While these protests were election-related, the authors argue that "they grew out of a broad set of social, economic, and political transformations that had culminated in 2005" (Branch and Mampilly 2015, p. 151). Much like in the North African case where countries experienced mass demonstrations during the Arab Spring, "these transformations led a wide array of primarily urban groups—professionals, workers, intellectuals and students, youth in and out of school, and the informal networks of spanning political society—to accumulate a set of grievances" against ruling elites (Branch and Mampilly 2015, p. 151). While such events in Sub-Saharan Africa may have been part of the foundation on which the events in North Africa unfolded, the "Arab Spring", in turn, inspired similar pro-democratic protests in Nigeria, Sudan, and Uganda (Branch and Mampilly 2015). At the same time, authoritarian leaders in these countries stepped up security measures in response to the revolutions in North Africa, making it likely that the third protest wave ebbed shortly thereafter in Sub-Saharan Africa (see, e.g., Izama and Echwalu 2011, pp. 69–70).

Figure 3.1 shows that the developments of political mobilization over time were driven less by explicitly pro-democratic protests, and more by direct engagements with ruling elites which brought forward the socio-economic grievances of citizens. In Fig. 3.1, the absolute number of political mobilizations by societal groups is indicated by the black line. It is composed of pro-democratic mobilizations (white bars) and socio-economic mobilizations (grey bars). The white bars show much less fluctuation over time than the grey bars. The changes in the overall numbers of political mobilizations are mostly produced by shifts in the number of socio-economic mobilizations. This is especially the case for the second major peak around 2000 and smaller high points between the three major peaks. The first and third major peaks around 1991 and 2012, respectively, proceed in parallel with increases in pro-democratic mobilizations. This suggests that outside continent-wide protest waves, concerns with the democratic process or human rights are often not central to national protest movements.

Figure 3.1 also shows that mobilizations of the political opposition are much less important than political mobilizations by societal groups, at least in terms of their number. This is in line with the expectations based on the discussion of the mobilization capacity of oppositional political elites and societal groups in Sect. 3.4. In multi-party systems where the electoral dominance of ruling elites is overbearing, opposition parties can neither develop strong ties to their constituencies, nor gain an "electoral foothold" (Donno 2011, p. 28). In such a situation, "civil society is a particularly crucial locus for pluralism and challenging state power" (Hearn 1999, p. 4).

Comparatively small in number, too, are major pro-government mobilizations of civilian supporters and proactive attacks of the security apparatus on government-critical individuals and organizations. Besides Angola and Guinea, such political mobilizations by ruling elites are not frequent in any of the countries on the subcontinent. The absolute numbers for such events vary between none and six per year for the whole of Sub-Saharan Africa. In addition, the Social Conflict in Africa Database provides information on the repressive measures taken by the security apparatus in response to political mobilizations by societal groups and the political opposition.

In Fig. 3.2, the number of political mobilizations by societal groups in Sub-Saharan Africa for a given year are provided alongside the share of such events that were violently repressed by ruling elites. Whereas the black line represents the number of political mobilizations by societal groups per year, the stacked grey and white bars represent the share of these events that were repressed with lethal force (dark grey bar), non-lethal force (light grey bar) or not violently repressed (white bar). On average, ruling elites responded to 33.50% of political mobilizations by societal groups in a given year with repressive measures, of which 6.40% were lethal and 27.10% were non-lethal. The annual share of political mobilizations by societal groups that were met with repressive measures varies between 18.18% in 1995 and 50.34% in 2011.

As Fig. 3.2 shows, the share of political mobilizations by societal groups that are met with lethal and non-lethal repression often increases with the number of political mobilizations by societal groups in a given year. This may reflect an attempt by authoritarian ruling elites to regain control over public space. It is also noteworthy that at the height of the second and third continent-wide protest waves in 1991 and 2012, respectively, the share of repressed political mobilizations drops compared to the previous year. This may suggest that at these points in time the repressive capacities of authoritarian ruling elites were outmatched by the numerous mobilizations by societal groups and opposition actors.

3.6 Summary

In this chapter, it was argued that to adequately describe the power dynamics in electoral authoritarian regimes requires an appreciation of the capacity of collective political actors to mobilize money, time, and material goods outside the channels of political institutions. While ruling elites have strong advantages over oppositional political elites and societal groups in both maintaining and building up mobilization capacity, the analysis concluded that societal groups represent the most important alternative source of political power in electoral authoritarian regimes in Sub-Saharan Africa.

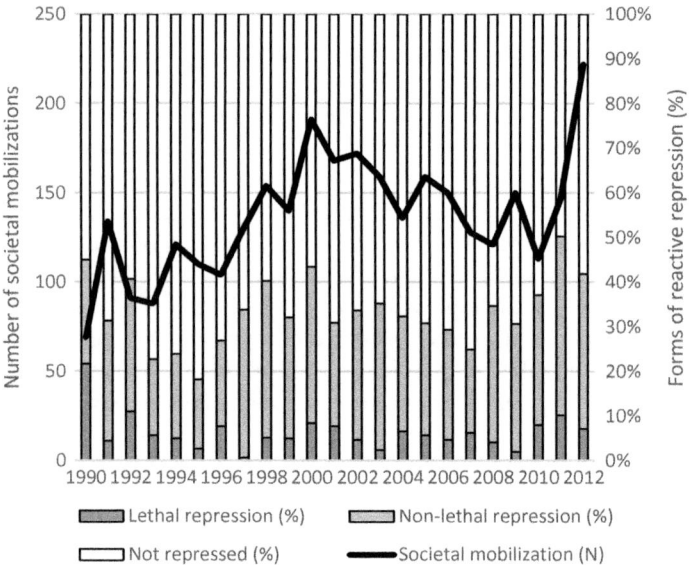

Fig. 3.2 Repression of political mobilizations by societal groups in Sub-Saharan Africa. *Notes* Numbers on the vertical axis on the left are absolute numbers of political mobilizations by societal groups in countries in Sub-Saharan Africa with over one million inhabitants (N = 42). The vertical axis on the right provides percentages for the different forms of repressive measures that political mobilizations were met with in a given year. Non-lethal repression comprises instances in which security forces used tear gas or arrests to repress political mobilizations. For reactive repressive measures to be counted as lethal, deaths must have been reported

Section 3.1 argued that electoral authoritarianism begets low state capacity, both in terms of the reach of state institutions and their ability to assert the principals of legal-rational bureaucracy vis-à-vis patrimonial power networks. This means that extra-institutional, patrimonial power trumps institutional power in the democratization process, and neo-patrimonial power networks dominate political conflict during democratization. Hence, only when both sources of political power are analyzed, can the trajectories of political struggles in electoral authoritarian regimes be understood.

In Sect. 3.2, an understanding of political power was introduced that appreciates both institutional positions and neo-patrimonial power networks as sources of political power. It is based on the premise that a group can only realize its interests in a political struggle when it can overcome its collective action problem. From this vantage point, political power was defined as an actor's ability to project a credible mobilization threat into the political arena. It was demonstrated that this mobilization threat is rooted in a collective actor's capacity to mobilize adherents in the face of adversity. In collective action research, a group's mobilization capacity is synonymous with the solutions to the collective action problem that are available to it.

Section 3.3 discussed such solutions to the collective action problem, and their implications for the mobilization of adherents. It was shown that both institutions and networks provide such solutions. Four mobilization tactics that actors can engage into mobilize people and their resources were defined: Intra-network communication, public communication, organization building, and direct engagement with neutral bystanders and one's opponents. It was argued that among these tactics, direct engagement is the most complex to employ.

Based on this theoretical framework, Sect. 3.4 provided an analysis of the political power of three principal actors in African electoral authoritarian regimes: Ruling elites, oppositional political elites, and societal groups. It was argued that due to their control over state structures and the economy, ruling elites have strong advantages over their opponents in both maintaining and building up the capacity to mobilize time, money, and material goods in their struggle to maintain the status quo. It was further demonstrated that neo-patrimonial authoritarian politics create an environment that is most detrimental to the ability of opposition parties to develop constituency ties and organizational capacity. The analysis concluded that while societal groups face mobilization problems through repression themselves, they nonetheless often represent the only alternative source of political power with national significance in electoral authoritarian regimes. It was argued that mobilization power and threat are important aspects of their role in the democratization process.

In Sect. 3.5, political mobilizations were introduced as an indicator for a collective actor's mobilization threat. Political mobilizations are public direct engagements by ruling elites, oppositional political elites, and societal groups with their opponents. Data on such public collective actions were used to investigate trajectories of political mobilizations by these actors in Sub-Saharan Africa. The analysis showed that the number of public direct engagements by societal groups with ruling elites on the subcontinent increased throughout the 1990s. In 2000, it reached a first peak, only to surpass this level again in 2012. It also showed that developments of political mobilization over time were driven less by explicitly pro-democratic protests than direct engagements with ruling elites that brought forward socio-economic grievances of citizen. It demonstrated the importance of spontaneous and violent mobilizations in the struggle against ruling elites. In line with the previous discussion of the mobilization capacity of oppositional political elites and societal groups, the numbers of political mobilizations suggest that political oppositions typically pose a smaller mobilization threat to ruling elites than societal groups.

References

Amenta E, Caren N, Chiarello E, Su Y (2010) The political consequences of social movements. Ann Rev Soc 36:287–307. https://doi.org/10.1146/annurev-soc-070308-120029

Axelrod RM (2006) The evolution of cooperation. Basic Books, New York

Bayart JF (1986) Civil society in Africa. In: Chabal P (ed) Political domination in Africa: reflections on the limits of power (pp. 109–125, Annual meeting of the African Studies Association, Vol. 26), Cambridge University Press, Cambridge

Berazneva J, Lee DR (2013) Explaining the African food riots of 2007–2008: an empirical analysis. Food Policy 39:28–39. https://doi.org/10.1016/j.foodpol.2012.12.007

Bergen G (2007) Labor, democracy, and development in Senegal. In: Kraus J (ed) Trade unions and the coming of democracy in Africa. Palgrave Macmillan, New York, pp 35–60

Bermeo N (1997) Myths of moderation: confrontation and conflict during democratic transitions. Comp Polit 29(3):305–322

Bleck J, van de Walle N (2011) Parties and issues in Francophone West Africa: towards a theory of non-mobilization. Democratization 18:1125–1145. https://doi.org/10.1080/13510347.2011. 603473

Branch A, Mampilly ZC (2015) Africa uprising: Popular protest and political change (African arguments). Zed Books, in association with International African Institute, Royal African Society, World Peace Foundation, London

Bratton M, van de Walle N (1992) Popular protest and political reform in Africa. Comp Polit 24(4):419–442

Bratton M, van de Walle N (1997) Democratic experiments in Africa: regime transitions in comparative perspective (Cambridge studies in comparative politics). Cambridge University Press, Cambridge

Bunce VJ, Wolchik SL (2006) Youth and electoral revolutions in Slovakia, Serbia, and Georgia. SAIS Rev 16(2):55–65

Bunce VJ, Wolchik SL (2011) Defeating authoritarian leaders in postcommunist countries. Cambridge University Press, Cambridge

Bush R (2010) Food riots: poverty, power and protest. J Agrarian Change 10:119–129. https://doi. org/10.1111/j.1471-0366.2009.00253.x

Chabal P, Daloz JP (1999) Africa works: Disorder as political instrument. International African Institute in association with James Currey, Oxford; Indiana University Press, [London], Bloomington

Coleman JS (2000) Foundations of social theory, 3rd edn. Belknap Press of Harvard University Press, Cambridge, Mass

Collin M (2001) This is Serbia calling: Rock'n'roll radio and Belgrade's underground resistance. Serpent's Tail, London

della Porta D, Diani M (2006) Social movements: An introduction (2nd ed). Malden, Blackwell, Massachusetts

Diamond LJ (1999) developing democracy: toward consolidation. Johns Hopkins University Press, Baltimore

Dicklitch S, Lwanga D (2003) The Politics of being non-political: human rights organizations and the creation of a positive human rights culture in Uganda. Human Rights Q 25:482–509

Donno, D (2011) Elections and democratization in authoritarian regimes. Paper prepared for presentation at Duke University's Seminar on Global Governance and Democracy. University of Pittsburgh, Pittsburgh

Dulani B (2011) Democracy movements as bulwarks against presidential usurpation of power: lessons from the third-term bids in Malawi, Namibia, Uganda and Zambia. Stichproben. Wiener Zeitschrift für kritische Afrikastudien 11(20):115–139

Eisenstadt T (2000) Eddies in the third wave: protracted transitions and theories of democratization. Democratization 7(3):3

Erdmann G (1999) Parteien in Afrika Versuch eines Neuanfangs in der Parteienforschung [Political parties in Africa. towards a new beginning in political party research]. Afr Spectr 34:375–393. https://doi.org/10.2307/40174815

Erdmann G, Engel U (2007) Neopatrimonialism reconsidered: critical review and elaboration of an elusive concept. Commonwealth Comp Polit 45:95–119. https://doi.org/10.1080/14662040601135813

Etzioni A (1975) A comparative analysis of complex organizations: On power, involvement, and their correlates. Free Press, New York

Finkel, SE, Pérez-Linán A, Seligson, MA (2006) Effects of U.S. foreign assistance on democracy building: results of a cross-national quantitative study. United States Agency for International Development, Washington, DC

Francisco RA (2010) Collective Action Theory and Empirical Evidence. Springer Science+Business Media LLC, New York, NY

Freeman J (1979) Resource mobilization and strategy: a model for analyzing social movement organization actions. In: Zald MN, McCarthy JD (eds) The dynamics of social movements: resource mobilization, social control, and tactics. Winthrop Publishers, Cambridge, Mass., pp 167–189

Geddes B (1999) What do we know about democratization after 20 years?: annual review of political science. Annu Rev Polit Sci 2(1):115–144

Gerschewski J (2013) The three pillars of stability: LEgitimation, repression, and co-optation in autocratic regimes. Democratization 20:13–38. https://doi.org/10.1080/13510347.2013.738860

Goldstone JA, Tilly C (2001) Threat (and Opportunity): popular action and state response in the dynamics of contentious action. In: Aminzade RR, Goldstone JA, McAdam D, Perry EJ, Sewell WH, Tarrow SG, et al. (eds) Silence and voice in the study of contentious politics (pp. 179–194, Cambridge studies in contentious politics). Cambridge University Press, Cambridge

Gould J (2006) Strong Bar, Weak State? Lawyers, Liberalism and State Formation in Zambia. Dev Change 37:921–941. https://doi.org/10.1111/j.1467-7660.2006.00507.x

Gross N (2009) A pragmatist theory of social mechanisms. Am Soc Rev 74(3):358–379

Gueye M (2013) Urban guerrilla poetry: the movement Y'en a Marre and the socio-political influences of hip hop in Senegal. J Pan Afr Stud 6(3):22–42

Gurr TR (1974) Why men rebel (4th edn., Princeton paperbacks). Princeton, Princeton University Press, NJ

Gyimah-Boadi E (2004) Civil Society and Democratic Development. In: Gyimah-Boadi E (ed) Democratic reform in Africa: the quality of progress. Lynne Rienner Publishers, Boulder, Colo, pp 99–119

Harsch E (2009) Urban protest in burkina faso. Afr Aff 108:263–288. https://doi.org/10.1093/afraf/adp018

Hearn, J (1999) Foreign Political Aid, Democratization and Civil Society in Uganda in the 1990s. CBR Working Papers, 53. Center for Basic Research, Kampala

Hechter M (1988) Principles of group solidarity (California Series on Social Choice & Political Economy, 11). University of California Press, Berkeley

Heilbrunn JR (1993) Social origins of national conferences in benin and togo. J Mod Afr Stud 31:277–299. https://doi.org/10.1017/S0022278X00011939

Hyden G (1997) Civil society, social capital, and development: dissection of a complex discourse. Stud Comp Int Dev 32(1):3–30

Izama A, Echwalu E (2011) Season of Dissent. Transition, pp 58–71. https://doi.org/10.2979/transition.106b.58

Jalali R (2005) Foreign aid and civil society: how external aid is detrimental to southern NGOs and social movements. Democracy Soc. 2(2)

Japp KP (1984) Selbsterzeugung oder Fremdverschulden: Thesen zum Rationalismus in den Theorien sozialer Bewegungen. Soziale Welt 35(3):313–329

Kailitz S, Tanneberg D (2015) Legitimation, Kooptation, Repression und das Überleben von Autokratien „im Umfeld autokratischer Wahlen". Eine Replik auf den Beitrag von Hans Lueders und Aurel Croissant. Zeitschrift für Vergleichende Politikwissenschaft 9:73–82. https://doi.org/10.1007/s12286-015-0233-1

Kandelaki, G (2006) Georgia's Rose Revolution: a participant's perspective. United States Institute of Peace, Washington

Kasfir N (1998) Civil society, the state and democracy in Africa. In: Kasfir N (ed) Civil society and democracy in Africa: critical perspectives. Cass, London, pp 123–149

Klandermans B (1993) A theoretical framework for comparisons of social movement participation. Sociol Forum 8(3):383–402

Kuran T (1991) Now out of never: the element of surprise in the East European revolution of 1989. World Polit 44(1):7–48

Lichbach MI (1994) Rethinking rationality and rebellion: theories of collective action and problems of collective dissent. Rationality Soc 6:8–39. https://doi.org/10.1177/1043463194006001003

Lichbach MI (1995) The rebel's dilemma (Economics, cognition, and society). University of Michigan Press, Ann Arbor

Linz JJ, Stepan A (1996) Problems of democratic transition and consolidation: Southern Europe, South America, and post-communist Europe. Johns Hopkins University Press, Baltimore, Md

Rakner Lise, van de Walle Nicolas (2009) Opposition weakness in Africa. J Democracy 20:108–121. https://doi.org/10.1353/jod.0.0096

Marwell G, Oliver P (1984) Collective action theory and social movements research. Social Movements, Conflicts and Change 7:1–27

Marwell G, Oliver P (1993) The critical mass in collective action: A micro-social theory (Studies in rationality and social change). Cambridge University Press, Cambridge [England], New York, NY, USA

Marwell G, Oliver P, Prahl R (1988) Social networks and collective action: a theory of the critical mass. III. Am J Sociol 94(3):502–534

McAdam D, Tarrow SG, Tilly C (2001) Dynamics of contention (Cambridge studies in contentious politics). Cambridge University Press, Cambridge

McCarthy JD, Zald MN (1977) Resource mobilization and social movements: a partial theory. Am J Sociol 82(6):1212–1241

Merkel W (2004) Embedded and defective democracies. Democratization 11:33–58. https://doi.org/10.1080/13510340412331304598

Merkel W (2010) Systemtransformation: Eine Einführung in die Theorie und Empirie der Transformationsforschung (2nd ed., Lehrbuch). VS Verlag für Sozialwissenschaften, Wiesbaden

O'Donnell GA, Schmitter PC (1986) Transitions from authoritarian rule: Tentative conclusions about uncertain democracies, The Johns Hopkins University Press, Baltimore

OECD-DAC Secretariat (2013) Flows of official development assistance to and through civil society organizations in 2011. Organisation for Economic Co-operation and Development, Paris

Oliver P, Marwell G (1988) The paradox of group size in collective action: a theory of the critical mass. II. Am Sociol Rev 53:1–8

Oliver P, Marwell G (2001) Whatever happened to critical mass theory? A Retrospective Assess. Sociol Theory 19(3):292–311

Oliver P, Marwell G, Teixeira R (1985) A theory of the critical mass. I. interdependence, group heterogeneity, and the production of collective action. Am J Sociol 91(3): 522–556

Olson M (1990) The logic of collective action in soviet-type societies. J Sov Nationalities 1(1):8–27

Olson M (2003) The logic of collective action: Public goods and the theory of groups (21st edn., Harvard economic studies, Vol. 124). Harvard University Press, Cambridge, Mass

Osaghae E (1999) Democratization in sub-saharan Africa: faltering prospects, new hopes. J Contemp Afr Stud 17:5–28. https://doi.org/10.1080/02589009908729636

Petersen RD (2001) Resistance and rebellion: lessons from Eastern Europe (Studies in rationality and social change). Cambridge University Press, Cambridge

Przeworski A (1986) Some problems in the study of the transition to democracy. In: O'Donnell GA, Schmitter PC, Whitehead L (eds) Transitions from authoritarian rule: comparative perspectives. The Johns Hopkins University Press, Baltimore, pp 47–63

Przeworski A (1991) Democracy and the market: political and economic reforms in Eastern Europe and Latin America (Studies in rationality and social change). Cambridge University Press, Cambridge

Przeworski A (1992) The games of transition. In: Mainwaring SP, O'Donnell GA, Valenzuela JS (eds) Issues in democratic consolidation: the new South American democracies in comparative perspective. University of Notre Dame Press, Notre Dame, Ind, pp 105–152

Rapoport A, Chammah AM (1970) Prisoner's dilemma: A study in conflict and cooperation (1st edn., Ann Arbor paperbacks, AA 165). University of Michigan Press, Ann Arbor

Remi Aiyede E (2003) The dynamics of civil society and the democratization process in Nigeria. Canadian Journal of African Studies/Revue Canadienne des Études Africaines 37(1):1

Rucht D (1990) The strategies and action repertoires of new movements. In: Dalton RJ, Kuechler M (eds) Challenging the political order: new social and political movements in Western Democracies. Polity Press, Cambridge, MA, pp 156–175

Rucht D (2008) Protest als Kommunikation. In: Gosewinkel D, Schuppert GF (eds) Politische Kultur im Wandel von Staatlichkeit (pp. 337–356, WZB-Jahrbuch, Vol. 2007). edition sigma, Berlin

Rucht D (2009) Von Zivilgesellschaft zu Zivilität: Konzeptuelle Überlegungen und Möglichkeiten der empirischen Analyse. In: Frantz C, Kolb H (eds) Transnationale Zivilgesellschaft in Europa. Waxmann, Münster, New York, München, Berlin, pp 75–102

Rucht D, Neidhardt F (2007) Soziale Bewegungen und kollektive Aktionen. In: Joas H (ed) Lehrbuch der Soziologie, 3rd edn. Campus-Verlag, Frankfurt am Main, pp 627–651

Salehyan I, Hendrix CS, Hamner J, Case C, Linebarger C, Stull E et al (2012) Social conflict in Africa: a new database. Int Interact 38:503–511. https://doi.org/10.1080/03050629.2012.697426

Saunders R (2007) Trade union struggles for autonomy and democracy in Zimbabwe. In: Kraus J (ed) Trade unions and the coming of democracy in africa. Palgrave Macmillan, New York, pp 157–197

Schelling TC (1980) The strategy of conflict. Harvard University, Cambridge, Mass

Schmitter PC (1997) Civil society East and West. In: Diamond LJ, Plattner MF, Chu YH, Tien HM (eds) Consolidating the third wave democracies (pp. 239–262, A Journal of democracy book). Johns Hopkins University Press, Baltimore

Schock K (2005) Unarmed insurrections: People power movements in nondemocracies (Social movements, protest, and contention, Vol. 22). University of Minnesota Press, Minneapolis, Minnesota

Sharp G (2003) From dictatorship to democracy: a conceptual framework for liberation. Albert Einstein Institution, Boston, Mass

Slater D (2009) Revolutions, crackdowns, and quiescence: communal elites and democratic mobilization in Southeast Asia. Am J Sociol 115:203–254. https://doi.org/10.1086/597796

Snow DA, Rochford EB, Worden SK, Benford RD (1986) Frame alignment processes, micromobilization, and movement participation. Am Sociol Rev 51(4):464–481

Thompson MR, Kuntz P (2004) Stolen elections: the case of the Serbian October. J Democracy 15:159–172. https://doi.org/10.1353/jod.2004.0074

Uddhammar E, Green E, Söderström J (2011) Political opposition and democracy in sub-Saharan Africa. Democratization 18:1057–1066. https://doi.org/10.1080/13510347.2011.603466

Ulfelder J (2005) Contentious collective action and the breakdown of authoritarian regimes. Int Polit Sci Rev/Revue int de Sci politique 26(3):311–334

United States Agency for International Development (2015) The 2014 CSO Sustainability Index for Sub-Saharan Africa. United States Agency for International Development, Washington, DC

von Lieres B (2014) Citizenship from below: the politics of citizen action & resistance in South Africa & Angola. In: Obadare E, Willems W (eds) Civic agency in Africa: Arts of resistance in the 21st century. James Currey; Boydell & Brewer Inc, Woodbridge, Suffolk, Rochester, NY, pp 49–62

Weipert-Fenner I, Wolff J (2015) Socioeconomic contention and post-revolutionary political change in Egypt and Tunisia: a research agenda. Working Papers, 24. Peace Research Institute Frankfurt, Frankfurt am Main

Zelimir K, Djuric S, Cvetkovic V (2015) Sports fan violence in Serbia: shadow of turbulent sociopolitical circumstances. In: Albrecht JF, Dow MC, Plecas D, Das DK (eds) Policing major events: Perspectives from around the world (pp. 75–88, International Police Executive Symposium co-publications). CRC Press, Boca Raton, FL

Chapter 4
No Protest, No Choice: Political Mobilizations and Electoral Competitiveness in Sub-Saharan Africa

Since 1989, regularly holding multi-party elections has become so widespread a practice in authoritarian regimes across Sub-Saharan Africa that it seems safe to say that "democratization while holding elections" will be the main avenue by which future gains in democratization will be achieved. The following are therefore central questions that research on democratization in Sub-Saharan Africa should seek to answer: How does a political regime move away from a situation in which power is concentrated in the hands of a small ruling elite that exploits its control over the state and the economy to ensure electoral victories whenever and however necessary? How does a political regime move towards a situation where that same ruling elite finds itself in meaningful electoral competition with other political elites?

In this chapter, it will be argued that when societal groups mobilize in electoral authoritarian regimes in Sub-Saharan Africa, they increase the electoral success of oppositional political elites and drive the democratization process. Given the sobering assessment regarding democratic progress in most countries on the subcontinent, the analysis points to the limited mobilization capacity of societal groups as an important explanatory factor for the widespread phenomenon of "elections without democratization" on the African subcontinent. In other words, if citizens in electoral authoritarian regimes do not protest, elections do not provide them with a meaningful choice.

The present chapter provides the link between the analysis of collective action and democratization in Sub-Saharan Africa. First, the chapter argues that the distribution of political power provides a proximate explanation for democratic regime transformations. When power between ruling elites, oppositional political elites, and societal groups becomes more evenly distributed, democratization may emerge as an unintentional byproduct of the political struggle of self-interested political elites. Therefore, for authoritarian regimes to democratize political power must be redistributed out of the hands of a small authoritarian elite to oppositional political elites and societal groups. From a collective action perspective, political power is gained in a political struggle of mobilizations and counter-mobilizations. If collective action entrepreneurs have the "fortuna" and "virtu" (O'Donnell and Schmitter

© Springer Nature Switzerland AG 2020
W. Stuppert, *Political Mobilizations and Democratization in Sub-Saharan Africa*,
Advances in African Economic, Social and Political Development,
https://doi.org/10.1007/978-3-030-22792-0_4

1986, pp. 4–5) to use their current mobilization capacity to engage in mobilization tactics that increase their political power, the power balance may change, and democratization may result.

Second, it will be argued that an increasing mobilization threat from societal groups promotes the power of oppositional political elites in two ways: socioeconomic mobilizations that provide a political platform to the opposition, and pro-democratic mobilizations that assert the constitutional framework and the regulatory responsibility of the state. It has been previously demonstrated that neo-patrimonial authoritarian politics in Sub-Saharan Africa create an environment in which oppositional political elites have little mobilization capacity. Instead, societal groups represent the most important alternative source of political power in electoral authoritarian regimes on the African subcontinent. The two mechanisms show how their mobilizations are linked to electoral competition between political elites.

Third, the chapter will present the research design utilized to test the effects of societal mobilization on democratization processes in Sub-Saharan Africa. Electoral competitiveness will be introduced as a measure for the gradual "democratization while holding elections" of authoritarian electoral regimes. As the main explanatory factors, indicators for the relative mobilization threat of ruling elites, oppositional political elites, and societal groups will be presented. Based on these indicators, six research hypotheses will be formulated, and the methodological design for the quantitative research will be specified and discussed.

Fourth, the chapter will present case studies on the role of societal mobilizations in three major shifts in electoral competitiveness in different countries in Sub-Saharan Africa. It will also present the results of four multiple linear regression analyses of data on all direct national multi-party elections held by electoral authoritarian regimes in Sub-Saharan Africa between 1990 and 2012. The empirical findings will be discussed in light of the research hypotheses and the literature on democratic transitions.

4.1   Democratization and the Balancing of Power

This section introduces the distribution of political power as a proximate explanation for democratic regime transformations. It proceeds from the idea that a political regime is a set of procedures that determines the relations between states and citizens, and prescribes who may engage in politics and how (Tilly 2007, p. 12). These procedures also determine the distribution of power in a polity (Bratton and van de Walle 1997, p. 9). This means that a political regime is a form of social order with a characteristic distribution of political power. From this viewpoint, an autocracy is a form of social order where political power is concentrated in the hands of a small authoritarian elite. In a democracy, political power, as the sum of institutional and extra-institutional power, is much more equally distributed between ruling elites, oppositional political elites and societal groups, and must be for the system to be accepted by the most powerful factions among the political elite.

While the claim regarding the concentration of power in an autocracy seems uncontroversial, the contention that a democracy must be underpinned by a much more equal distribution of power between elite factions and society is in need of explanation. This claim is based on the premise that for democracy to take hold electoral contests must be the preferable alternative for political elites to solve their political conflicts. This not only requires them to be able to mutually veto violations of the political process through political mobilizations, but also requires a civil society that wields sufficient mobilization capacity to pose a credible mobilization threat to violators of the rules of the political game, so that political elites can demobilize.

If self-interested political elites are assumed, it can also be assumed that they organize as participants in a democratic process for executive recruitment only if preferable alternatives cannot be realized. Arguably, if an elite faction could dominate the political system with their overwhelming human and material resources, they would strive to remove the uncertainty of the democratic institutional setup. Only if this is not possible is democracy attractive to political elites, because of the "institutionalized uncertainty" it provides for the regulation of political conflicts. Accepting temporary rule of another elite faction without giving up the chance to rule in the future is preferable to a state of constant resource-depleting mobilization and counter-mobilization, but not preferable to a situation in which one's own side, having enough extra-institutional mobilization capacity, would be able to dominate the political struggle with certainty.

It has been argued that in order to maintain uncertainty in the political process, a strong institutional framework is needed. To be this "(albeit imperfect) agent of coalitions formed to assure compliance" (Przeworski 1991, p. 23) of all participants in the democratic political game, the state must be politically neutral and have the necessary regulatory capacity. It has to be neutral vis-à-vis collective political actors in the sense that it does not allow for the one-sided enforcement of the substantive interests of any of them, and it must have the capacity to monitor participants' behavior and sanction their violations of democratic rules.

However, who assures that the agent which political coalitions have formed to assure compliance acts as a neutral arbiter of the political process? Or, more specifically, who keeps the ruling coalition in control of the state from changing the terms of the democratic contract and removing uncertainty from the political process? If one limits the discussion to elite factions involved in the political process, one would have to conclude that only if the extra-institutional power of non-ruling elites matched the institutional power of ruling elites would democracy represent a stable arrangement among elites. Only if non-ruling elites posed a credible threat to upend the institutional framework in the event the terms of the democratic contract are violated would democracy represent an intra-elite equilibrium.

Thinking of democracy exclusively as an intra-elite equilibrium would imply that elite factions had to remain in a state of permanent mobilization, that is, maintain a wide patronage network, so that extra-institutional checks and balances are continuously provided. This is because gaining control over a state entails a gain in political power for ruling elites that is hard to match for oppositional political elites. Moreover, a balance between ruling elites can always turn into a kleptocratic state-capture agreement. To ensure that the power of ruling elites remains checked, the state neutral, and the system democratic, societal groups must pose a significant mobilization threat to political elites. Only then is there a stable equilibrium and can a situation be maintained in which political elites can safely demobilize: Political power rests with a democratic set of rules instead of with the power networks of elites (Przeworski 1991, p. 14).

It will therefore be argued that for authoritarian regimes to democratize, political power has to be redistributed out of the hands of a small authoritarian elite to oppositional political elites and societal groups. Similar to the design axiom "form follows function," the design of a system of governance follows the distribution of political power in a polity. This design is not intentional, in that it would be picked deliberately by political actors among a set of options. Instead, for a given set of parameters, a type of regime represents what could be called a "chaotic attractor" of the dynamic system of governance, i.e., a "state space" to which trajectories of political development starting anywhere in a given region of possible distributions of political power converge (Brown 1996; Mackenzie 2005).

If self-interested political elites are assumed, it cannot be argued that a member of an authoritarian political elite would opt for the democratic variant of governance over the autocratic one by his or her own free choosing. This would require the assumption that he or she is normatively motivated. One does not need to assume enlightened politicians, however, to explain how democratization comes about. The trick is to switch perspectives, and not see democratization as a normative conflict about different systems of governance, but as one where self-interested elite factions and societal groups are involved in a struggle for power, with power understood as a collective actor's ability to realize its group-specific interests (Przeworski 1986, p. 57). Therefore, the basis of the democratization process is a conflict about who gets to govern, and with how much discretion.

Assuming self-interested political elites does not deny that genuinely pro-democratic political entrepreneurs may exist who are truly motivated to improve the lives of their fellow countrymen by mobilizing for democracy. However, as Przeworski (1991, p. 24) claims, "a theory of democracy based on the assumption of self-interested strategic compliance is plausible and sufficient". Democratization is not presented as "the original or primary aim" of the power struggle between different groups—this would imply the independent role of ideology or values of political actors. Instead, it will be demonstrated that the emergence of democracy can be made plausible "as a fortuitous by-product of the struggle" (Rustow 1970, p. 353) between contending parties.

Vanhanen (1997, p. 23) expressed a similar idea with his "Darwinian" democratization theory, although his lack of collective action vocabulary makes his reasoning sound circular. He maintains that in the struggle to obtain scarce resources, people use sanctions. These sanctions require the use of "power resources," such as economic resources, or the ability to use physical force (Vanhanen 1997, p. 24). Democratization, then, "takes place under conditions in which power resources have become so widely distributed that no group is any longer able to suppress its competitors or to maintain its hegemony" (Vanhanen 1997, p. 24).

The present study will not assume that changes in the distribution of political power immediately result in changes in the political system. Before democratic institutions will play a significant role in the regulation of political conflict, political actors must converge in their expectations regarding the degree of dominance they can reach in a political struggle, since they chose political strategies based on each other's expected behavior. The onset of a genuine process of democratization only becomes possible, therefore, after an extended period of time in which none of the political actors who aspire to rule in a given territory are able to dominate the others (or build a dominant coalition) to the extent that their claim to power is conceded to by all contenders. Strategic options to establish political hegemony must have been largely exhausted, or at least must be believed to be exhausted, by those who would be able to pursue them. The frequent interruptions of electoral series through coups and revolutions in places such as Guinea-Bissau or Niger show that the convergence of expectations among political elites may require repeated attempts by different powerful factions to grasp power by extra-institutional means before elections as a means to recruit political leadership will be accepted by all powerful elite factions.

This convergence of expectations is Rustow's (1970, p. 355) "prolonged and inconclusive political struggle," which he claims to be a necessary condition for the establishment of democracy. According to Rustow (1970, p. 352), such a struggle is only conceivable if the forces that take part in the struggle are "well-entrenched," and if the issues raised in the political struggle "have a profound meaning to them". This "hot family feud" (Rustow 1970, p. 355) is needed to provide the grounds for successful democratic regime changes. Democratization, then, is the "fortuitous by-product" (Rustow 1970, p. 353) of such a struggle.

From a collective action perspective, the characteristics of "well-entrenched" and "profound motivation" point to two sets of solutions to the collective action problem for the political actors that take part in the "hot family feud": Organizational structures and community (Lichbach 1994, 1995). Both enable political entrepreneurs to sustain a steady following and to generate a constant inflow of support in terms of time, money, and material goods. They are forms of extra-institutional power that collective actors can be said to possess if they developed, for example, organizational structures or ties to communities that allow them to appeal to joint norms in their attempt to mobilize resources. Thus, Rustow's "prolonged and inconclusive political struggle" can be fruitfully interpreted from this perspective as a struggle over such solutions to the collective action problem (Lichbach 1995). Institutional power is based on hierarchies which enable collective actors, inter alia, to impose, monitor, and enforce contracts. This institutional form of power becomes more salient in the political struggle, the more political institutions are consolidated.

Hence, the broader theoretical framework offered by collective action theory allows us to locate the characteristics of political actors that in Rustow's understanding are conducive to sustainable mobilization in a larger spectrum of solutions to the collective action problem. It also allows us to go beyond geographically and historically contingent examples, such as the "social classes" mentioned by Rustow (1970, p. 352), to analyze political struggles that provide the grounds for successful democratization wherever and whenever they occur.

As discussed earlier, power in these struggles means control over solutions to the collective action problem. More precisely, it means the ability to pose a credible mobilization threat to others in a struggle for political power. A collective actor's mobilization threat is intimately linked to its mobilization capacity, that is, its command over solutions to the collective action problem. Hence, what the process of the institutionalization of democracy needs as a starting condition is a situation in which the ability to mobilize contributions in terms of time, money, and material goods of no participating political actors is enough to establish control over a territory and its resources. In more common political science terms, we need a conflict among elites or elite coalitions that aspire to govern in which no side is powerful enough to dominate the others.

Rustow (1970, p. 354) assumes that "the serious and prolonged nature of the struggle is likely to force the protagonists to rally around two banners". This may be the case because the political struggle between parties contending for power over a territory rarely takes place in the institutional vacuum of failed states. If there is a state, however, authoritarian ruling elites will take advantage of its resources and institutions—they will employ their institutional political power—to keep the upper hand in the struggle over solutions to the collective action problem. This creates a situation in which all factions among the oppositional political elite have similar experiences of repression at the hands of the same repressive apparatus. These dynamics make the forging of anti-regime movements, or at least the establishment of intensified cooperation between otherwise politically inimical opposition actors more likely, since "intergroup conflict between regime and opposition begets intragroup cooperation" (Lichbach 1995, p. 102).

Achieving a power balance between authoritarian ruling elites and oppositional political elites is a necessary, but not a sufficient condition for the establishment of a democracy. Rustow (1970, p. 361) writes that eventually there must be a moment of decision by the participating political actors to recognize the unsolvable character of the struggle under the present state of mutual belligerence and to embrace democracy as a solution to it. In Rustow's writing (1970, p. 355), this sounds like a moment of almost sage-like enlightenment: "What concludes the preparatory phase is a deliberate decision on the part of political leaders to accept the existence of diversity in unity and, to that end, to institutionalize some crucial aspect of democratic procedure". If this statement is true, and the endorsement of a normative stance such as "the existence of diversity in unity" is a necessary component of democratization processes, this would break with the aforementioned idea of democratization as an unintentional byproduct of the political struggle of self-interested political elites.

The step to accept democracy as the solution to the power struggle requires less enlightened leaders (and seems more probable) if more attention is paid to the role of mobilized citizens in the power struggle. Collective actors outside the realm of partisan politics can be equipped with mobilization capacity independently of participants in the struggle for political power. This mobilization capacity encompasses organizational structures and resources contributed by individuals with a common interest. In this sense, "rising levels of resources increase people's ability to place pressure on elites" (Welzel and Inglehart 2008, p. 130). Trade unions, for example, have proven to be powerful actors in democratization processes because of their ability to mobilize members for contentious political action and as voters in elections. As part of coalitions, they have shaped the outlines of the democratic regimes they helped to bring about. VonDoepp (1996), for example, highlights the importance of trade unions for democratization processes in Kenya and Zambia.

If there is no balance of mobilization capacity between political elites and societal groups, political compromises among powerful elite factions that do not entail the establishment of genuine multi-party democracy are feasible. Feasible alternatives to genuine multi-party democracy for powerful elite factions which try to solve their political stalemate are, for example, competitive one-party systems (Bratton and van de Walle 1997, p. 78; Brownlee 2007; Magaloni 2006) and oligarchic multi-party systems which are comprised of electoralist personalistic parties (Gunther and Diamond 2001, p. 28). Here, elections are held, but not competitive.

The relationships that are established between politicians and the unorganized, resource-poor electorate in such plebiscitary "façade democracies" do not allow for substantial vertical accountability. As Ihonvbere (1996, p. 23) noted for the African experience with electoral politics, it has been "clearly demonstrated" that "elections may take place, a multiplicity of parties may dominate the political terrain, but the elitist, exploitative, violent, manipulative, and in many instances pedestrian and predatory character of politics remains intact". In such "façade democracies," society is only involved in politics through top-down mobilization around elections. Momentary political support is secured in neo-patrimonial relationships. Most directly, it takes the form of vote buying. Promises of nepotism or ethnic favoritism can also establish more long-term relationships between politicians and the electorate. However, as (Lindberg 2009, p. 10) explains, in such neo-patrimonial relationships

> there are often only blurred or poorly defined expectations of behaviour on the part of the patron, whereas the client can be confronted with rather direct demands. The client's right to demand information and justification from the patron is sometimes very weak, or non-existent in these highly asymmetrical power relationships, and then it ceases to be an accountability relationship. [...] Thus, even if the client or a set of clients regularly can extort some form of compensation, protection, or personal favours from the patron, that does not make such relationships instances of accountability.

Only if the electorate has overcome their atomization in patron-client relationships and wielded independent mobilization capacity can they gain the ability to hold political elites accountable. Thus, public support for elite factions does not establish vertical accountability when societies are organizationally weak. In such plebiscitary regimes, therefore, contestation between elite factions remains insubstantial. Free to redefine their allegiances post-electorally, elites go into opposition with the purpose of positioning themselves for co-optation. This may happen through party coalitions or through individual floor-crossing ("political nomadism"), which is so common in African politics (Loada and Santiso 2002, p. 4).

Hence, if there is no balance of mobilization capacity between political elites and societal groups, elite factions may solve their conflicts by dividing society into two groups: Politico-economic elites with almost exclusive access to state and market and the governed "rest". The spoils of governance are the basis for a kleptocratic elite pact to exploit the nation. Neo-patrimonial relationships guarantee that some parts of the electorate share in some of the spoils some of the time, and simultaneously that compensations for electoral support remain insubstantial.

If it is genuine political competition that emerges from the "hot family feud," what is needed is not only a balance of power between elite factions, but also between societal groups and elite factions. For this, societal groups with an independent mobilization capacity of their own must exist. In this sense, "the chances of democracy must be seen as fundamentally shaped by the balance of class power" (Rueschemeyer et al. 1992, p. 47). If there is a substantial independent mobilization capacity among societal groups, there is a potential power basis for emerging political actors outside the circles of ruling elites, whether they emerge from splits of ruling elites or as new anti-governmental political entrepreneurs. Only if these societal groups are able to lend to and retract their support from elite factions, can different parties to the intra-elite political conflict emerge for which some form of genuine representative democracy will be a workable compromise.

To sum up, a trajectory towards democratization requires a political struggle where none of the political actors that aspire to rule in a given territory are able to dominate the political arena. This requires political actors with a minimum mobilization capacity to thwart attempts at their domination by others. At the same time, there must be societal actors that balance out the mobilization capacity of those actors that organize as participants in the formal political process. Only then the will "process of establishing, strengthening, or extending the principles, mechanisms, and institutions that define a democratic regime" (Garreton Merino 1995, p. 146) progress.

As long as the distribution of power does not develop in this way, multi-party elections may be introduced and regularly held, but these elections will not become more competitive over time. Instead, such electoral authoritarian regimes will remain "systems in which opposition parties are supposed to lose elections" (Schedler 2009, p. 303). Under these circumstances, with no viable political alternatives provided, vertical accountability cannot be established. If, however, societal groups build up mobilization capacity while authoritarian national multi-party elections are regularly held, they can—through their credible mobilization threats—help to bring out intra-elite conflict and strengthen oppositional elites in those elections.

This theoretical approach does not assume that the distribution of political power transforms into gains in democratization in a mechanistic way. If we assume that democratization takes place as the "fortuitous by-product" (Rustow 1970, p. 353) of a political struggle for dominance, and not as the intended outcome of pro-democratic political entrepreneurs, we must allow for inertia and divergences. The causal claim is weaker: For a given distribution of political power—including extra-institutional and institutional power—a type of regime represents a point of convergence. Sooner or later, similar distributions of power will lead to similar political systems. For electoral authoritarian regimes, this means that changes in the distribution of political power, as indicated by official election results, will transform into a gradual strengthening of democratic governance over time. Figure 4.1 illustrates these points. Here, the changing distributions of political power between ruling elites ("R"), oppositional political elites ("O"), and societal groups ("S") are depicted as shares of a pie. The

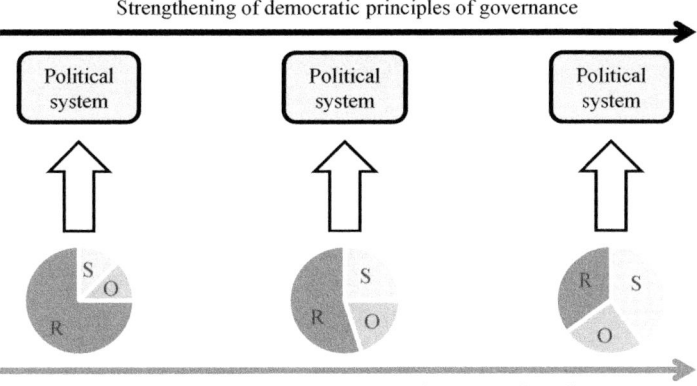

Fig. 4.1 Macro-theoretical model for the explanation of democratization processes. *Notes* The pie charts illustrate changing distributions of political power between ruling elites ("R"), oppositional political elites ("O"), and societal groups ("S")

more even these distributions become, the more democratic principles of governance will be strengthened.

Democratization processes have an element of self-reinforcement. To some extent, societal groups' increased mobilization capacity can be the result of previous gains in democratization. This is because "democratization efforts allowing increasingly competitive elections in authoritarian regimes supply previously excluded groups with an arena in which to begin organizing drives" (Almeida 2003, p. 349). Also, instances in which, e.g., protest groups successfully wrought pro-democratic concessions from a regime, as well as past electoral victories, change the calculus of potential activists who might, due to a higher probability of winning attached to anti-regime mobilization, be more willing to mobilize against the regime in the future (Lichbach 1995, p. 67). However, there is no mechanistic way in which past mobilization successes or an opening of public space to oppositional elite factions and societal groups automatically lead to an increase in mobilization capacity. Such opportunities must be effectively used by collective action entrepreneurs to increase their mobilization threat by using the right mobilization tactics at the right moment in time.

Here, collective action theory as discussed in Chap. 3 may provide the micro-theoretical underpinning for the macro-theoretic relationship of increasing power balance and democratization. From this perspective, the present distribution of political power in the current political system influences the availability of solutions to the collective action problem for each actor. This mobilization capacity can be used by actors to engage in mobilization tactics. Political actors can engage in four mobilization tactics to increase their mobilization threat: Intra-network communication, public communication, organization building, and direct engagements with one's

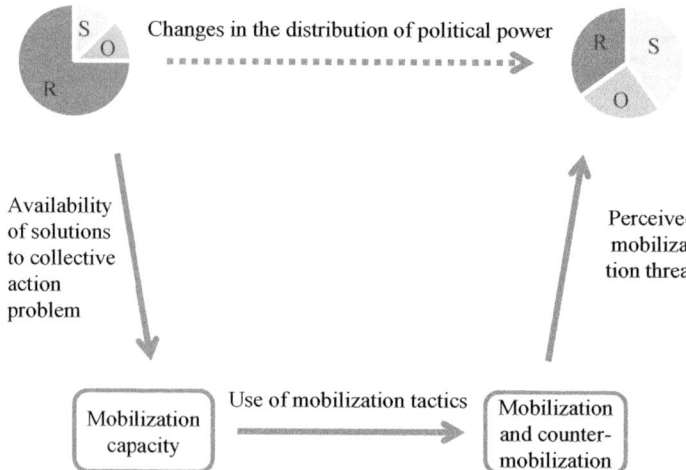

Fig. 4.2 Micro-theoretical model for the explanation of changes in political power. *Notes* The pie charts illustrate changing distributions of political power between ruling elites ("R"), oppositional political elites ("O"), and societal groups ("S")

opponents and neutral bystanders. Their employment will lead to mobilizations and counter-mobilizations by other actors. Based on this interaction, an actor's mobilization threat is built up and maintained. This, in turn, produces a specific distribution of power among actors participating in the political struggle on the macro level. Figure 4.2 illustrates these points. It should be noted that the nexus between mobilization capacity, the employment of mobilization tactics, and the mobilization threat that emanates from mobilizations is more complicated than shown in this figure. All three elements recursively influence each other. This recursivity could be depicted as an endless concatenation of the causal chain displayed in the graphic.

The combination of both models provides a theory of democratization that is rooted in collective action theory. On the macro level, the theory posits that every distribution of political power between ruling elites, oppositional political elites, and societal groups will, with lags and initial divergences, converge in a political system that reflects this power. If the neo-patrimonial power networks of ruling elites dominate the political struggle, it will produce a political system where a small circle of members of the ruling elite has the capacity to set the rules of the game and command security forces. Such a situation is depicted by the first pie chart in Fig. 4.1, in which the ruling elites have the largest share, and both societal groups and oppositional political elites have very small shares. These shares change over time through the actions and interactions of the participants in the political struggle on the micro level. A given political system and distribution of political power determine the availability of solutions to the collective action problem to each actor. Engaging in mobilization tactics leads to mobilizations and counter-mobilizations between the actors. Based on these interactions, actors build up a mobilization threat that determines the power that is available to them to realize their group-specific interests, i.e., their political power. This altered distribution of political power will then lead to changes in the political system over time. If societal groups and oppositional political elites are able to increase their power relative to ruling elites, these changes will consist in the strengthening of democratic principles of governance, i.e., democratization.

4.2 Societal Groups and the Changing of the Balance of Power

Democratization takes place when political power between ruling and oppositional political elites, as well as political elites and societal groups, becomes more evenly distributed. In Chap. 3, it has been argued that despite the limitations of societal groups in fulfilling democratic functions, they represent the most important alternative source of political power in electoral authoritarian regimes in Sub-Saharan Africa. While collective action theory provides us with a novel perspective from which to appreciate the role of civil society in democratization, the conceptual framework of mobilization capacity and mobilization tactics needs to be applied to the interaction of societal groups and oppositional political elites to understand the role of the former in the democratization process. After all, by definition, societal groups are not themselves competing for power over political institutions, and democratization requires a balancing of power between oppositional political elites and ruling elites inside the institutional framework in order to progress. In the following subsections, two parallel mechanisms will be described by which mobilization capacity can become increasingly evenly distributed between the principal actors in the democratization processes of electoral authoritarian regimes in Sub-Saharan Africa. In the first, societal groups and oppositional political elites interlock their efforts to mobilize adherents, and expansions of societal groups' mobilization capacity promote opposition power. In this case, societal groups engage in socio-economic mobilization. In the second, societal groups assert the constitutional framework and the regulatory responsibility of the state through their work on human rights and the democratic process. In this case, societal groups engage in pro-democratic mobilization. Both mechanisms require societal groups to build up a credible mobilization threat that increases the perceived costs of their suppression and gives them political space to maneuver.

4.2.1 Building up Opposition Power

As it has been demonstrated in Sect. 3.4.2, the organizational weaknesses and weakened community ties of opposition parties in electoral authoritarian regimes arise from a political process marked by neo-patrimonialism and repression. Patrimonial politics leads to personalistic leadership on the side of both ruling and opposition parties, and with that to a lack of public discourse around substantial policy issues. It also leads to opposition parties' exclusion from access to the resources of both the state and the national economy. International donors do not offer an alternative source of funding, as they typically follow a doctrine of non-partisanship when it comes to support for the democratic process in electoral authoritarian regimes. State repression represents an additional obstacle to meaningful public discourse about political alternatives, since preference falsification leads to mutual ignorance among opposition supporters, and outspoken regime critics face personal sanctions. Raising the cost of individual contributions to opposition parties, state repression also diminishes the possibilities opposition parties have to build strong organizations.

This means not only that the mobilization capacity of opposition parties in electoral authoritarian regimes in Sub-Saharan Africa is regularly too weak to pose a credible threat to ruling elites, but also that oppositional parties are in an unfavorable position relative to improving their mobilization capacity on their own. However, directly and indirectly, oppositional political elites can profit from societal groups' mobilization capacity. First, societal groups provide oppositional political elites with protected spaces to promote their skills and networks. As leaders in civil society organizations, and as participants in the work of advocacy and lobby organizations, oppositional political elites can improve their leadership skills and establish connections with representatives of national and international organizations. Second, societal groups build political platforms based on mobilizations around socio-economic issues, the dissemination of government-critical information, the strengthening of people's proactive understanding of citizenship, and their perception of self-efficacy. These political platforms can be used by opposition parties to appeal to their constituencies.

To play this supportive role, neither civil society organizations nor opposition parties have to intentionally enter into collaboration. In fact, both the non-partisanship mantra of international donors and the exposure of opposition parties and their allies to state repression act as strong disincentives for open collaboration between societal groups and oppositional political elites in electoral authoritarian regimes. However, as much as democratization can be a "fortuitous by-product" of the struggle between elite factions, mutual benefit can be the result of societal groups and oppositional political elites each pursuing their own, independent agendas.

From the perspective of oppositional elites, neither the platform building function of societal groups nor the protected space they provide for aspiring political leaders to groom their skills and networks requires oppositional political elites to purposefully align their agenda to that of societal groups. However, when deciding whether to openly challenge the government, political entrepreneurs and disaffected members of the ruling elite will quite naturally take into account the presence or absence of a power base independent of the incumbents and their patronage network. As Przeworski (1986, p. 56) explains, "where some perspectives of an 'opening' […] have appeared, they have always involved some ruling groups that sought political support among forces that until that moment were excluded from politics by the authoritarian regime". This same process is behind the frequent observation that "if the elite divides against itself, its factions appeal to the masses for support" (Huntington 1965, pp. 420–421).

Historically, student unions, trade unions, and churches have been identified as important forces behind the promotion of intra-elite competition in Sub-Saharan Africa through the sustained mobilization of their adherents (Bratton and van de Walle 1992). However, much more fluid protest movements with less clear-cut agendas can provide a political platform for challengers of the ruling elite, too. Such protest movements often center on economic grievances and are driven as much by established civil society organizations as by the urban underclass (Branch and Mampilly 2015, p. 19). As Bratton and van de Walle (1997, p. 103) explain,

> economic protests signified the existence of a pool of disgruntled urbanites who had been alienated by government policies and performance but who lacked leadership, organization, or a clear political agenda. This mass constituency was ripe for appropriation by ambitious leaders who could articulate an appealing message of political change.

Karatnycky and Ackerman (2005) confirmed the role of ordinary citizens' protest in democratization for a wide variety of cases in diverse historical and cultural settings. Later in the democratization process, when electoral politics are more firmly established and societal protests are less disruptive, the economic agenda set by such protests can still serve as an important populist political platform, as, for example, the success of the electoral strategy of the oppositional Patriotic Front in Zambia shows (Resnick 2012; Larmer and Fraser 2007).

As long as societal groups are too weak to provide a platform for a sustainable challenge to the ruling elite, aspiring opposition leaders will either seek a career in the ruling party or hide out and nurture their skills and networks in civil society organizations. As Heilbrunn (1993, p. 277) explains, disaffected elites in authoritarian regimes who have been excluded from the patronage networks often established "independent bases of power in voluntary associations beyond the immediate reach of the state". When political careers in the opposition fail, human rights organizations and other internationally-linked societal groups provide opposition politicians with safe havens before a new attempt can be made at contesting ruling elite power.

Societal groups, too, do not have to intend to support oppositional political elites to promote their mobilization capacity. The collective action perspective on their role in the democratization process shows that they not only contribute to opposition power through human rights work or activities with the explicit goal of improving the freedom and fairness of the electoral process. By mobilizing latent collective entities as actual collective actors, societal groups help to form a citizenry that formulates political claims directed at the government and articulates demands for state responsiveness. This represents a contribution to the establishment of an alternative political platform which opposition parties can appropriate to reach out to potential constituencies. Playing this role does not require societal groups to dovetail with the political aspirations of the opposition.

In fact, too close a cooperation between societal groups with oppositional political elites diminishes the positive impact of societal groups on the democratization process. Tying their mobilization capacity to the political agendas of opposition parties means that once a change in government does take place, the independent mobilization capacity of society is reduced, and the new ruling elite may continue authoritarian policies where the old one left off. For example, after the opposition came to power in Zambia in 2012, civil society experts lamented the docility of societal groups in reaction to a legislative project pursued by the new Patriotic Front that aimed to restrict NGO activities. According to a governance advisor for a bilateral donor in Zambia interviewed by the author in 2012, this was "because these are guys who have been together. They have been singing the same song. [In opposition, the Patriotic Front] would articulate what civil society wanted and use it. And the PF was used by CSOs to champion certain causes" (personal interview, 14 November 2012, Zambia). Only if societal groups retain their partisan independence and cultivate their own mobilization capacity are they able to turn the competition among political elites into a foundation for vertical accountability through competitive elections. This is because only when they are able to lend and retract their political support in accordance with their own agenda are societal groups able to influence the agenda of political parties, both ruling and oppositional.

4.2.2   Safeguarding Democratic Institutions

In electoral authoritarian regimes, opposition parties are mostly preoccupied with their own survival as participants in the electoral process. This means that responsibility for safeguarding the rules of the democratic game largely falls to societal groups. As Dulani (2011, p. 124) describes:, "In countries where the ruling parties hold commanding legislative majorities, [social movements in Sub-Saharan Africa] have had to play the role of unofficial opposition, seeking to hold governments accountable and sometimes preventing them from abusing their majorities". Again, this is only partially a task that societal groups perform with the explicit aim of advancing the democratization process. Safeguarding political rights and civil liberties is first and foremost a way for them to secure the necessary space to articulate grievances and push them onto the agenda of the political elite.

Civil society organizations safeguard this space through programs on human rights monitoring and the strengthening of the democratic process. For example, they take on roles as researchers into human rights abuses, attorney's offices for victims of state repression, or election monitors. By publicly protesting arbitrary state action, societal groups increase the costs of violations of political rights and civil liberties for the ruling elite. All of these activities assert the constitutional framework and the regulatory responsibility of the state. Moreover, when societal groups strengthen institutional checks and balances, they prevent political elites from entering kleptocratic pacts. By curtailing the discretionary power of ruling elites, societal groups therefore counter the influence of the ruling elite's neo-patrimonial networks on state action in Sub-Saharan Africa. Thus, they strengthen the institutional framework, that is, the potency of the principals of legal-rational bureaucracy in state institutions. The more the state becomes neutral in a partisan sense, the more institutional power becomes sufficient to rule, and ruling elites as well as oppositional political elites will demobilize their costly patrimonial power networks. Extra-institutional power becomes less important for political survival, and eventually, elite-initiated mass-based mobilization is diminished to the mobilization of voters in elections.

This means that societal groups regularly have to prove their capacity to mobilize citizens and patrons when their democratic rights are violated in order to influence the process by which authoritarian ruling elites decide whether to continue violating democratic rights and repress, or play according to the democratic rule set and tolerate. As Bermeo (1997) puts it, "if anti-regime forces of any sort succeed in elevating the sense of struggle and raising the costs of suppression, they affect half the decision calculus and win half the battle". Thus, "while civil society will not single-handedly create democracy, or always be internally democratic, it does provide an autonomous public sphere of collective political activity whose very existence has the potential to limit the state's reach and create some element of political accountability and means of political participation" (Orvis 2001, p. 18).

4.3   Specifying a Test of the Mobilization-Democratization Link

The central tenet of this book is that societal mobilization leads to democratization. The preceding section has shown how collective action by societal groups may increase the mobilization capacity of oppositional political elites, and thus promote electoral competition. The present section will specify the research design utilized to test this. First, it will argue that the protracted democratization processes of electoral authoritarian regimes require electoral competitiveness as a yardstick to measure their progress. It will then detail how competitiveness has been measured in authoritarian elections in Sub-Saharan Africa. Second, it will present indicators for the relative mobilization threat of ruling elites, oppositional political elites, and societal groups. Third, six hypotheses will be specified and then empirically tested using four multiple linear regression analyses of data on all direct national multi-party elections held by electoral authoritarian regimes in Sub-Saharan Africa between 1990 and 2012.

To use the competitiveness of elections as a measure of the democratization of electoral authoritarian regimes implies a departure from an understanding of the democratization process as a sequence of phases. Instead, today's democratization processes will be understood as "protracted transitions" (Eisenstadt 2000; Barkan 2000) that may extent over many cycles of multi-party elections. Such elections may display democratic qualities to a varying extent. The most important among these qualities, it will be argued, is their competitiveness.

In literature on transitions, traditionally three phases of the process between the end of an autocratic regime and the establishment of a democratic regime were distinguished. The first phase spans the time from the first sustained challenges to autocratic rule until the regime fully disintegrates. Some call it the liberalization phase

(O'Donnell and Schmitter 1986, p. 7), others prefer the more neutral term "end of the autocratic regime" (Merkel 2010, p. 95). Part of this phase is the regime transition in the narrow sense as the interval between the end of an old and the beginning of the establishment of a new regime (Merkel 2010, pp. 94–95). The first phase ends when political decisions cease to be at the discretion of an autocratic elite, and start to be taken in the framework of democratic institutions (see, e.g., O'Donnell and Schmitter 1986, p. 7; Merkel 2010, p. 105). This implies that the question of where the regime transition in a broader sense, i.e., the process between the dissolution of the old and the establishment of the new political order, is leading to is already decided. The next phase is either called the democratization (O'Donnell et al. 1986; Przeworski 1991) or the institutionalization (Merkel 2010) phase, and often equated with the preparation and eventual holding of founding elections (see, e.g., O'Donnell and Schmitter 1986; Linz and Stepan 1996; Bratton and van de Walle 1997). It seems that scholars largely and tacitly assumed that such an institutional arrangement signified a consensus among the main political actors to rule the country democratically. Hence, "according to the standard wisdom of the transitions literature, elections had little to do with the transition process except as indicators of its successful completion" (Lindberg 2009, p. 4). After founding elections, the new democratic regime was said to enter its "consolidation" phase. In that third and last phase, the "accidental arrangements, prudential norms and contingent solutions that have emerged during the uncertain struggles of the transition" have to be transformed "into institutions, that is, into relationships that are reliably known, regularly practiced and normatively accepted by those persons or collectivities defined as the participants/citizens/subjects of such institutions" (Schneider and Schmitter 2004, p. 4).

In the bi-polar world of the Cold War, where democracy was one viable option among several forms of regimes, it may have been true that the preparation and eventual holding of founding elections marked a clear new, democratic trajectory for governance in a country. In a post-Cold War world, however, where holding national multi-party elections has become the sine-qua-non for the political survival of democratic and autocratic ruling elites alike, this assumption is no longer tenable. In the present world order, the introduction of multi-party elections may signify different steps in a transition in different countries and under different regimes (Carothers 2002, p. 12). Geddes ((2003, p. 66), see also 1999), for example, claims that personalist autocratic regimes are likely to introduce multi-party elections under domestic or international pressure and be "ready to renege on agreements at the first opportunity". Here, when holding such elections, the regime tries to make as few concessions to the democratic process as is necessary for "mimicking the democratic form" (Diamond 2002, p. 24), i.e., electoral campaigning for oppositional parties will be restricted, civil rights curtailed, and the elections rigged as much as possible and necessary under domestic and international surveillance. Hence, the introduction of multi-party elections does not necessarily signify either the end of the autocratic regime or that "agreement [...] about political procedures to produce an elected government" (Linz and Stepan 1996, p. 3) has been reached.

If the introduction of national multi-party elections cannot be linked to a specific moment in the democratization process, the idea that there is a meaningful sequencing of the process in phases collapses. Multi-party elections may continue autocratic rule by different means or indeed signify the end of the institutionalization process. Hence, in democratization processes today, liberalization, institutionalization, and consolidation—understood as the "normative acceptance" of democratic governance—represent rather intertwined threads than a sequence of phases.

Such "protracted transitions" (Eisenstadt 2000; Barkan 2000) can extend over decades, are at times without a clear trajectory, and can be marked by setbacks and sudden advancements. This is nothing new. In fact, countries in the first wave of democratization took many years to achieve the standards of electoral democracy. After the quick installment of democratic regimes in the second and at the beginning of the third wave, we may well witness a "fourth wave" (McFaul 2002) of long-term democratization unfolding. The main difference in comparison to the first wave would be that this time the extension of suffrage came first, followed by "extremely gradual, incremental processes of liberalization" (Carothers 2002, p. 15). This has been described by Dahl (1998, p. 38) as the thorniest way to democracy long before the onset of the "fourth wave".

Instead of sequencing the democratization process into separate phases, this book will study it as "the process of establishing, strengthening, or extending the principles, mechanisms, and institutions that define a democratic regime" (Garreton Merino 1995, p. 146). The democratization of electoral authoritarian regimes will be investigated with the understanding that a country can witness the rise and fall of several such regimes in succession. They come into being by preparing their first *de jure* multi-party elections and end either when elections are abolished, that is, when elected political representatives are forced out of office in an unconstitutional manner, or when the democratization process is successful, that is, an "agreement [...] about political procedures to produce an elected government" (Linz and Stepan 1996, p. 3) is reached. When is such an agreement reached? Elections that are held in authoritarian regimes vary in the extent to which they adhere to democratic qualities. However, even when fulfilling minimum democratic standards in the way they are organized, the freedom and fairness of elections in electoral authoritarian regimes are constrained by the fact that they are held in a situation in which, generally, ruling elites do not fully respect political rights and civil liberties. All substantial restrictions on political rights and civil liberties, in turn, have consequences for the freedom and fairness of elections. Thus, authoritarian ruling elites create a "tilted playing field" long before the process of organizing upcoming national multi-party elections starts, and international observers arrive to assess it. This is achieved, for example, through the imprisonment of leading opposition politicians, restrictions of the right to assembly, increasing control over media, or partisan staffing of the election commission. Hence, we can only speak of the end of an electoral authoritarian regime, and the successful transition to a democracy once direct national multi-party elections are organized in a regime that is already known to fully respect political rights and civil liberties at the time when the preparation of elections begins.

How do we measure the progress of democratization processes between the introduction of multi-party elections and the holding of fully democratic elections? A central feature of electoral authoritarian regimes is the lack of electoral competitiveness. In these regimes, election results overstate support for those holding power. This is because ruling elites know that among the citizens they govern there are many potential dissidents who would join protest movements or even rebellions. If this was not the case, they would not have to curtail political rights and civic liberties. This leads to large-scale "preference falsification" (Kuran 1991, p. 17). In such a situation, both protests and elections become important signals for potential dissidents to overcome their mutual ignorance. Hence, ruling elites are forced to tightly control the display of political support in the public sphere, and this includes elections. Authoritarian ruling elites cannot tolerate a strong showing of opposition candidates in elections. When holding elections, authoritarian ruling elites must therefore claim "widespread, enduring, and intense support" to discourage public manifestations of anti-regime sentiments (Lichbach 1995, p. 78). Thus, most authoritarian ruling elites start election manipulation long before election day. Hence, if electoral competitiveness does increase, it not only signals shifts in electoral support, but in political power as well. Put differently, "election results in authoritarian contexts tend to ratify rather than redistribute the power that competing groups wield" (Brownlee 2007, p. 9).

The more opposition candidates and parties are supported by citizens in the run-up to elections and have this support registered through the official electoral process, the more authoritarian ruling elites have lost control over the election process and the more political space they concede to the opposition. Thus, increasing competitiveness leads to more institutionalized uncertainty for both ruling elites and oppositional political elites. Whereas ruling elites will reassess the probabilities they attach to a possible defeat in the future, oppositional political elites will see increasing chances to take over power through elections. This increased uncertainty for the elites translates into increased accountability for citizens. Arbitrary governance is curtailed by the expectation of punishment through mobilization well before the actual defeat of incumbents at the polls.

This means that electoral competitiveness, measured as the distribution of electoral support between ruling elites and oppositional political elites in official election results, can be used as a yardstick for the progress of the democratization process of electoral authoritarian regimes. This does not imply that for the political process to be understood to democratize every election should be ever closer to a result that would effect a change in government. Ultimately, competitiveness is about the perception of elites, since it is the uncertainty created among them when a change in government becomes more likely that increases vertical accountability. It is likely that this perception does not increase and decrease with each percentile change in election outcomes. At the same time, the ruling elites' perception of the likelihood of losing an election will be more complex an estimate than simple extrapolation from past elections.

Crucially, however, the electoral process itself is the indicator for the progress of the democratization process. Two aspects of it seem important for an assessment of its competitiveness. First, how much control do ruling elites have over it? Second, how powerful are opposition candidates and parties? From this viewpoint, free and fair elections with no promising alternatives to incumbents are as undemocratic as authoritarian elections in which powerful opposition candidates compete.

Ruling elites will blatantly manipulate elections so that they don't have to admit defeat or send a signal of weakness. At the same time, we can assume that they will only do this if they need to. This means that the higher the ruling elites' perceived risk that they will lose is, the less free and fair the electoral process will be. As Lindberg (2009, p. 36) explains for the Zimbabwean case, there often is "an inverse relationship between the level of real competition and the trustworthiness of official results". Conversely, this means that the less uncertain ruling elites are about their reelection, the less undue control over the electoral process they will exert.

Elites will strive to minimize outright manipulation of the electoral process because there is a price on last-minute cheating. This price varies with the degree to which ruling elites depend on favorable foreign relations with, e.g., pro-democratic donors and societal groups with strong mobilization capacity. If, for example, international election observation missions are present and the regime's dependency on foreign aid is high, blatant vote fraud may lead to cutbacks in internationally-financed development programs or economic embargos. Domestically, opposition groups in politics and society may increase the expected costs of cheating for ruling elites through pre-electoral demonstrations that raise the specter of so-called "electoral revolutions" in the aftermath of stolen elections (Tucker 2007). Most authoritarian ruling elites, therefore, start election manipulation long before election day. Given the wide variety of options at the disposal of autocratic ruling elites to secure a favorable election outcome, one could conclude the following: Only the uninformed and unprepared, the incapable, or the woefully sophomoric among the incumbents in electoral authoritarian regimes need to blatantly manipulate elections around election day. Those who plan and strategize are able to avoid such a showdown.

More mindful ruling elites create an environment in which elections produce favorable outcomes. If we talk about national multi-party elections in electoral authoritarian regimes, we speak of elections held under circumstances in which—by definition—respect for political rights and civil liberties is lacking. All substantial restrictions on political rights and civil liberties have consequences for the freedom and fairness of elections. They impact the likelihood that grievances are articulated and opposition to government policies is formed. Yet, preventive measures, such as the "disappearance" of opposition politicians, are by their nature impossible to assess in terms of their consequences on the competitiveness of elections.

Therefore, the degree of control that ruling elites have over the electoral process cannot be assessed as an independent aspect of the competitiveness of elections for both empirical and theoretical reasons. We have no way of knowing by observation to which degree potential opposition candidates would have had a chance to compete if they had emerged, or how much of a following they would have had if ruling elites had respected political rights and civil liberties. What we are able to observe, however, is the level of actual competition in elections, that is, the degree to which ruling elites have to concede control over the political process of executive recruitment to their opposition in politics and society.

To measure electoral competitiveness, elections will be understood as competition between, on the one side, powerholders and their parties, and those opposition parties and candidates that decide to contest the elections on the other. Differentiating between powerholders and the political opposition is complicated by the fact that ruling elites in electoral authoritarian regimes often create several parties to lend their political dominance the semblance of multi-party politics. The criterion that has been used to differentiate between parties loyal to the ruling elite and opposition parties is therefore whether they presented themselves as alternative power centers to the voters. This means that, first, publicly-announced electoral coalitions that involve the largest ruling party are regarded as powerholders, even if not all of the parties in the coalition have previously been part of the government. Second, former partners of the largest ruling party have to convincingly distance themselves from the government leadership in their election campaigns in order to be counted as opposition parties and candidates. Note that it is irrelevant for this differentiation whether challengers to the ruling elite have democratic credentials. Ousted authoritarian rulers who preside over the former party of power are counted as much opposition candidates as small, urban, pro-democratic movement parties.

Based on the assignment of each contesting party and candidate to the category of ruling elites or oppositional political elites, the official election results were used to determine the extent of electoral competitiveness. Inevitably, the official results of authoritarian elections are a distorted reflection of the political preferences of the citizenry. This is not only due to voter abstinence or biased electoral rules, but also to the neo-patrimonial influence that ruling elites can exert over the political process in general, and the electoral process in particular. A share of 30% of votes for the opposition in an authoritarian election could therefore be, e.g., the result of the violent repression of the opposition and the manipulation of the tallying process. This means that we assume that if the electoral process had been truly free and fair, the opposition would have garnered many more votes in the election. The same share of votes could, however, also be the result of a free and fair election, without, alas, the participation of those opposition parties that would have turned political apathy into protest votes. This absence of the opposition party could be the result of opposition leadership having been jailed or murdered long before electoral campaigning started. Finally, a share of 30% for the opposition could also be the result of authoritarian ruling elites using their neo-patrimonial influence over mass media and the state administration to win over voters through propaganda and pork-barrel politics.

In short, we do not know to which degree the results of authoritarian elections reflect the expressed political preferences of voters, and even less the political preferences that the citizenry did not express, or those preferences that it would have expressed if it had had access to reliable information on the political agendas of the contestants. We only know that authoritarian governance necessarily produces election results that factor in the control of ruling elites over the political process. This, however, makes the official election results a good indicator for the degree to which electoral competition was able to foster uncertainty in the political system, and thus to increase vertical accountability. Whether ruling elites manipulated the tallying process, or whether they suppressed opposition votes through vote buying, propaganda, or repression to arrive at a 30% opposition vote share in the official election results, these 30% indicate to their own followers, the citizenry, and their opponents the degree to which ruling elites had to give way to the power of the political opposition. The higher the share for the opposition, the more uncertain powerholders and their followers will be with regard to their ability to stay in power.

Electoral competitiveness will be expressed as the share of contested seats that powerholders and their parties garnered in parliamentary elections and the share of votes incumbents received in the first round of presidential elections, respectively. To account for differences in the dynamics of electoral competition between parliamentary and presidential elections, a dichotomous variable that differentiates between the two types of elections will be included among the controls in multiple linear regression analyses.

To measure electoral competitiveness in parliamentary elections, the share of contested seats will be used, rather than the share of votes for two reasons. First, the way that votes transform into parliamentary seats varies between legislative elections in different countries, and this changes what opposition votes mean in terms of the threat they pose to the ruling elite. It is this, the threat, however, that determines the degree to which elections establish the basis for vertical accountability. The prize in the legislative contest is not the vote, but—executive power aside—representation in the legislature. If opposition parties take seats in the legislature, this threatens the access of individual representatives of the ruling elite to state coffers and provides a modicum of horizontal accountability. In a first-past-the-post system for parliamentary elections, garnering 30% of the popular vote may mean that the opposition did not come close to winning a single seat in parliament. If the system is, in turn, based on proportional representation, 30% of the vote could mean that the opposition gains a sizeable "electoral foothold," and a number of members of the ruling elite lose their privileges and allowances as parliamentarians. Moreover, with increased legislative representation, the political opposition improves its possibilities to monitor the legislation process and implementation of government policies in parliamentary committees. Second, electoral commissions in authoritarian regimes often do not publish final election results for parliamentary elections. The composition of the parliament after the elections, however, is necessarily public knowledge. In the case of parliamentary elections, the extent of the political support enjoyed by the ruling elite is therefore often signaled by the legislative representation of the opposition, rather than the share of the popular vote they received.

In the case of presidential elections, the distribution of votes in the first rather than the second round of the elections will be used. First, this is because not all election systems in Sub-Saharan Africa provide for the possibility of a second round in presidential elections. Second, if a second round takes place, given the authoritarian nature of the electoral regimes under study, more often than not the decision is between the authoritarian incumbent and one opposition candidate. The share of the votes of the ruling elite candidate will then most likely be higher than in the first round. This, in turn, would mean that although a run-off election signals that electoral competition is stronger than if it did not have to take place, if electoral competitiveness was measured by the outcome of the second round, it would be assessed as weaker. Lindberg (2006b, p. 40) makes a similar point:

Many presidential elections in Africa demand an absolute majority and provide for two-round electoral systems. Since the runoff election is between the two most successful candidates from the first round, winning shares in the runoff tend to be inflated, while the figures from the first round are more representative of the actual level of competition.

Finally, the share of seats and votes that powerholders and their allies receive will be employed to measure electoral competitiveness, instead of the shares of seats and votes of the largest opposition party or the strongest opposition candidate. First and foremost, by using the share won by the largest opposition party or strongest opposition candidate, the ability of the opposition to form electoral coalitions or unite behind a joint presidential candidate would be measured. It could be argued that opposition unity is an important factor in the threat that the opposition poses to the ruling elite's claim to power. After all, a cohesive opposition is much harder for ruling elites to break up or partially co-opt than an opposition that consists of parties that are at loggerheads with each other. However, parliamentary factions of different opposition parties can and often do cooperate after the elections, and parties that each fielded their own counter-candidate in a presidential election often unite behind the strongest one in the second round. Irrespective of this, it may well be that opposition unity is an important factor in the decision of citizens to cast a vote for the opposition, but this effect of opposition unity is accounted for when employing election results as the indicator for electoral competitiveness.

To assess which parties and candidates belong to the ruling elite and which represent the de facto political opposition, well over 600 publications have been consulted, among which were election observation mission reports, academic papers, and country reports by international research projects. For each election, at least two sources have been compared. Official election results have been collected from these sources and from the African Elections Database (Nunley 2012).

Electoral competitiveness has been measured for all direct national multi-party elections for the parliament or the presidency in Sub-Saharan Africa between 1990 and 2012 that were held under the conditions of non-democratic governance. The qualifications "direct" and "national" imply that only elections in which national representatives are elected through citizens directly are included. Indirect elections, such as in the case of the Senate in Gabon, where local counsellors cast their votes to elect senators, are not included in this definition. Neither are elections on the sub-national level. Elections that have been held in territories that are not internationally recognized, such as Somaliland, are not part of the study population either.

An election was considered multi-party only if the field of contenders was not fully determined by the ruling party or president. If opposition parties chose to boycott an election, the election was still considered a multi-party election. If, however, all parties that did not declare their support of the ruling party were excluded from the electoral contest by law, as was the case in the Nigerian presidential and parliamentary elections in 1998, or only parties that were created by the government were allowed to contest the election, as was the case in Nigeria's 1992 and 1993 elections, then the elections were not regarded as multi-party even though more than one party contested them. These elections were therefore excluded from the study population.

Included in the definition of multi-party elections, in turn, are the so-called "no-party" presidential elections in Sudan and Uganda in 1996 (Mugaju and Oloka-Onyango 2000). No-party elections were elections in which only individuals who had no party affiliation were allowed to compete. Parties were prohibited from playing an active role in politics (Carbone 2003). Nonetheless, in no-party elections, the field of contenders is not fully determined by the ruling party. This sets them apart from one-party elections. In no-party *presidential* elections, an individual opposition candidate, if successful, would have been enough to provide significant political change. For example, in Uganda's 1996 presidential elections, two of the three candidates clearly represented political alternatives to the incumbent (William 1997). No-party presidential elections provided a meaningful outlet for the preferences of dissident voters. Opposition candidates in no-party legislative elections, on the other hand, cannot agitate for a change in government because they have to compete as "independents," and so cannot develop a joint alternative political platform from the incumbents. While the two no-party *presidential* elections in Sudan and Uganda in 1996 have been included in the study population, no-party *legislative* elections have been excluded from it.

To measure the degree to which governance was considered democratic at the time of the preparation of elections, the latest Freedom House rating for the respective country was employed which did not cover the period of six months before polling day. This was done so that election-related activities did not influence the Freedom House rating. Thus, rating the governance of ruling elites as democratic because of an election-related thaw in the relations between the ruling elites and their opposition in preparation of the arrival of international election observation missions is avoided. Only elections where the regime had already received the status "free" from Freedom House for the year preceding electoral campaigning were counted as non-authoritarian. All other elections were considered authoritarian and are part of the study population.

To measure the mobilization threat that ruling elites, oppositional political elites, and societal groups pose to each other before elections, the public direct engagements of these actors with their opponents will be used as an indicator. Political mobilizations are public direct engagements of ruling elites, oppositional political elites, and societal groups with their opponents. Information on political mobilizations by ruling elites, oppositional political elites, and societal groups is taken from the Social Conflict in Africa Database (Salehyan et al. 2012). To be able to clearly delineate cause and effect with regard to electoral competitiveness, measures for the relative mobilization threat of the principal actors in the democratization process exclude political mobilizations during electoral campaigns. Following the operationalization by Lindberg (2006a, p. 35), the campaign phase is defined as a period of six months before polling day. It is assumed that campaign activities usually start at this time. Campaigning is a crucial part of the electoral contest already. From that moment onwards until the elections, opposition parties mobilize adherents as participants of the electoral contest. During the campaign, the effects of societal groups' mobilization threat and the less antagonistic roles they play for the strengthening of opposition parties already play out. Including mobilizations of the principal actors in the democratization process during election campaigns would therefore create a situation in which the line between cause and effect becomes blurry. Therefore, to operationalize the mobilization threat of ruling elites, oppositional political elites, and societal groups, the number of political mobilizations occurring 18 to six months before election day will be used.

The main empirical hypothesis of the book is that the stronger the mobilization threat from societal groups is, the more competitive authoritarian elections in Sub-Saharan Africa are. In the following paragraphs, more nuanced hypotheses regarding the effect of the mobilization threat of the principal political actors on electoral competitiveness are formulated. These will be tested in four regression models. The expected impact of the mobilization threat posed by societal groups on the democratization process through regular direct public engagement is in the first instance an increased protection of the political space in which societal groups operate. By raising the costs of their suppression, societal groups make ruling elites more likely to tolerate public acts of dissent and accommodate public demands for reform. Opposition parties profit from this curtailing of the ruling elite's neo-patrimonial power as well. Stronger societal groups with more room to maneuver indicate more room for oppositional political elites to nurture their leadership skills and networks and reach out to constituencies. For this reason, it is generally assumed that the more public protest by societal groups is directed towards the ruling elite, the better the performance of opposition parties in authoritarian elections.

Hypothesis 1: The higher the frequency of public direct engagements by societal groups with ruling elites in the time before the onset of electoral campaigning, the higher the electoral competitiveness in authoritarian elections.

From the previous discussion of the role of societal groups in the democratization process, we can further conclude that the types of issues that societal groups raise in publicly visible confrontations with ruling elites are important for their impact on the democratization process. Direct engagements will have an impact on the mobilization capacity of oppositional political elites if societal groups bring forward demands on the state with regard to specific socio-economic grievances, such as economic development, environmental protection, education, or public health care. Through this "socio-economic mobilization," they will contribute to public discourse on governance and government policies. This, in turn, is one important part of the establishment of political platforms that opposition parties can employ to reach out to potential constituencies. When societal groups address the political process rather than substantial politics in their direct engagements with ruling elites, their impact on electoral competitiveness is less immediate. By protesting the violations of political rights and civil liberties, societal groups do not directly facilitate the buildup of mobilization capacity among oppositional political elites. After all, an improved political playing field needs a strong political opposition in order to increase electoral competitiveness.

Hypothesis 2: Public direct engagements with ruling elites in which societal groups raise socio-economic issues will have a stronger impact on electoral competitiveness than pro-democracy mobilizations.

When societal groups address the state and government with their public direct engagements, they increase their mobilization threat in the eyes of ruling elites, and thus contribute to an intensification of electoral competitiveness in electoral authoritarian regimes. However, societal groups can also mobilize against each other. From a collective action perspective, it would be expected that such public direct engagements weaken the overall mobilization threat that societal groups pose to ruling elites. Much like elite splits weaken authoritarian ruling coalitions by facilitating collaborations with societal groups, mobilizations of one societal group against another will give ruling elites opportunities to accommodate the demands of less government-critical groups and diminish the overall mobilization capacity of societal groups. Where elite splits decrease the probabilities that security forces attach to the ruling elite winning a conflict with their opponents, and hence decrease the resolve of the army and the police to use repression in defense of the government, societal conflicts have a contrary effect. They increase the perceived ability of ruling elites to win the political conflict and make collaboration between the security apparatus and the political leadership more likely.

Hypothesis 3: The higher the frequency of public direct engagements of one societal group with another in the time before the onset of electoral campaigning, the lower the electoral competitiveness in authoritarian elections.

The collective action perspective also leads to expectations regarding the impact of ruling elites' mobilizations on electoral competitiveness. Mobilizations of the ruling elite in the public sphere, such as pro-government rallies or attacks of the security forces on societal groups and the political opposition, increase the mobilization threat that ruling elites pose to their opponents. Pro-government mobilizations of civilian supporters reinforce the impression among citizens that the ruling elite enjoys widespread support in the population. With that, the likelihood increases that mutual ignorance among would-be dissenters will be maintained, and potential support for the opposition will express itself as political apathy rather than pro-opposition activism. Proactive attacks of the security apparatus on government-critical individuals and organizations, in turn, decrease the availability of solutions to the collective action problem to societal groups and the political opposition, and thereby increase the mobilization capacity of the ruling elite relative to the mobilization capacity of their opponents.

Hypothesis 4: The higher the frequency of public direct engagements of ruling elites with societal groups or the opposition in the time before the onset of electoral campaigning, the lower the electoral competitiveness in subsequent authoritarian elections.

Similar to societal groups, the collective action perspective leads us to the hypothesis that the political opposition also contributes to a strengthening of electoral competitiveness by increasing their mobilization threat through public direct engagements with the ruling elite and the bystander public in the time before elections. Given the unfavorable context for the development of the mobilization capacity of the political opposition in electoral authoritarian regimes, however, their activities are expected to be largely confined to the mobilization of citizens in elections. Comparative research on parties in Sub-Saharan Africa seems to confirm this expectation (see, e.g., Erdmann 1999). During the electoral process, opposition parties stage public direct engagements when they organize political rallies. In addition to this, they are also active during the electoral process when they communicate their political messages through the mass media channels available or establish a network of party representatives for election observation. By declaring their contestation of the elections, they threaten to turn the pre-electoral mobilization capacity of societal groups and their own ability to mobilize party militants into a direct attack on ruling elite dominance.

To adequately conceptualize the role of opposition parties in the framework of this research design, the impact of two different aspects of the mobilization threat of oppositional political elites on electoral competitiveness will be tested. First, it will be tested whether the mobilization threat projected by opposition parties through public direct engagements has a positive effect on electoral competitiveness. The hypothesis is that, for the same reasons as in the case of societal groups, it will.

Hypothesis 5: The higher the frequency of public direct engagements of opposition parties with ruling elites in the time before the onset of electoral campaigning, the higher the electoral competitiveness in authoritarian elections.

Second, the extent to which major opposition parties and candidates declare their participation in the elections by legally registering for the electoral contest was measured. The non-participation of opposition parties and candidates occurs for two reasons. First, there is self-chosen non-participation, such as when individual parties or candidates withdraw because of weak political support, or the political opposition declares a boycott of the election. Second, there is forced non-participation, such as when individual parties and candidates are unable to meet established legal criteria, or ruling elites have certain opposition parties or candidates banned. Problems of weak political support and legal issues aside, we can assume that behind the non-participation of opposition parties are strategic considerations by opposition parties and ruling elites that weigh short-term and long-term consequences. If major opposition parties boycott elections, we may assume that they attempt to turn anti-government into anti-regime mobilization: They give up on a gradual democratization process and agitate for a revolutionary end to the current regime. At the same time that they reinvest their energy into a revolution with uncertain outcomes through their non-participation, opposition parties forgo the chance to transform the pre-electoral mobilization threat posed by societal and political groups into electoral competitiveness. As Lindberg (2006b, p. 162) explains, election boycotts "may serve well to discredit the established regime, but they are of little practical use in furthering greater openness". This is because without the participation of the political opposition "there is no choice, and when there is no choice, the public cannot exercise its discretion to indirectly rule via representation" (Lindberg 2006b, p. 150). If opposition parties decide to participate in elections instead, "even if the conditions are not fully free and fair," they have a chance to "gradually build strength both within legislatures and in society in general, in anticipation of winning subsequent elections"

(Lindberg 2006b, p. 162). Given the organizational weakness of African opposition parties, it seems especially doubtful that their boycott contributes to a revolutionary regime change, let alone a regime change that brings along a more democratic regime. Based on data on opposition behavior and democratization in all countries in Sub-Saharan Africa between 1989 and 2003, Lindberg (2006b, p. 155) concludes that opposition participation "is clearly associated with the transformation of electoral autocracies into democracies over a sequence of multi-party elections". Thus, by precluding an increase in electoral competitiveness through their non-participation, opposition parties are missing an opportunity to contribute to the democratization of electoral authoritarian regimes.

Regardless of the "tragedy" of self-chosen, non-participation as pro-democratic protest (Lindberg 2006b), the threat of a boycott by major opposition parties may be made with the intent to push forward reforms of the electoral process rather than promote a revolution. In this case, a threat to boycott would be a bluff by an opposition that tries to improve the conditions under which they participate in the elections. Having to follow through with it, however, reveals the weakness of their own mobilization threat and that of societal groups. Ruling elites who are able to organize and hold elections despite such a threat and its implementation prove, in turn, their dominance over the political struggle. Election results will indicate this dominance with very high shares of votes for the ruling party and its candidates. Bans of individual opposition parties or their candidates by ruling elites indicate a similar state of affairs. If ruling elites are able to follow through with such a political ban, that is, if elections are held without the participation of the banned parties, they assert their position of power in the interaction with oppositional political elites and societal groups. This will result in reduced electoral competitiveness, as it is unlikely that all supporters of a banned party will shift their electoral support to another opposition candidate.

Hypothesis 6: The more major opposition parties declare their participation in elections at the outset of the electoral process, the higher the electoral competitiveness in authoritarian elections.

To investigate these hypotheses, several multiple linear regression analyses will be conducted. The cases for these multivariate analyses are authoritarian direct national multi-party elections for either the parliament or the presidency on the African subcontinent between 1990 and 2012. 284 such elections have been held in Sub-Saharan Africa in that period, of which 148 were parliamentary and 136 were presidential elections. If a country has a two-chamber parliament, elections for each of the chambers that were held on the same date were counted as one election.

The data on authoritarian elections in Sub-Saharan Africa used for the empirical analyses contains repeated observations (i.e., elections) of the same fixed political units (i.e., countries). Generally, it takes the form of time-series cross-section data. As repeated elections in one country cannot necessarily be treated as independent observations, ordinary least squares or generalized least squares methods may perform poorly in estimating regressions of time-series cross-section data (Steiner and Martin 2012, p. 250).

However, the data is strongly "cross-sectional dominant" (Stimson 1985). The number of countries in Sub-Saharan Africa with authoritarian elections is 42, while the average number of authoritarian elections per country is only five. (Note that 94 elections are general elections where a presidential and a legislative election occur at the same time.) Cross-sectional dominant data present less concern for autocorrelation, that is, for correlation of repeated observations with earlier instances of themselves (Fortin-Rittberger 2015, p. 392). At the same time, methods that could statistically model such features of the data require a minimum number of repeated observations per unit, so that averaging operations over time are meaningful. For this reason, Beck (2001, p. 274) argues that "one ought to be suspicious of TSCS methods used for, say, $T < 10$". In the data utilized herein, all but one unit has less than ten observations. In 21 countries, less than five elections were held.

With few repeated observations and a relatively large number of units, the data is structurally similar to panel data. Therefore, generalized least squares will be recurred to in order to estimate the effect of the mobilization threat of societal groups on electoral competitiveness, and correct for unit heterogeneity. Two solutions are commonly discussed to deal with unit heterogeneity: Fixed effects or random effects. Fixed-effects models have the disadvantage of decreasing the degrees of freedom of the regression model and the efficiency of the variables of interest (Steiner and Martin 2012, p. 251). Random-effects models, on the other hand, make additional assumptions regarding unobserved unit heterogeneity in the data (Fortin-Rittberger 2015, p. 396). Another drawback is that regression coefficients based on random-effect models are harder to interpret substantively, as they represent average changes in the dependent variable when the independent variable changes across time *and* between countries by one unit (Fortin-Rittberger 2015, p. 396).

A Hausman test is often recommended to determine which solution to choose (Greene 2011, p. 419). It tests the null hypothesis that differences between the coefficients obtained with a fixed-effects and a random-effects model are not systematic. If it is rejected, the more restrictive fixed-effects model should be used. For all four multiple linear regression models that were specified, the Hausman test was nonsignificant, i.e., the null hypothesis could not be rejected. Table A.8 provides the test statistics for all four models. In line with these results, generalized least squares with random effects were used to estimate the regressions.

4.4   Political Mobilizations and Electoral Competitiveness

In previous chapters, it has been shown that the story of democratization in Sub-Saharan Africa is one of uncompetitive politics, where the outcome of elections is regularly a foregone conclusion. This lack of electoral competitiveness is strongly linked to broader democratic deficiencies, such as the protection of civil liberties. At the same time, it was demonstrated that despite the inimical conditions of neo-patrimonial electoral authoritarian regimes, political mobilizations of societal groups on the subcontinent have time and again led to sustained mobilizations that effected lasting political consequences. Moreover, the quantitative data suggest that societal groups in Sub-Saharan Africa have increased their mobilization capacity over time.

In the present chapter, the evidence on trends in political mobilization and electoral competitiveness will be combined to test the book's central hypothesis, namely, that the stronger the mobilization threat by societal groups at the outset of the electoral process is, the more competitive authoritarian elections in Sub-Saharan Africa are. It was hypothesized that the mobilization threat posed by societal groups achieves this mainly in two ways. First, it improves the conditions for civic activism and electoral competition, because by their threat to mobilize against ruling elites, societal groups raise the costs of their suppression and that of the violation of political rights and civil liberties by any actor. Second, through the political or socio-economic issues their mobilizations bring forward, societal groups provide a political platform for oppositional political elites on which the latter can base their electoral campaigns. Based on these mechanisms, six hypotheses were formulated regarding the effects of the relative mobilization threats of societal groups, the political opposition, and ruling elites on the competitiveness of authoritarian elections.

Before these hypotheses are tested with quantitative data, it will be demonstrated in three case studies how societal mobilizations produce important shifts in electoral competitiveness. These case studies serve to highlight the different ways in which the mobilization threat posed by societal groups may translate into increased electoral competitiveness in founding and later elections. The three case studies show that such a threat does not have to be revolutionary to propel democratization processes, as when pro-democracy movements sweep away authoritarian rulers. By strengthening the position of the political opposition through socio-economic mobilizations and cooperation, the mobilization threat by societal groups may also lead to increased electoral competitiveness below the threshold of electoral turnovers, and thereby to pro-democratic political reform.

Subsequently, multiple linear regression analyses of all authoritarian elections in Sub-Saharan Africa between 1990 and 2012 will provide quantitative evidence for the influence of the mobilization threat by societal groups on electoral competitiveness. The results show that when societal groups engage in political mobilizations, and especially socio-economic mobilizations, they increase the chances that electoral competitiveness increases. A detailed discussion of the results of four regression models will relate the empirical evidence to the six quantitative research hypotheses.

4.4.1   How Political Mobilizations Effect Electoral Competitiveness

In the following pages, three case studies will show how the mobilization threat by societal groups in the pre-election period of authoritarian elections translates into electoral competitiveness in different ways under different circumstances. The focus is not on the role of pro-democracy movements in regime change, that is, it is not on the process by which often broad-based revolutionary movements lead to the introduction of multi-party politics. While political mobilizations by societal groups seem to have played an important role in democratic regime changes across Sub-Saharan Africa, this book focuses on the role of societal mobilization for the strengthening of the political opposition in the gradual democratization of electoral authoritarian regimes while preparing for or regularly holding elections. To illustrate the processes behind such incremental political change, the case studies will look at political mobilizations of societal groups in the period before the onset of electoral campaigning for three different elections, and the ways in which those mobilizations influenced the political power of opposition parties.

The three cases are the events leading up to founding elections in Zambia in 1991 and their aftermath, the third legislative elections in Burkina Faso in 2002, and the eight presidential elections in Senegal in 2012. The case studies will show how violent and non-violent political mobilizations by societal groups can promote electoral competitiveness directly and indirectly, in close collaboration with or distanced from oppositional political elites, in extra-ordinary as well as in regular elections. The examples will also highlight additional observable implications of the book's main hypothesis regarding the role of the mobilization threat of societal groups for electoral competitiveness, such as the importance of trade unions for broader protest movements, the urban origin of most political mobilizations, and the weakness of civil society after protest-driven electoral turnovers.

In Zambia, the decision to hold multi-party elections in 1991 marked the end of a successful political struggle against the ruling elites of the one-party regime. At the same time, preparations for these elections required a continuation of the struggle under new conditions. When the long-term president of Zambia's one-party state, Kenneth Kaunda, announced the holding of the country's first multi-party elections in September 1990 for the following year, he was reacting to mounting pressure for reform that started with food riots in Lusaka and led to the formation of a broad-based movement for multi-party democracy (Bartlett 2000; Erdmann and Simutanyi 2003). While such an announcement is an important step in the transition to democracy, sufficiently insulating the ensuing process of institutional reform from the influence of the authoritarian incumbents is a necessary condition for competitive founding elections. Concurrent and subsequent transitions to multi-party politics under the tutelage of authoritarian leaders in Sub-Saharan Africa show that top-down democratization processes often lead to a continuation of single-party authoritarian politics in a multi-party disguise. Founding elections in Djibouti (1992), Equatorial Guinea (1993), Togo (1993), or Rwanda (2003) are cases in point. Here, leaders of one-party regimes "exploited the powers of incumbency to dictate the rules of the political game by manipulating electoral laws, monopolizing campaign resources, or interfering with the polls" to effectively prevent electoral competition by the political opposition that they had just decreed into existence (Bratton and van de Walle 1997, p. 121). As the Zambian example shows, truly competitive founding elections under the participation of the "old guard" may be achieved through extra-ordinary mobilization and collaboration of societal groups with oppositional political elites. In particular, it shows how the labor movement—which in the pursuit of democratic reform had already proven its capability to bring the country's economy to a halt—provided essential mobilization capacity to the political challengers of the ruling party (Erdmann and Simutanyi 2003, p. 11).

Oppositional political elites coalesced under the umbrella of the Movement for Multi-party Democracy (MMD). Formed as an advocacy group in July 1990, it registered as a political party in January 1991, shortly after the necessary legislation was passed. The MMD counted among its members business owners, clerics, academics, and intellectuals, as well as the leadership of trade unions (Bartlett 2000). In early 1991, the Zambian Congress of Trade Unions (ZCTU) officially declared its allegiance to the MMD. At that moment, "all trade union offices all over the country immediately became recruiting centers for the movement while trade union leaders openly campaigned for public support to defeat Kaunda" (Ihonvbere 1996, p. 117) and the ruling United National Independence Party (UNIP). Such organizational structures of societal groups proved vital to counter-weigh the "overinflated UNIP party machinery from the ward chairmen up" that had evolved in 27 years of single-party rule (Andreassen et al. 1992, p. 21) not only for recruitment, but also during campaigning. Political rallies by various societal groups in favor of multi-party democracy were instrumental in promoting the agenda of change. Ihonvbere (1996, p. 123) cites a former member of parliament of the MMD as saying that "the unions, churches, schools, and businesses helped to spread the message of the MMD to the remotest parts of Zambia".

Moreover, while Zambian opposition parties were busy forming a leadership, building organizations, and—with the help of societal groups—reaching out to potential constituencies, attempts by the ruling elite to shape the emerging electoral process to their advantage had to be fought off repeatedly. Here, too, the support of societal groups was crucial. In June 1991, for example, a commission instituted by the ruling party UNIP made proposals for constitutional amendments that would have vested a lot of power in the presidency under the new multi-party system, including the right to impose martial law. Before the background of violent clashes between workers, students, the urban underclass, and UNIP supporters, church leaders stepped in and negotiated a joint constitutional review process in which the opposition "was able to push through significant amendments to the new constitution, thereby introducing important checks and balances within the political structure" (Andreassen et al. 1992, p. 16). Attempts at tilting the playing field for UNIP included intimidation of MMD supporters. This included threats of revenge for the lack of electoral support by UNIP officials, violent attacks of known MMD members, and the deployment of paramilitary forces. While the deterrent effect of local counter-mobilizations by societal groups in containing state-sponsored violence is hard to pinpoint, on the national level, coalitions of civil society organizations provided important channels for the voicing of local grievances and facilitated consultations between UNIP and the MMD that led to calls by both party leaderships to remain calm and peaceful (Andreassen et al. 1992, p. 41).

For the electoral process itself, the mobilization of societal groups was important in providing for a free and fair contest. Two local monitoring groups emerged in the pre-election period: The Zambian Independent Monitoring Team (ZIMT) and the Zambian Election Monitoring Coordination Committee (ZEMCC). Together, the two monitoring groups trained and deployed over 6000 local election observers (Andreassen et al. 1992, ix). Reportedly, however, only ZEMCC was able to place monitors at polling stations throughout Zambia (Andreassen et al. 1992, p. 58). Overall, the churches played an important role in the recruitment of election observers and in the provision of facilities for trainings across the country (Ihonvbere 1996, p. 135). The ZEMCC's appeal and success in particular "was very much based on the fact that theirs was a broad-based organization, which was able to use the highly efficient and trusted grassroots infrastructure of the churches" (Andreassen et al. 1992, p. 58).

In founding elections where societal groups were not able to cast such a broad and dense net of local election monitors over the entirety of the country, incumbents often tinkered with election results, especially in rural areas where international election observers had not been present, and thus secured their survival in office. In Zambia, however, the MMD's support, as registered in the official election results, "was widespread, rural and urban, and did cut across ethnic groups" (Ihonvbere 1996, p. 125). It led to an overwhelming victory by the political opposition. In the new parliament, the UNIP lost all but 16.67% of its seats, and its presidential candidate, Kenneth Kaunda, was defeated by a wide margin, with 24.24% for the incumbent compared to 75.76% of the votes for MMD leader Frederick Chiluba.

The Zambian example also displays a typical post-transition phenomenon: A demobilization by a large part of civil society in the wake of founding elections. This phenomenon has its roots in a reduction of the solutions to the collective action problem available to societal groups. While a victory for the pro-democracy movement, the election to power of the MMD paralyzed civil society in the country. First, as a local observer expressed, with the MMD in power, civil society organizations "felt it was 'their' government in power" and did not expect to have to mobilize against it (Mumba 2010, p. 8). A realignment among societal groups is needed before broad-based political mobilizations against the new government become possible. This process of reorientation was reported, too, by local experts when power changed hands again between the government and the opposition in Zambia in general elections in 2011 (personal interview, 14 November 2012, Lusaka). Second, with many influential figures in Zambian civil society now in government, societal groups lacked experienced leadership to mobilize successfully. Third, the new ruling elites, although they were drawn from the ranks of trade unions in many instances, soon turned against their former power base when the latter started organizing against government policies (Mumba 2010, p. 9). As an important figure in the MMD later noted, the labor movement might have been targeted by the MMD government precisely because the new president was a former leader of the ZCTU and therefore took the mobilization threat of trade unions seriously: "He used the labor movement as a ladder to become president. So, you wouldn't have wanted another person that uses the same ladder" (personal interview, 27 November 2012, Lusaka). The government's interference with the labor movement led to political conflicts among trade unions with regard to their stance towards the MMD, which paralyzed the leadership and led to a split of the movement in 1994 (Erdmann and Simutanyi 2003, p. 40).

While democratic governance deteriorated after 1991 until civil society had found its footing again, violations of political rights and civil liberties never reached the levels of systematic repression of societal groups that had been common under Kaunda's one-party regime. As Elemu (2010, p. 21) explains, "Kaunda promoted an ideology that ensured strict party and state control in all spheres of society. [...] What existed is similar to what has been conceptualised as 'state-led civil society'". After society had regrouped, civil society organizations flourished, despite harassments from MMD sources (Commonwealth Human Rights Initiative 1996, p. 17). Hundreds of new organizations were formed and old ones increased their mobilization capacity. The church, for example, built structures with, in some parts of the country, "a more pervasive presence than the government" (Duncan et al. 2003, p. 39). Service delivery NGO's played an increasingly important role in filling the gap in basic service delivery, which provided civil society with important avenues for constituency outreach (Erdmann and Simutanyi 2003, p. 42). The "experience and confidence gained over the past decade" (Erdmann and Simutanyi 2003, p. 43) then culminated in the formation of the Oasis Forum, a broad-based coalition of civil society organizations that stopped Frederick Chiluba's bid to change the constitution and stand for a third term as the president of Zambia (Dulani 2011).

Burkina Faso's second multi-party parliamentary election in 2002 took place in a much less fluid political situation than the Zambian founding elections. Public direct engagements by societal groups in Burkina Faso in the months before electoral campaigning addressed an assertive authoritarian ruling elite that had gained considerable experience in countering electoral threats. The country's president at the time, Blaise Compaoré, had gained power in a coup in 1987. Before a sustained protest movement for democratic reforms could emerge, under his leadership, the ruling party Front Populaire (PF) introduced presidential and legislative multi-party elections that led to his unassailable election and re-election in 1991 and 1998, and to overwhelming presidential majorities in the parliament after legislative elections in 1992 and 1997. As Loada and Santiso (2002, p. 3) explain, "the democratization process thus remained largely in check, in the straightjacket of a predominant ruling party".

Nevertheless, the 2002 parliamentary elections would prove substantially more competitive than the previous parliamentary elections in 1997. After having won 90.99% of the seats in the 1997 electoral contest, in 2002, with 57 of the 111 mandates, the ruling party Congrés pour la Démocratie et le Progrès (CDP) barely managed to retain an absolute majority in parliament. In view of the political reform the election had triggered and the seismic shift in electoral support, "many political commentators asserted that the country was in a critical moment of its political evolution" (Hilgers 2010, p. 353). Given the massive gain in political power by the opposition, in 2003 observers wondered whether Blaise Compaoré would last in office until the next presidential election (Hilgers and Mazzocchetti 2006, p. 6).

Burkina Faso's highly competitive second parliamentary election was preceded by sustained, broad-based political mobilizations by societal groups. Through their protest, they promoted an agenda for political reform that was taken up by oppositional political elites, and facilitated coordination and cooperation among civil society organizations and political parties. The joint mobilization threat of the social and political opposition forced political concessions by ruling elites, and built an electoral platform for oppositional political elites that strongly resonated with the electorate. Thus, the Burkinabé example shows that below the threshold of revolutionary overthrow and electoral turnover, societal mobilization can result in increased electoral competitiveness in electoral authoritarian regimes.

The political mobilizations by societal groups in the pre-election phase took their origin in the spontaneous protests that followed the assassination of the independent Burkinabé journalist Norbert Zongo in 1998. These demonstrations and riots gave birth to the "Trop c'est trop!" (Enough is enough) movement that led to a peak of political mobilizations in Burkina Faso in 2000. The movement's central demand was a comprehensive investigation into the death of the government-critical journalist. This quickly turned into a broader call for the end of a "culture of impunity" in Burkina Faso, in which ruling elites committed crimes without punishment (Hagberg 2002, p. 221). Soon, the movement's rallying cry "enough is enough" referred to a range of excesses of the ruling elite and the consequences of its governance, such as severe poverty, corruption, and political hegemony (Harsch 1999, p. 395). The strength of the protest movement and the breadth of its political demands "astounded even veteran opposition politicians and took many of them off guard" (Harsch 1999, p. 399). At that time, the main opposition parties enjoyed little support, and had struggled "with demoralization and lack of unity and direction for several years" (Harsch 1999, p. 399). With 9.11% of the mandates, their representation in parliament was at an historic low.

While opposition politicians joined the demonstrations and spoke at rallies, they were not able to direct the movement's course (Harsch 1999, p. 400). As the organizational core of the movement emerged the "Collectif d'organisations democratiques de masse et de partis politiques," a coalition of four clusters of societal groups: Human rights organizations, previously "non-political" organizations that had been politicized by the assassination and the violence in its aftermath, a group of opposition parties, and associations of students and pupils (Ouédraogo 2006, p. 16). Thus, the Collectif united the social and political opposition to the CDP. It carried on the demands of the movement, but it also claimed to represent "the real country" and thus directly challenged Compaoré's claim to power (Hagberg 2002, p. 226). The Collectif organized a series of demonstrations and strikes, "so as to maintain the mobilisation and keep the pressure on 'the power'" (Hagberg 2002, p. 222). These direct public engagements of the Collectif were not intended to be violent, but boundaries with riots and lootings of state property were fluid. Often, the violent repression of peaceful marches triggered counter-violence, making the capital Ouagadougou sometimes look like "a city under siege" (Hagberg 2002, p. 224).

While it created "intense pressure" on the government through street action (Loada and Santiso 2002, p. 6), at the same time, the Collectif provided ruling elites with a negotiating partner. This allowed for a process of consultation and concertation in the two years leading up to the parliamentary elections in which a series of political reforms were enacted. Thus, the mobilization threat of societal groups led to concessions by ruling elites that increased the space for the political opposition to mobilize. The reform package included a revision of the election code, a reinstitution of presidential term limits, and the inclusion of opposition parties in the government. As Loada and Santiso (2002, p. 6) explain, "these developments reflect an important change in the political culture and attitude of the CDP, brought about by the mobilization of civil society and opposition parties against impunity and authoritarianism".

Thanks to the political reforms and the joint agenda set by societal groups in the streets, opposition parties made marked gains in the election (Harsch 2009, p. 275). With 64.1%, turnout was 8% higher than in the previous legislative election. The parties organized in the Collectif increased the share of the votes they were able to garner in the election considerably. This led some parties to win additional legislative mandates, while others gained representation in the Burkinabé parliament for the first time. Thus, the parliamentary elections confirmed the gain in political power that the opposition had achieved in the pre-election period through its renewed connection with societal groups (Hilgers and Mazzocchetti 2006, p. 10).

Political mobilization decreased considerably after the 2002 elections. Ruling elites reacted to the demobilization in predictable ways. They "neutralized" the political reforms they were forced to concede in the years prior. Electoral reforms were reviewed in 2004 and changed to the disadvantage of smaller parties, the presidential two-term limit was declared non-retroactive in 2005, and the case of the murder of the independent journalist that inspired the "Trop c'est trop" movement was closed in 2006 (Hilgers 2010, p. 353). Only in 2014 were Blaise Compaoré and his ruling party finally ousted. The popular uprising that led to his overthrow, however, "did not arise ex nihilo" (Chouli 2015, p. 325). Instead, "the decline of the Compaoré regime can be traced back to the assassination of journalist Norbert Zongo in 1998 and its political effects" (Frere and Englebert 2015, p. 298). Political mobilizations in the aftermath of Zongo's death "marked a turning point in the fight against political impunity and led to a real growth of popular mobilizations" over time (Chouli 2015, p. 326). Despite intermittent demobilizations, networks, organizations, and framings survived, and provided the grounds for renewed mobilizations at a later time. Thus, the 2014 Burkinabé "insurrection" clearly showed continuities with previous uprisings, both in terms of leading organizations and the social and political struggles at its core (Chouli 2015, p. 325).

The political mobilizations by societal groups in the run-up to Senegal's eighth presidential election in 2012 had much more immediate consequences. The election was overshadowed by the attempts of president Abdoulaye Wade to consolidate his power through constitutional amendments and repression. Senegal was one of only four countries on the African subcontinent that had already established a multi-party electoral regime when the wave of democratic regime changes swept across Sub-Saharan Africa in the early 1990s. The inception of its current series of elections dates to 1983. For most of that time it was heralded as a rare example of a functioning democratic polity in Sub-Saharan Africa (Villalón 1994, p. 163). Wade had replaced the long-term president Abdou Diouf in a peaceful electoral turnover in Senegal's fifth cycle of multi-party elections in 2000. His election to the presidency was seen as a proof that the country's democratic system had matured (Resnick 2013, p. 629). One year later, the Parti Socialiste du Sénégal (PS), which had governed the country since 1960, lost its legislative majority to Wade's Parti Démocratique Sénégalais (PDS) in parliamentary elections.

However, from 2005 onwards, protests against the rising cost of basic commodities and Wade's failure to deliver on his campaign promise of more jobs for Senegal's youth threatened the hold on power of both the president and the PDS. In reaction to this, Senegal's new ruling elites tried to curtail the political space for societal and political opposition. Knowing well what brought him into power, Wade's efforts to establish control over societal mobilizations focused on the media and political NGOs (Hartmann 2014, p. 174). The ruling elite's attempts at an authoritarian roll-back led to Freedom House down-grading the country's status to "partially free" in 2007. This rating was kept until Senegal's eight presidential elections in 2012. In the meantime, the country witnessed more attempts of the ruling elite to effect an authoritarian concentration of political power. While the electoral process had been protected against interference by a wave of violent mass protests, opposition parties successfully reached out to the electorate in the 2012 presidential elections. Yet, with Macky Sall, a late comer to the anti-government protests and a former prime minister under Wade, won the presidency in the run-off election. Thus, the Senegalese example shows that, first, violent protest is not inimical to the consolidation of democracy, and that, second, while societal groups and opposition parties may benefit from coordination and cooperation, individual candidates are able to profit from the mobilization threat and agenda-setting power of civil society as well, if they do not seek close collaboration with societal groups.

Pre-electoral political mobilizations started on 23 June 2011 with mass protests against a proposal for a constitutional amendment that Wade submitted to the parliament at short notice. The protests were organized by a movement called "Y'en a Marre" (Fed up), which was made up of Senegalese musicians and journalists. The constitutional amendment would have lowered the necessary majority to win the presidency in the first round to 25% of the votes, and created the post of a popularly-elected vice-president. It was rumored that the latter was a move to create a public office for Wade's son to prepare him for a take-over of the presidency when his father had exhausted the constitutional term limits.

Several thousand, mostly young people heeded the movement's call for protests, which quickly turned violent. Faced with the unexpected mass mobilization, the government withdrew the proposal for the constitutional amendment on the same day. As much as it is likely that the anger expressed in the massive street violence was not caused by the constitutional amendment alone, it is unlikely that ruling elites would have conceded victory to the movement had it not feared the youth's potential for further violence. Instead, long-standing grievances, such as high unemployment and frequent power outages, created an explosive atmosphere in which the movement's rallying cry acted as an ignition spark (Hartmann 2012, p. 7).

On the same day as the mass protests and the withdrawal of the proposal, civil society organizations and opposition parties founded the "Mouvement 23-Juin" (M23), named after the date of the mass uprising. In July 2011, Wade announced his intention to run for a third term, arguing that the two-term limit was added to the constitution after he had ascended to the presidency and hence did not apply to him (Gueye

2013, p. 26). The movement publicly declared its resolve to prevent Wade's candidature "with all means available" (Hartmann 2012, p. 7). While it ultimately failed in this, the movement served as an important discussion forum and coordinating body for demonstrations and strike activities of societal groups and political parties. The M23 also decided to support a joint presidential candidate. In December 2011, three months before the presidential elections, it publicly announced its support for Moustapha Niasse, a long-term opposition politician. This led to tensions between the movement and other presidential hopefuls who had supported the political mobilizations of the movement (Hartmann 2012, p. 7). Despite these tensions, in the remaining time before the elections, the movement transformed itself into a vocal political coalition in support of the candidates that emerged from its midst (Mari 2012).

However, in the first round of the presidential elections in February 2012, Macky Sall emerged as the leading opposition candidate. With 26.58% of the votes, he came in second after Wade with 34.81%. Moustapha Niasse, the movement's main candidate, garnered only 13.20% of the votes. Sall was not directly involved in the "Y'en a Marre" or M23 movements. While Niasse and other opposition politicians participated in mass protests and engaged in civil disobedience alongside the movements' political activists, Sall toured the country on his own election campaign (Resnick 2013, p. 633). Yet, he clearly profited from the political mobilizations of the broad-based civic movement. First, he based his own campaign on the movements' anti-authoritarian and pro-poor platform. He focused on the problem of high food prices and frequent power outages that the "Y'en a Marre" movement had forcefully put on the political agenda (Resnick 2013, p. 634). Second, in the second round of the presidential election, Sall secured the support of political candidates closer to the M23 in exchange for promising to implement policies central to the movement's agenda (Hartmann 2014, p. 182). With the support of these candidates behind him, Sall won the presidency in the run-off against Wade with 65.80% of the votes.

The three examples show that political mobilizations by societal groups promote electoral competitiveness directly and indirectly. Indirectly, political mobilizations promote electoral competitiveness by protecting the political space in which both societal groups and opposition parties are able to mobilize. In Zambia and Senegal, violent protests helped to prevent constitutional changes that would have cemented the control of incumbents over the electoral process. In Zambia, for example, the country-wide deployment of election monitors by societal groups forestalled manipulations of the voting process, while in Senegal protests prevented constitutional amendments that were designed to keep the incumbent in power.

Directly, political mobilizations promote electoral competitiveness by contributing to the electoral appeal of oppositional political elites. In all three examples, the protests of societal groups created government-critical political platforms on which opposition parties could build their agendas for change. The grievances at the heart of the protests ranged from economic issues, such as unemployment and the rising costs of basic commodities, to issues of morality, such as the lack of punishment for human rights violations by ruling elites. Also, in all three cases, mass mobilizations facilitated collaboration between societal groups and oppositional political elites. In

Zambia, food riots and strikes against neo-liberal reforms turned into pro-democracy protests, and ultimately led to the formation of the Movement for Multi-party Democracy. In Burkina Faso, the "Trop c'est trop" protests promoted the formation of the Collectif, which renegotiated the terms of the competition for the upcoming parliamentary elections. In Senegal, the "Y'en a Marre" movement gave way to the "Mouvement 23-Juin," which united civil society organizations and opposition parties around a joint political agenda. A third way in which political mobilizations promote electoral competitiveness directly, through the strengthening of the political opposition, is by contributing mobilization capacity to the electoral campaigns of oppositional political elites. In Zambia, trade unions lent their organizational structures to the MMD for recruitment, and the labor movement, as well as the churches, promoted the MMD's agenda for change in the hard-to-reach Zambian countryside. In Senegal, the "Mouvement 23-Juin" campaigned for its own presidential candidates. While these candidates failed in the first round of the elections, they played a crucial role in Senegal's second electoral turnover by transferring their political support to the remaining opposition contender in the run-off elections.

The three examples also show that the effects of political mobilizations in the democratization process are not limited to moments of transition and founding elections. Societal groups have so far received most of the little attention they have been paid in transition literature for their role in such situations of extra-ordinary politics. The Zambian example shows that the extra-institutional mobilization power of societal groups is important for the success of opposition parties in founding elections when they compete with the powerful organizations of ruling parties and their exclusive access to state institutions in the transforming one-party state. However, as the examples of the Burkinabé and Senegalese elections in 2002 and 2012 show, in later elections, too, societal groups play important roles as arbiters in the political game and in building government-critical political platforms for opposition politics. The case studies show that as long as democratic institutions do not supersede the logics of neo-patrimonial politics, the extra-institutional mobilization power of societal groups remains an important deterrent to ruling elites violating political rights and civil liberties. They also show that as long as political competition is marked by the use of state resources and repression through ruling elites, organizationally weak opposition parties that are the constant target of state repression need the support of civil society organizations to reach out to the electorate.

Moreover, the examples demonstrate that political mobilizations by societal groups do not have only positive effects on electoral competitiveness when they adhere to norms of civility. While much has been written about the role of civil society as a non-partisan force that strengthens democracy by promoting tolerance, non-violence, and civic-mindedness, the examples described above show that violent mobilizations combined with self-interested opposition politicians can lead to progress in the democratization process, too. The cases suggest that violent political mobilizations pose a threat to ruling elites that paves the way for the organized political opposition to negotiate for political reforms.

The case studies also show that positive effects of public mobilizations by societal groups on the electoral appeal of the political opposition do not necessitate a close collaboration of societal groups and oppositional political elites. The Senegalese example suggests that mass uprisings may contribute to a political climate in which popular demands are taken up by opposition candidates for opportunistic reasons. The Zambian example indicates that more sustainable outcomes in terms of democratic reforms can be achieved when societal groups keep a certain distance between themselves and opposition parties. Thus, they may continue to pressure for promised reforms after opposition candidates who purported to promote their agendas have ascended to power.

4.4.2   *Political Mobilization as a Cause for Electoral Competitiveness*

In Sect. 4.3, six quantitative hypotheses regarding the effect of political mobilizations by societal groups, oppositional political elites, and ruling elites on electoral competitiveness were formulated. In this section, in order to test these hypotheses, four multiple linear regression models will be applied to data on all authoritarian elections in Sub-Saharan Africa between 1990 and 2012. For all these models, electoral dominance is the dependent variable. This variable expresses electoral competitiveness as the share of votes or seats in parliamentary and first-round presidential elections, respectively, that were won by those holding executive power at the time of the election. This means that the lower electoral dominance, the higher electoral competitiveness. From this, it follows that predictors with negative coefficients increase electoral competitiveness, while those with positive coefficients decrease electoral competitiveness. Descriptive statistics for the variables and indicators that were included in the models are provided in Table A.9 in the appendix.

All four models feature measures for the quality of the electoral process, the electoral framework, the extent of authoritarian ruling elites' experience with multi-party elections, and economic development as control variables. Each model also includes the electoral participation of opposition parties as one of two indicators for the mobilization threat posed by oppositional political elites to powerholders. In model 1, an indicator for the intensity of social conflict was added to this set of variables. This indicator represents the number of public direct engagements in the twelve-month period before the onset of electoral campaigning by all principal actors in electoral authoritarian regimes. Instead of this aggregate indicator, model 2 includes four separate indicators for public direct engagements: Three for political mobilizations by societal groups, oppositional political elites, and ruling elites, respectively, and a fourth measuring the extent of societal conflict between societal groups. Model 3 further disaggregates political mobilizations by societal groups, and includes one indicator for their pro-democratic mobilizations and one for their socio-economic mobilizations in the pre-election period. Model 4 offers an alternative way to disaggregate the political mobilizations by societal groups. It differentiates between organized and spontaneous political mobilizations by societal groups in the pre-election period.

Table 4.1 shows the results of the multiple linear regression analyses for the four models. It provides the coefficients for the indicators in the models and the levels of their statistical significance. Since generalized least squares with random effects were used for estimation, the coefficients are not easy to interpret substantively. The coefficients represent the average change in electoral competitiveness when the indicator changes across time and between countries by one unit. Moreover, the values are not standardized.

Model 1 has been estimated for reasons of comparison with the theoretically meaningful models 2–4. All four models are statistically significant. The latter three models explain 40.4% of the variance in electoral dominance. Thus, they make an important contribution to our understanding of electoral competitiveness in electoral authoritarian regimes.

The results for model 1 show that it is not the intensity of social conflict that drives electoral competitiveness. When public direct engagements, such as demonstrations, riots, or strikes, are not differentiated according to actors and targets, no significant relationship between such mobilizations and electoral competitiveness emerges. This is important to keep in mind for the interpretation of the results of later models, as it makes the empirical case for a more differentiated treatment of public direct engagements in quantitative analyses. The participation of opposition parties in the election emerges as a very strong predictor in this model. In absolute terms, the electoral contestation of all major opposition parties reduces the electoral dominance of powerholders by an average of 16%, compared to a situation where only some active opposition parties participate. The results of model 1 thus lend support to the sixth quantitative research hypothesis. It claimed that the more major opposition parties declare their participation in elections at the outset of the electoral process, the higher electoral competitiveness in authoritarian elections. This is clearly the case. In fact, the electoral contestation of opposition parties emerges as the strongest predictor of electoral competitiveness in all four models.

The experience of electoral authoritarian ruling elites with multi-party elections, in turn, increases their electoral dominance. This evidence is not in direct contradiction with Lindberg's hypothesis of "democratization by electoral practice," since in this case the dependent variable is only a partial regime of democracy. However, it suggests that all else being equal, the longer ruling elites preside over electoral authoritarian regimes, the more they consolidate their power over the electoral process rather than allow for political competition to emerge. On average, the votes or seats for powerholders in first-round presidential elections and parliamentary elections, respectively, increase by 3.47% with every additional direct national multi-party election held in an uninterrupted series. The third and last significant predictor in the first model is the quality of the electoral process. The results of the model indicate that the less ruling elites resorted to repressive measures in the run-up to elections and last-minute manipulations of the electoral process, the more competitive the elections were. All three significant predictors of the first model remain statistically significant in later models, too, and, except for the quality of the electoral process, do not substantially change in their predictive power.

Table 4.1 Mobilization threat and electoral competitiveness in Sub-Saharan Africa

Variable	Indicator	Model			
		1	2	3	4
Quality of electoral process	Composite indicator of election quality, ranging from 0 (low) to 1 (high)	−14.529**	−12.839**	−12.913**	−12.825**
Economic development	GDP per capita/PPP (in constant 2005 intern. dollars) in the year prior to elections	0.001	0.001	0.001	0.001
Electoral experience	Rank number of current election in uninterrupted election series	3.466**	3.224**	3.264**	3.233**
Electoral framework	Election type (parliamentary = 1, presidential = 2)	0.655	0.166	0.156	0.163
	Electoral rule (PR = 1, plurality = 2)	6.460	6.167	6.179	6.165
Intensity of social conflict	Public direct engagements by all principal actors, 18–6 months prior to elections	−0.197			
Mobilization threat	Electoral contestation by major opposition parties	−16.090***	−16.113***	−16.114***	−16.109***
	Political mobilization by oppositional elites		−2.736*	−2.753*	−2.745*
	Political mobilization by societal groups		−0.979***		
	• Pro-democratic mobilization			−0.918	
	• Socio-economic mobilization			−1.028*	
	• Organized mobilization				−1.005**
	• Spontaneous mobilization				−0.927
	Political mobilization by ruling elites		0.251	0.242	0.245
	Social conflict between societal groups		1.120***	1.118***	1.105**

(continued)

Table 4.1 (continued)

Variable	Indicator	Model			
		1	2	3	4
	Overall R^2	0.353	0.404	0.404	0.404
	Significance	0.000	0.000	0.000	0.000
	Cluster	32	32	32	32
	ρ	0.370	0.360	0.332	0.364
	N	205	205	205	205

Notes Models estimated by random-effects generalized least squares regressions, based on all authoritarian elections in Sub-Saharan Africa between 1990 and 2012. Dependent: Electoral dominance. $*p \leq 0.05$, $**p \leq 0.01$, $***p \leq 0.001$

Besides electoral experience, all other control variables in model 1 do not correlate significantly with the dependent variable. The level of economic development shows no relationship with electoral competitiveness. This is in line with the expectation that the effect of economic development on democratization will be largely mediated by the frequency of political mobilizations by societal groups and the political opposition. In multi-variate analyses which include measures for political mobilizations, economic development can be understood to express the residual explanatory value of the dispersion of "action resources" that were not employed for public direct engagements.

The low predictive power of election type suggests that presidential and parliamentary elections do not significantly differ with regard to the electoral dominance that ruling elites achieve on average. It should be noted, however, that this result is likely strongly influenced by two circumstances. First, most parliamentary elections in Sub-Saharan Africa use plurality voting systems. This makes the results of these elections biased towards larger parties similar to how the results of presidential elections are. Second, for presidential elections, the results of the first rounds were employed to operationalize electoral dominance, thus avoiding the concentration of votes produced by run-off elections. Added to the model along with election type, electoral rule indicates the residual differences that the use of plurality over proportional representation systems make for electoral dominance in parliamentary elections. Both control variables display similar properties in the remaining models: They are neither strong, nor statistically significant predictors of electoral competitiveness.

In model 2, public direct engagements in the twelve-month period before the onset of electoral campaigning are differentiated according to the actors initiating them, and by the principal opponents they target. The results show that when societal groups or oppositional political elites address ruling elites with their grievances in demonstrations, riots, or strikes, they significantly increase electoral competitiveness. Every political mobilization by societal groups decreases the share of seats or votes conferred to powerholders in the election by an average of 0.98%. In the case of mobilizations by the political opposition, the corresponding effect is a loss of electoral support of 2.74% for ruling elites.

These findings lend support to hypotheses 1 and 5. Hypothesis 1 claimed that the higher the frequency of political mobilizations by societal groups in the time before the onset of electoral campaigning is, the higher will be the electoral competitiveness in subsequent authoritarian elections. In hypothesis 5, it was suggested that political mobilizations by opposition parties have the same effect on electoral competitiveness. Given the fact that opposition protests are much rarer than those by societal groups, model 2 suggests that political mobilizations by societal groups are a particularly important driver of electoral competitiveness in Sub-Saharan Africa.

Significant, too, in the second model is the influence of social conflict between societal groups on electoral competitiveness. Here, the effect is negative. This is in line with hypothesis 3. It stated that the higher the frequency of public direct engagements of one societal group against another in the time before the onset of electoral campaigning is, the lower the electoral competitiveness in authoritarian elections.

As previously discussed, by mobilizing against each other, societal groups weaken the overall mobilization capacity of civil society, and invite authoritarian interventions to "divide and rule". Hence, the more societal groups engage in public, direct confrontations with other societal groups, the more ruling elites are able to assert their dominance over the electoral process. In model 2, where they have the strongest effect, each such mobilization leads to a 1.12% increase in electoral dominance by ruling elites.

Given that direct public engagements by societal groups have opposing effects on electoral competitiveness depending on whether they are targeting ruling elites or not, the results of the analysis suggest a nuanced position in the debate on the role of "social unrest" in democratization processes. Some democratization theorists propagate an altogether negative view of the role of mass-based actors in transitions. Based on such a view of mass mobilization, Karl (1990, p. 8), for example, concluded in her study of Latin-American transitions to democracy that "no stable political democracy has resulted from regime transitions in which mass actors have gained control even momentarily over traditional ruling classes". In a similar vein, Przeworski (1986, p. 63) states that "it seems as if an almost complete docility and patience on the part of organized workers are needed for a democratic transformation to succeed". While the results of the present analysis cast doubt on this negative view of social conflict in the transition process, neither are all forms of societal mobilization beneficial for it. Only a nuanced conceptualization of "social unrest" that differentiates between political mobilizations by societal groups and other forms of social conflict leads to meaningful conclusions.

Model 2 also shows that mobilizations by ruling elites, such as pro-government violence or demonstrations of their civilian supporters, do not significantly influence electoral competitiveness. This is in contradiction to hypothesis 4. Hypothesis 4 claimed that the higher the frequency of such mobilizations by ruling elites in the time before the onset of electoral campaigning, the lower the electoral competitiveness in subsequent authoritarian elections. While the relationship of these mobilizations with electoral dominance is positive, as predicted, it is weak and not significant. As discussed in Sect. 3.5, however, political mobilizations are a less adequate indicator for the mobilization threat of ruling elites than for that of societal groups and oppositional political elites. Reactive repression to mobilizational challenges is a much more frequent form of ruling elite mobilization, and it is not captured here for reasons of comparability with the indicators for the mobilization threat posed by other actors.

Model 3 further differentiates between those public direct engagements with ruling elites in which societal groups mobilized against violations of political rights and civil liberties (pro-democracy mobilizations) from those in which they addressed ruling elites with socio-economic grievances (socio-economic mobilizations). The results suggest that the latter kind of political mobilization is a slightly stronger driver of electoral competitiveness. Whereas socio-economic mobilizations reduce electoral dominance by on average 1.03%, pro-democracy mobilizations reduce electoral dominance by 0.92%. Moreover, only the coefficient for socio-economic mobilizations is statistically significant. Thus, these findings lend support to hypothesis 2, in which it was claimed that socio-economic mobilizations have a stronger impact on electoral competitiveness than pro-democracy mobilizations. In terms of effecting progress in the democratization process, the results suggest that the role of civil society in the build-up of opposition power is more important than its role in safeguarding democratic institutions. However, first, the differences in the effects are small. Second, in most pre-election periods in Sub-Saharan Africa, societal groups engage in both pro-democracy and socio-economic mobilizations. Therefore, the empirical analyses do not account for the role pro-democracy mobilizations might play in protecting the political space for civil society. This increased protection, in turn, may allow more societal groups to engage in socio-economic mobilizations.

Model 4 provides an alternative segmentation of political mobilizations by societal groups. Here, organized mobilizations are distinguished from "spontaneous" mobilizations where initiating actors cannot be identified. It shows that mobilizations that are initiated by an identifiable societal group or organization have a stronger effect on electoral competitiveness than spontaneous protests. Qualitative insights in individual protest movements suggest that the sequence of protests may play a role in the explanation of these differential effects. It seems that spontaneous and often violent mass protests frequently provide the mobilization threat that provides civil society organizations and opposition parties with a protected political space to mobilize and reestablish links with their constituencies. Those actors, however, provide the organizational capacity for sustained protest movements that carry grievances which were initially voiced in spontaneous uprisings and riots into the political arena. This means that similar to the role of pro-democracy mobilizations in providing the grounds for socio-economic mobilizations, the effect of spontaneous mobilizations on electoral competitiveness might be partially mediated by organized mobilizations, since the former type of protests promote the latter.

Taken together, the results show that the mobilization threat by societal groups is an important driver of electoral competitiveness. They support the hypothesis that the higher the frequency of political mobilizations by societal groups in pre-election times is, the higher the electoral competitiveness of authoritarian elections. In particular, socio-economic mobilizations limit the electoral dominance of ruling elites. Mobilizations by the political opposition play a similar role in the strengthening of electoral competitiveness. However, the declarations of opposition parties to contest the elections pose a greater mobilization threat to ruling elites. Social conflict between societal groups, in turn, diminishes the mobilization threat of civil society, and increases the electoral dominance of ruling elites.

4.5 Summary

The analyses in this chapter concluded that "ordinary citizens" play an important role in the democratization processes of electoral authoritarian regimes in Sub-Saharan Africa. By voicing grievances against ruling elites in protests, riots, and strikes, societal groups increase the political power of oppositional political elites and provide a basis for increasing electoral competitiveness. Considering the limited progress of democratization processes on the subcontinent, the study thus suggests that the weak mobilization threat of societal groups is a major explanatory factor for limited electoral competitiveness in Sub-Saharan Africa. The chapter advanced this argument in several ways.

Section 4.1 argued that democratization may emerge as an unintentional by-product of the political struggle of self-interested political elites when power between ruling elites, oppositional political elites, and societal groups becomes more evenly distributed. The democratization of authoritarian regimes, therefore, requires a redistribution of political power from a small authoritarian elite to oppositional political elites and societal groups. It was argued that mobilizations and counter-mobilization between these actors may result in such a redistribution of power.

Section 4.2 further specified this link by presenting two mechanisms through which the collective actions of societal groups may promote the power of oppositional political elites. While socio-economic mobilizations provide a political platform to the opposition, pro-democratic mobilizations assert the constitutional framework and regulatory responsibility of the state. Thus, societal groups contribute to the strengthening of electoral competition.

Sections 4.3 and 4.4 provide an empirical test of the effects of societal mobilization on democratization processes in Sub-Saharan Africa. According to the specifications of the research design in Sect. 4.3, six research hypotheses were tested in four multiple linear regression analyses of data on all direct national multi-party elections held by electoral authoritarian regimes in Sub-Saharan Africa between 1990 and 2012. In Sect. 4.4, the results of these analyses were presented and discussed. The results support the main hypothesis that the mobilization threat by societal groups is an important driver of electoral competitiveness. Thus, the results show that "ordinary citizens" have an important role to play in the democratization processes of electoral authoritarian regimes. By mobilizing in protests, riots, and strikes that are critical of the government, they provide a basis for increasing competition between factions of political elites.

References

Almeida PD (2003) Opportunity organizations and threat-induced contention: protest waves in authoritarian settings. Am J Soc 109:345–400. https://doi.org/10.1086/378395

Andreassen B, Geisler G, Tostensen A (1992) Setting a standard for Africa?: lessons from the 1991 Zambian Elections. Report, 5. Chr. Michelsen Institute, Bergen

Barkan JD (2000) Protracted transitions among Africa's new democracies. Democratization 7(3):227–243

Bartlett DMC (2000) Civil society and democracy: a zambian case study. J S Afr Stud 26:429–446. https://doi.org/10.1080/030570700750019655

Beck N (2001) Time-series cross-section data: what have we learned in the past few years? Annu Rev Polit Sci 4:271–293. https://doi.org/10.1146/annurev.polisci.4.1.271

Bermeo N (1997) Myths of moderation: confrontation and conflict during democratic transitions. Comp Polit 29(3):305–322

Branch A, Mampilly ZC (2015) Africa uprising: popular protest and political change (African arguments). Zed Books, in association with International African Institute, Royal African Society, World Peace Foundation, London

Bratton M, van de Walle N (1992) Popular protest and political reform in Africa. Comp Polit 24(4):419–442

Bratton M, van de Walle N (1997) Democratic experiments in Africa: regime transitions in comparative perspective (Cambridge studies in comparative politics). Cambridge University Press, Cambridge

Brown TA (1996) Nonlinear Politics. In: Kiel L, Elliott E (eds) Chaos theory in the social sciences. University of Michigan Press, Ann Arbor, MI, pp 119–137

Brownlee J (2007) Authoritarianism in an age of democratization. Cambridge University Press, Cambridge

Carbone GM (2003) Political parties in a 'no-party democracy'. Hegemony and opposition under 'Movement democracy' in Uganda. Party Polit 9(4): 485–502

Carothers T (2002) The end of the transition paradigm. J Democracy 13:5–21. https://doi.org/10.1353/jod.2002.0003

Chouli L (2015) The popular uprising in Burkina Faso and the transition. Rev Afr Polit Econ 42:325–333. https://doi.org/10.1080/03056244.2015.1026196

Commonwealth Human Rights Initiative (1996) Zambia: democracy on trial. New Commonwealth Human Rights Initiative, Delhi

Dahl RA (1998) Polyarchy: participation and opposition, 26th edn. Yale University Press, New Haven

Diamond LJ (2002) Thinking about hybrid regimes. J Democracy 13(2):21–35

Dulani B (2011) Democracy movements as bulwarks against presidential usurpation of power: lessons from the third-term bids in Malawi, Namibia, Uganda and Zambia. Stichproben. Wien Z für kritische Afrikastudien 11(20):115–139

Duncan A, Macmillan H, Simutanyi N (2003) Zambia: Drivers of pro-poor change: an overview. Oxford Policy Management, Oxford

Eisenstadt T (2000) Eddies in the third wave: protracted transitions and theories of democratization. Democratization 7(3):3

Elemu D (2010) The emergence and development of governance and human rights civil society in Zambia: a critical analysis. In: Mutesa F (ed) State-civil society and donor relations in Zambia. UNZA Press, Lusaka, Zambia, pp 19–44

Erdmann G (1999) Parteien in Afrika Versuch eines Neuanfangs in der Parteienforschung [Political parties in Africa. Towards a new beginning in political party research]. Afr Spectr 34:375–393. https://doi.org/10.2307/40174815

Erdmann G, Simutanyi N (2003) Transition in Zambia: the hybridisation of the third republic. Konrad Adenauer Foundation, Lilongwe, Malawi

Fortin-Rittberger J (2015) Time-series cross-section. In: Best H, Wolf C (eds) The SAGE handbook of regresion analysis and causal inference. Sage, Los Angeles, pp. 387–408

Frere M-S, Englebert P (2015) Briefing: burkina faso—the fall of blaise compaore. Afr Aff 114:295–307. https://doi.org/10.1093/afraf/adv010

Garreton Merino MA (1995) Redemocratization in chile. J Democracy 6:146–158. https://doi.org/10.1353/jod.1995.0009

Geddes, B (1999) Authoritarian breakdown: empirical test of a game theoretic argument. Atlanta

Geddes B (2003) Paradigms and sand castles: theory building and research design in comparative politics (analytical perspectives on politics). University of Michigan Press, Ann Arbor, Michigan

Greene WH (2011) Econometric analysis, 7th edn. Pearson Education, Harlow

Gueye M (2013) Urban guerrilla poetry: the movement Y'en a Marre and the socio-political influences of hip hop in Senegal. J Pan Afr Stud 6(3):22–42

Gunther R, Diamond LJ (2001) Types and functions of parties. In: Diamond LJ, Gunther R (eds) Political parties and democracy (pp. 3–39, Journal of democracy book). Johns Hopkins University Press, Baltimore, MD

Hagberg S (2002) 'Enough is Enough': an ethnography of the struggle against impunity in Burkina Faso. J Mod Afr Stud 40:217–246. https://doi.org/10.1017/S0022278X02003890

Harsch E (1999) Trop, c'est trop! Civil Insurgence in Burkina Faso, 1998–99. Rev Afr Polit Econ 26(81):395–406

Harsch E (2009) Urban protest in Burkina Faso. Afr Aff 108:263–288. https://doi.org/10.1093/afraf/adp018

Hartmann C (2012) Machtwechsel im Senegal—neue Chance für die Demokratie? GIGA Focus Afrika(2)

Hartmann C (2014) Zivilgesellschaft und politischer Wandel im Senegal. In: Eberlei W (ed) Zivilgesellschaft in Subsahara Afrika. Springer VS, Wiesbaden, Germany, pp 169–190

Heilbrunn JR (1993) Social origins of national conferences in Benin and Togo. J Mod Afr Stud 31:277–299. https://doi.org/10.1017/S0022278X00011939

Hilgers M (2010) Evolution of political regime and evolution of popular political representations in Burkina Faso. Afr J Polit Sci Int Relat 4(9):350–359

Hilgers M, Mazzocchetti J (2006) L'après-Zongo: Entre ouverture politique et fermeture des possibles. Politique africaine 101:5. https://doi.org/10.3917/polaf.101.0005

Huntington SP (1965) Political development and political decay. World Polit 17:386–430. https://doi.org/10.2307/2009286

Ihonvbere JO (1996) Economic crisis, civil society, and democratization: The case of Zambia. Africa World Press, Trenton, NJ

Karatnycky A, Ackerman P (2005) How freedom is won: from civic resistance to durable democracy. Freedom House

Karl TL (1990) Dilemmas of democratization in Latin America. Comp Polit 23(1):1–21

Kuran T (1991) Now out of never: the element of surprise in the east European revolution of 1989. World Polit 44(1):7–48

Larmer M, Fraser A (2007) Of cabbages and King Cobra: populist politics and Zambia's 2006 election. Afr Aff 106:611–637. https://doi.org/10.1093/afraf/adm058

Lichbach MI (1994) Rethinking rationality and rebellion: theories of collective action and problems of collective dissent. Rationality Soc 6:8–39. https://doi.org/10.1177/1043463194006001003

Lichbach MI (1995) The rebel's dilemma (Economics, cognition, and society). University of Michigan Press, Ann Arbor

Lindberg SI (2006a) Democracy and elections in Africa. Johns Hopkins University Press, Baltimore

Lindberg SI (2006b) Tragic protest: why do opposition parties boycott elections? In: Schedler A (ed) Electoral authoritarianism: the dynamics of unfree competition. Rienner, Boulder, Colo, pp 149–163

Lindberg SI (2009) Democratization by elections: a new mode of transition? In: Lindberg SI (ed) Democratization by elections: a new mode of transition. Johns Hopkins University Press, Baltimore, pp 1–21

Linz JJ, Stepan A (1996) Problems of democratic transition and consolidation: Southern Europe, South America, and post-communist Europe. Johns Hopkins University Press, Baltimore, Md

Loada A, Santiso C (2002) Landmark elections in Burkina Faso: towards democratic maturity? International Institute for Democracy and Electoral Assistance, Stockholm

Mackenzie A (2005) The problem of the attractor: a singular generality between sciences and social theory. Theor, Cult Soc 22:45–65. https://doi.org/10.1177/0263276405057190

Magaloni B (2006) Voting for autocracy: hegemonic party survival and its demise in Mexico (Cambridge studies in comparative politics). Cambridge University Press, Cambridge, New York

Mari F (2012) Ein Lehrstück in Demokratie. Welt-Sichten 5(5): 36–39

McFaul MA (2002) The fourth wave of democracy and dictatorship. World Polit 54:212–244

Merkel W (2010) Systemtransformation: Eine Einführung in die Theorie und Empirie der Transformationsforschung (2nd ed., Lehrbuch). VS Verlag für Sozialwissenschaften, Wiesbaden

Mugaju J, Oloka-Onyango J (eds) (2000) No-party democracy in Uganda: Myths and realities. Fountain Publishers, Kampala, Uganda

Mumba MH (2010) Civil society activism in Zambia: a historical perspective. In: Mutesa F (ed) State-civil society and donor relations in Zambia. UNZA Press, Lusaka, Zambia, pp 1–17

Nunley AC (2012). African elections database: a database of elections in Sub-Saharan Africa. http://africanelections.tripod.com/. Accessed 29 Mar 2019

O'Donnell GA, Schmitter PC (1986) Transitions from authoritarian rule: Tentative conclusions about uncertain democracies. The Johns Hopkins University Press, Baltimore

Ouédraogo S (2006) Collectif des organisations démocratiques de masse et de partis politiques contre l'impunité au Burkina Faso. Les Cahiers du CRISES, MS0601. Centre de recherche sur les innovations sociales, Québec

O'Donnell GA, Schmitter PC, Whitehead L (eds) (1986) Transitions from authoritarian rule: comparative perspectives. The Johns Hopkins University Press, Baltimore

Orvis S (2001) Civil Society in Africa or African Civil Society? In: Ndegwa SN (ed) A decade of democracy in Africa (pp. 17–38, International studies in sociology and social anthropology, Vol. 81). Leiden, Brill, Boston

Przeworski A (1986) Some problems in the study of the transition to democracy. In: O'Donnell GA, Schmitter PC, Whitehead L (eds) Transitions from authoritarian rule: comparative perspectives. The Johns Hopkins University Press, Baltimore, pp 47–63

Przeworski A (1991) Democracy and the market: political and economic reforms in Eastern Europe and Latin America (studies in rationality and social change). Cambridge University Press, Cambridge

Resnick D (2012) opposition parties and the urban poor in African Democracies. Comp Polit Stud 45:1351–1378. https://doi.org/10.1177/0010414012437166

Resnick D (2013) Continuity and change in senegalese party politics: lessons from the 2012 elections. Afr Aff 112:623–645. https://doi.org/10.1093/afraf/adt049

Rueschemeyer D, Huber E, Stephens JD (1992) Capitalist development and democracy. University of Chicago Press, Chicago

Rustow DA (1970) Transitions to democracy: toward a dynamic model. Comp Polit 2(3):337–363

Salehyan I, Hendrix CS, Hamner J, Case C, Linebarger C, Stull E et al (2012) Social conflict in Africa: a new database. Int Interact 38:503–511. https://doi.org/10.1080/03050629.2012.697426

Schedler A (2009) The contingent power of authoritarian elections. In: Lindberg SI (ed) Democratization by elections: a new mode of transition. Johns Hopkins University Press, Baltimore, pp 291–313

Schneider C, Schmitter P (2004) Liberalization, transition and consolidation: measuring the components of democratization. Democratization 11:1–32. https://doi.org/10.1080/13510340412000287271

Steiner ND, Martin CW (2012) Economic integration, party polarisation and electoral turnout. West Eur Polit 35:238–265. https://doi.org/10.1080/01402382.2011.648005

Stimson JA (1985) regression in space and time: a statistical essay. Am J Polit Sci 29:914–947. https://doi.org/10.2307/2111187

Tilly C (2007) Democracy. Cambridge University Press, Cambrigde

Tucker JA (2007) Enough! electoral fraud, collective action problems, and post-communist colored revolutions. Perspect Polit 5(3):535–551

Vanhanen T (1997) Prospects of democracy: a study of 172 countries. Routledge

Villalón LA (1994) Democratizing a (Quasi) democracy: the senegalese elections of 1993. Afr Aff 93:163–193. https://doi.org/10.2307/723839

VonDoepp P (1996) Political transition and civil society: the cases of Kenya and Zambia. Stud Comp Int Dev 31(1):24

Welzel C, Inglehart R (2008) The role of ordinary people in democratization. J Democracy 19(1):126–140

William M (1997) Money and power in Uganda's 1996 elections. Afr J Polit Sci 2(1):168–179

Chapter 5
Conclusions

Why did the democratization processes of electoral authoritarian regimes in Sub-Saharan Africa make so little progress, despite the fact that by 2012, most countries on the subcontinent had a history of multi-party politics that spanned more than two decades? In pursuit of an answer to this question, the book develops a novel theoretical framework for the explanation of democratization processes. This framework assumes a gradual process of democratization. It purports to explain the democratization of electoral authoritarian regimes across a series of election cycles. When successful, these regimes undergo a process that can be called a "constitutional evolution" in which democratic principles of governance are strengthened while elections are regularly held. It also purports to explain democratic regime change without the normative motivations of democrats. Instead, it attempts to explain democratization as a "fortuitous by-product" (Rustow 1970, p. 353) of the political struggle between different elite factions, and between elites and "ordinary citizens".

The theoretical framework comprises two levels of analysis. On the macro level, it explains changes in the political system with the distribution of political power between ruling elites, oppositional political elites, and societal groups. It claims that when the distribution of such power between the three types of collective actors becomes more equal, democratic principles in the political system are strengthened. In particular, it claims that a state must be reached in which the political power of societal groups suffices to prevent intra-elite pacts to exploit the state, and in which oppositional political elites can prevent ruling elites from pacifying the polity by force. Only then a "prolonged and inconclusive political struggle" (Rustow 1970, p. 355) takes place that can lead to the acceptance of free and fair elections as the means of selecting powerholders. The more political power is balanced between political elites and societal groups, as well as between ruling elites and oppositional political elites, the more uncertainty becomes institutionalized in the political system, and the more vertical accountability is established. Both are core principles of a procedural-minimum conception of democracy, and both crucially hinge on competitiveness as a central aspect of democratic electoral practice.

© Springer Nature Switzerland AG 2020
W. Stuppert, *Political Mobilizations and Democratization in Sub-Saharan Africa*,
Advances in African Economic, Social and Political Development,
https://doi.org/10.1007/978-3-030-22792-0_5

On the micro level, the theoretical framework provides a detailed description of the processes by which political power is gained and maintained. Based on the assumption of self-interested actors, it introduces the collective action problem as a fundamental concept for the explanation of the interactions of contenders in a polit-ical struggle. According to this analytical perspective, a given political system and the prevalent distribution of political power determine the availability of solutions to the collective action problem to each actor in the political struggle. The sum of these solutions represents an actor's mobilization capacity. Based on this capacity, an actor will be able to engage in mobilization tactics, which are themselves public goods and underlie the collective action problem. Four different mobilization tactics were differentiated: Intra-network communication, public communication, organiza-tion building, and direct engagements with one's opponents and neutral bystanders. Engaging in mobilization tactics leads to mobilizations and counter-mobilizations between actors. Based on these interactions, actors build up a mobilization threat that determines their power to realize group-specific interests, that is, their political power.

This theoretical framework offers a new perspective on the role of civil soci-ety in democratization processes. First, it provides a broader perspective on who is important in civil society. The book's view of people power does not focus on eli-tist civil society organizations in Sub-Saharan Africa. Instead, it includes the urban underclass and other non-formalized actors. As mobilization capacity is a central concept in the theoretical framework, trade unions, student unions, and urban youth are expected to play important roles in their countries' democratization processes. Second, the focus on mobilization threat as the basis for the involvement of civil society in the democratization processes highlights the importance of the ability of societal groups to intensify political conflict. By directly engaging ruling elites, soci-etal groups promote the power of oppositional political elites. Through mobilizations around socio-economic grievances, they help to build a political platform on which oppositional political elites can reach out to potential constituents. Through mobi-lizations that focus on human rights and elections, they also safeguard the electoral process from violations by ruling elites. Thus, societal groups promote electoral competitiveness, and contribute to democratization.

For an empirical evaluation of this theoretical framework, the book employs data on all authoritarian elections in Sub-Saharan Africa between 1990 and 2012. Progress in the democratization processes is measured as the extent of the competitiveness of direct national multi-party elections. As indicators for the mobilization threat posed by societal groups and the political opposition to ruling elites at the outset of these elections, the frequencies of their political mobilizations, i.e., their public direct engagements with ruling elites in demonstrations, strikes, and riots, are used. Six quantitative research hypotheses were formulated:

- Hypothesis 1: The higher the frequency of public direct engagements by societal groups with ruling elites in the time before the onset of electoral campaigning, the higher the electoral competitiveness in authoritarian elections.

- Hypothesis 2: Public direct engagements with ruling elites in which societal groups raise socio-economic issues will have a stronger impact on electoral competitiveness than pro-democracy mobilizations.
- Hypothesis 3: The higher the frequency of public direct engagements of one societal group with another in the time before the onset of electoral campaigning, the lower the electoral competitiveness in authoritarian elections.
- Hypothesis 4: The higher the frequency of public direct engagements of ruling elites with societal groups or the opposition in the time before the onset of electoral campaigning, the lower the electoral competitiveness in subsequent authoritarian elections.
- Hypothesis 5: The higher the frequency of public direct engagements of opposition parties with ruling elites in the time before the onset of electoral campaigning, the higher the electoral competitiveness in authoritarian elections.
- Hypothesis 6: The more major opposition parties declare their participation in elections at the outset of the electoral process, the higher the electoral competitiveness in authoritarian elections.

The empirical evaluation of the theoretical framework proceeded in three parts. First, data on electoral competitiveness and democratic governance in Sub-Saharan Africa was analyzed to provide the context for the investigation into the determinants of electoral competitiveness. The analysis finds that while the advent of multi-party politics led to significant improvements in political rights and civil liberties across Sub-Saharan Africa, the continued holding of direct national multi-party elections —despite displaying important aspects of democratic practice—did not involve substantial gains in democratic freedoms. Instead, electoral competitiveness is found to be strongly associated with democratic governance. This suggests that because electoral competitiveness is low and electoral turnovers are rare in Sub-Saharan Africa, democratic governance does not take hold.

Second, the book investigated trends in political mobilizations by societal groups and the political opposition across Sub-Saharan Africa. It found that after multi-party politics had been ushered in by a continent-wide protest wave in the early 1990s, societal groups continued to mobilize in public direct engagements with ruling elites despite harsh repressive counter-measures. According to the analysis, spontaneous, often violent protests by the urban underclass represent a substantial part of the political mobilizations of societal groups. The analysis also showed that mobilizations by the political opposition are relatively few in number when compared to those of societal groups.

Third, the evidence on trends in political mobilization and electoral competitiveness were combined to test the effects of societal mobilization on the competitiveness of authoritarian elections in Sub-Saharan Africa. Three case studies of direct national multi-party elections in different countries at different points in the democratization process show that violent and non-violent political mobilizations by societal groups can promote electoral competitiveness directly and indirectly, in close collaboration with or at a distance from oppositional political elites, in founding as well as in later elections. Multiple linear regression analyses on all authoritarian elections in

Sub-Saharan Africa between 1990 and 2012 show that the mobilization threat by societal groups is an important driver of electoral competitiveness. The results also lend support to the second, third, fifth, and sixth hypotheses. The fourth hypothesis, namely that the higher the frequency of mobilizations by ruling elites in pre-election times is, the lower the electoral competitiveness in subsequent authoritarian elections, is not supported by the results. While the relationship of these mobilizations with electoral dominance is positive, as predicted, it is very weak and not significant.

The book's empirical findings show that ordinary citizens play an important role in the democratization processes of electoral authoritarian regimes in Sub-Saharan Africa. Beyond their contributions to the activities of an "organized, disciplined, and non-violent" civil society (Branch and Mampilly 2015, p. 7), their continued participation in demonstrations, strikes, and riots balances out the neo-patrimonial power of ruling elites over the electoral process, helps opposition parties to mobilize, and thus strengthens electoral competitiveness. This is a clear counterpoint to transition theorists who have claimed that "an almost complete docility and patience" (Przeworski 1986, p. 63) on the part of societal groups is necessary for a democratic transformation to succeed. Instead, without continued political mobilizations by societal groups in which they address ruling elites with their grievances, it seems that democratization processes are bound to stagnate.

These findings have important implications for the design and implementation of programs in international democracy assistance. Both the book's theoretical approach to the explanation of democratization processes and the empirical investigation into the determinants of electoral competitiveness stress the importance of the mobilization threat of societal groups for the promotion of democratization. Among the many actors in civil society, this analytical perspective throws those groups and organizations into relief that have the capacity to mobilize time, money, and material resources, and are willing to use this capacity to address ruling elites with the grievances of their constituents, regardless of whether those grievances relate to the political process, or are socio-economic in nature.

With regard to current approaches to democracy promotion, this suggests not so much a re-evaluation of the importance of supporting civil society in general, but a reconsideration of which parts of civil society to support, and how. Supporting civil society to further democratization has been a major concern of the international aid community since the global spread of multi-party politics in the beginning of the 1990s (Dicklitch 1998, p. 2). Ever since, international aid has provided civil society in Sub-Saharan Africa with support for pro-democratic activism, such as election monitoring, human rights work, advocacy, and civic education of unprecedented proportions (see e.g. Dicklitch 2001; Ottaway 2000). However, most of the money international donors spend on democracy assistance goes to civil society organization in Sub-Saharan Africa that are created with the preferences of international donors in mind: Professional, non-partisan organizations with university-educated staff that are well-versed in the language of development programs and projects (Hearn 1999, p. 2). This type of organization belongs to but one subset of societal organizations in African societies. To evaluate their potential to build up a credible mobilization threat, two dimensions can be applied to societal groups in African civil societies.

The first dimension relates to the predominant source of the groups' mobilization capacity, and the second to their propensity to get involved in domestic politics. First, there are those organizations that owe their existence to the financial donations, material support, and training programs of the international donor community, and that regularly try to influence government policy through their advocacy work and civic education programs. Second, there are donor-dependent organizations that are not only non-partisan, but non-political, such as service delivery organizations in the health or education sector. Both types of organizations are "free-floating on donors' funds" (Ottaway 2000, p. 81). They "remain artificial creations with weak roots in the community" (Ottaway 2000, p. 79). Instead of speaking for the constituencies they ostensibly represent, they "are organizations whose leaders have taken it upon themselves to define and represent the interests of people" (Ottaway 2000, p. 83). That is, they are not representing societal groups that they could mobilize. However, there are a third type of organization that Africans have formed and continue to form of their own initiative and with their own means. These are lobby organizations such as labor unions, student associations, or professional organizations, whose mobilization capacity relies on the contributions of their members in terms of time and money. These organizations represent their members in the political process through public demonstrations and strikes, and in negotiations with the government. Fourth, there are community-based organizations, such as burial associations, credit clubs, and other local voluntary organizations that are organized around the socio-economic interests of their members. These organizations, however, have been thoroughly depoliticized by the single-party and military African regimes of the 1970s and 1980s (Ottaway 2000, p. 81).

The outcomes of the efforts of the international aid community have been limited. While diplomatic action and economic sanctions may have prevented some authoritarian excesses at some points in time, the facilitation of steady progress in the democratization process through international support for the development of local civil society has largely failed. As Bunce and Wolchik (2011, p. 24) report, there "is a consensus among many analysts that such assistance has had positive effects, but largely at the margins". The present study suggests that international democracy assistance has failed for two reasons. First, donors have regrettably restricted their support to professional organizations that are apt at formulating policies, but that are poorly equipped to generate the mass support that could force the government to reconsider its positions. Not only may donors thus have limited the impact of their own funding on democratic regime change, they may also have depleted the pool of leaders that would have been available for lobby organizations, "as enterprising individuals move to the greener pastures foreign assistance creates" (Ottaway 2000, p. 100). In consequence, they may have damaged the development of mobilization capacity in local civil societies far beyond the immediate impact of their support programs on recipient organizations. Second, donor organizations have enforced a mantra of non-partisanship among recipient civil society organizations that not only encourages those organizations to avoid the sphere of "politics" as defined by ruling elites, but also impedes their ability to directly and indirectly support mobilizations of the political opposition. Instead of addressing corruption and mismanagement as the root causes of the socio-economic grievances of the people, many donor-dependent organizations have taken an approach that is essentially non-confrontational, focusing their work instead, for example, on civic education (Dicklitch and Lwanga 2003, p. 497). This, in turn, limits the possibilities of opposition parties to build a platform of alternative policy ideas on the advocacy work of civil society organizations.

What might a more successful strategy for international democracy assistance look like? The book's empirical findings suggest that a credible mobilization threat is not only posed by mobilizations around universal human rights and democracy. Instead, strikes, demonstrations, and spontaneous riots that express socio-economic grievances appear to play a quintessential part in building up such a threat. Naturally, the suggestion for international donors cannot be to provide trainings and financial support to urban youth so that the latter may more effectively disrupt the government—although in the so-called "electoral revolutions" in post-communist authoritarian regimes in Eastern Europe, some international donors have done exactly that, and with success (see, e.g., Bunce and Wolchik 2006, p. 59; Kuzio 2006, p. 370). Given the political and administrative constraints under which donors regularly operate, it is difficult for them to channel funds to groups that are not formalized, party-affiliated, or toy with violent activism.

The findings of the present study do not suggest that international development community should stop providing funds to professional, "orderly" advocacy organizations. As Ottaway (2000, p. 90) explains, while "radical movements have the muscle to make the government feel threatened and thus to force it to consider change [...] more professional groups may be more adept at turning the cry for change into specific policy demands when the time actually comes to enact reforms". This idea has been discussed earlier as a "positive radical flank effect" (see page 61). Instead, lobby organizations suggest themselves as additional recipients of foreign support in the framework of international democracy assistance. These organizations have regularly provided political direction at very early points in the formation of mass-based protest movements across Sub-Saharan Africa. During the democratic regime changes in the early 1990s, for example, trade unions and student associations were instrumental in channeling the socio-economic grievances of the citizenry into demands for political reform (Bratton and van de Walle 1992, p. 423). Although trade unions in Sub-Saharan Africa have often suffered, like the Zambian labor movement, from "deep reductions in the formal workforce, the privatization of formerly state-owned enterprises, and divisions internal to the movement" (Pletcher 1999, p. 206), the leadership that unions have been able to give to popular struggles as well as their own organizational power "suggest that they will continue to play a leading role in popular politics" (Beckman and Sachikonye 2010, p. 20). As Kraus (2007, p. 256) concludes, "The real significance of trade unions for democratic life in Africa is that they are virtually the only group representing the popular classes that has continuing organizational influence at the national level and poses challenging questions about rights of mass access to public resources". Their strong opposition to Structural Adjustment Programs by the International Monetary Fund and the World Bank and other neo-liberal reform agendas, however, has marginalized them in the field of international development. Thus, international financial support could prove vital in strengthening them organizationally. It could focus, for example, on worker education or the development of labor policies.

Student associations, on the other hand, while urban-based and elitist, represent a strongly politicized youth and a pool of experienced political leaders from which many of the future politicians in Sub-Saharan Africa are recruited. Elections of the student leadership on campuses often resemble a miniature version of national elections, with the same parties vying for public offices, posters all over the campus, and political rallies. Through the links of their members to families across the country, student associations could be employed in national get-out-the-vote campaigns, election monitoring, or broad-based public consultation processes. In addition to this, they themselves would be a valuable target of capacity trainings, in support of their future careers in the leadership of civil society organizations and political parties. Yet, as of now, donor organizations often sideline these associations in favor of youth organizations with little actual membership and few self-initiated activities when they want to provide civic education to youth in Sub-Saharan Africa.

While this shows that the empirical findings of the present study have important implications for international democracy assistance, the book's research into the effects of societal mobilizations on the democratization process has clear limitations. It invites further tests and extensions with regard to at least three points.

First, the availability of time-series data on politics in Sub-Saharan Africa for the period before 2006 is very limited. This represented an important limitation, especially regarding the multiple linear regression analyses that could be conducted. For example, no meaningful indicators for the legitimacy of governments, the extent of neo-patrimonialism, or the repressive actions of political regimes were available that would have covered the early 1990s. The more years pass, the more feasible it becomes to choose a later period for investigation into the determinants of electoral competitiveness, for which more indicators are available as controls or for the operationalization of alternative explanatory factors.

Second, the indicators that have been used to measure the role of societal groups in democratization processes limit the role of these groups to the political mobilizations they engage in. While this represents an important aspect of the influence of societal groups on democratization processes in electoral authoritarian regimes, it represents only the public, confrontative side of their activities. For example, their role in providing a protected space for aspiring political leaders to groom their skills and networks, or their role in safeguarding the electoral process through election monitoring has thus not been quantitatively investigated. Comparative studies that focus on the interactions of societal groups and opposition parties in Sub-Saharan Africa would represent an important extension of the present research, as well as comparative studies of the effect of societal groups on the democratic qualities of the electoral process. Also, the indicators that have been used for political mobilizations by societal groups capture only major mobilizations. The Social Conflict in Africa Database, while providing an important comparative insight into the frequencies of political mobilizations in Sub-Saharan Africa, by no means provides a full picture of protest activity in the respective countries. Here, additional event data could further our understanding of the relationship between different types of political mobilizations and different political outcomes.

Third, the empirical investigation presented in this book focused on the link of the micro level to the macro level of the theoretical framework. While it showed that the mobilization threat of societal groups, understood as the frequency of their political mobilizations in the pre-election period, is an important predictor of electoral competitiveness as a feature of the political system, the corollary effects of electoral competitiveness on other aspects of democratic practice were not included in the regression models. This would have required a more sophisticated quantitative analysis. The micro level, in turn, was only investigated in a cursory fashion in the framework of case studies. Here, additional quantitative data could be collected to include indicators of mobilization capacity into a multi-level model. For example, the number of organizations in civil society in a given country and at a given time could be measured, which would allow for an investigation of the predictive quality of the extent of organizational structures available to societal groups for the frequency of their political mobilizations.

References

Beckman B, Sachikonye LM (2010) Trade unions and party politics. In: Beckman B, Buhlungu S, Sachikonye LM (eds) Trade unions and party politics: labour movements in Africa. Human Sciences Research Council Publishers, Cape Town, pp 1–22

Branch A, Mampilly ZC (2015) Africa uprising: popular protest and political change (African arguments). Zed Books, in association with International African Institute, Royal African Society, World Peace Foundation, London

Bratton M, van de Walle N (1992) Popular protest and political reform in Africa. Comp Polit 24(4):419–442

Bunce VJ, Wolchik SL (2006) Youth and electoral revolutions in Slovakia, Serbia, and Georgia. SAIS Rev 16(2):55–65

Bunce VJ, Wolchik SL (2011) Defeating authoritarian leaders in postcommunist countries. Cambridge University Press, Cambridge

Dicklitch S (1998) The elusive promise of NGOs in Africa: lessons from Uganda. Macmillan, Houndmills, Basingstoke, Hampshire

Dicklitch S (2001) NGOs and democratization in transitional societies: lessons from Uganda. Int Polit 38:27–46. https://doi.org/10.1057/palgrave.ip.8892611

Dicklitch S, Lwanga D (2003) The politics of being non-political: human rights organizations and the creation of a positive human rights culture in Uganda. Human Rights Q 25:482–509

Hearn J (1999) Foreign political aid, democratization and civil society in Uganda in the 1990s. CBR working papers, 53. Center for Basic Research, Kampala

Kraus J (2007) Conclusion: trade unions and democratization in Africa. In: Kraus J (ed) Trade unions and the coming of democracy in africa. Palgrave Macmillan, New York, pp 255–286

Kuzio T (2006) Civil Society, youth and societal mobilization in democratic revolutions. Communist Post-Communist Stud 39:365–386

Ottaway M (2000) Social movements, professionalization of reform, and democracy in Africa. In: Ottaway M, Carothers T (eds) funding virtue: civil society aid and democracy promotion. Carnegie Endowment for International Peace, Washington, D.C., pp 77–104

Pletcher JR (1999) Agriculture and the dual transition in Zambia. J Developing Areas 33:199–222. https://doi.org/10.2307/4192847

Przeworski A (1986) Some problems in the study of the transition to democracy. In: O'Donnell GA, Schmitter PC, Whitehead L (eds) Transitions from authoritarian rule: comparative perspectives. The Johns Hopkins University Press, Baltimore, pp 47–63

Rustow DA (1970) Transitions to democracy: toward a dynamic model. Comp Polit 2(3):337–363

Appendix

See Table A.1.

Table A.1 Democratization in Sub-Saharan Africa, annual country averages

Year	Polity IV	Freedom House	Freedom House: Political Rights	Freedom House: Civil liberties
1990	−4.78 (4.97)	5.36 (1.30)	5.62 (1.41)	5.11 (1.28)
1991	−2.53 (5.38)	4.90 (1.49)	5.19 (1.73)	4.62 (1.35)
1992	−1.33 (5.82)	4.65 (1.55)	4.89 (1.81)	4.40 (1.39)
1993	−0.63 (5.85)	4.73 (1.60)	4.81 (1.94)	4.65 (1.35)
1994	−0.11 (5.74)	4.75 (1.65)	4.69 (1.99)	4.81 (1.39)
1995	−0.02 (5.60)	4.57 (1.69)	4.56 (2.00)	4.58 (1.47)
1996	−0.07 (5.42)	4.56 (1.69)	4.60 (2.01)	4.52 (1.46)
1997	−0.33 (5.30)	4.60 (1.66)	4.69 (1.99)	4.52 (1.44)
1998	−0.43 (4.94)	4.44 (1.56)	4.58 (1.96)	4.29 (1.32)
1999	0.24 (4.76)	4.47 (1.55)	4.50 (1.88)	4.44 (1.34)
2000	0.72 (4.88)	4.44 (1.57)	4.48 (1.90)	4.40 (1.35)
2001	1.07 (5.03)	4.43 (1.49)	4.42 (1.73)	4.44 (1.35)
2002	1.52 (5.12)	4.32 (1.52)	4.35 (1.80)	4.29 (1.34)
2003	1.37 (5.08)	4.24 (1.59)	4.38 (1.83)	4.10 (1.43)
2004	1.63 (5.22)	4.18 (1.61)	4.31 (1.80)	4.04 (1.47)
2005	1.87 (5.23)	4.10 (1.62)	4.23 (1.85)	3.98 (1.49)
2006	2.04 (5.29)	4.14 (1.63)	4.27 (1.86)	4.00 (1.49)
2007	2.20 (5.23)	4.16 (1.60)	4.27 (1.86)	4.04 (1.44)

(continued)

© Springer Nature Switzerland AG 2020
W. Stuppert, *Political Mobilizations and Democratization in Sub-Saharan Africa*,
Advances in African Economic, Social and Political Development,
https://doi.org/10.1007/978-3-030-22792-0

Table A.1 (continued)

Year	Polity IV	Freedom House	Freedom House: Political Rights	Freedom House: Civil liberties
2008	2.04 (5.36)	4.21 (1.64)	4.35 (1.88)	4.06 (1.49)
2009	2.02 (5.12)	4.32 (1.62)	4.46 (1.81)	4.19 (1.52)
2010	2.28 (5.01)	4.32 (1.65)	4.46 (1.84)	4.19 (1.55)
2011	2.40 (5.08)	4.30 (1.65)	4.42 (1.84)	4.19 (1.55)
2012	2.15 (4.94)	4.42 (1.67)	4.51 (1.90)	4.33 (1.54)

Notes Means for all countries in Sub-Saharan Africa (N = 48). Standard deviations are provided in brackets. Freedom House scores are on a scale of 7 to 1, where 7 indicates the worst and 1 the best freedom rating. The combined Polity IV autocracy-democracy score ranges from −10 to +10, with −10 indicating a strongly autocratic and +10 a strongly democratic regime

See Table A.2.

Table A.2 Democratization in Sub-Saharan Africa per year after founding elections

Year	Polity IV	Freedom House	Freedom House: Political Rights	Freedom House: Civil liberties
Introduction	0.90 (5.30)	4.43 (1.38)	4.34 (1.71)	4.51 (1.17)
+1	0.82 (5.23)	4.37 (1.51)	4.27 (1.79)	4.46 (1.35)
+2	0.92 (5.15)	4.34 (1.52)	4.24 (1.79)	4.44 (1.42)
+3	0.41 (5.22)	4.46 (1.51)	4.39 (1.85)	4.54 (1.29)
+4	0.41 (5.10)	4.48 (1.57)	4.44 (1.87)	4.51 (1.36)
+5	−0.08 (4.70)	4.54 (1.51)	4.59 (1.82)	4.49 (1.31)
+6	0.54 (4.69)	4.45 (1.45)	4.51 (1.73)	4.39 (1.27)
+7	0.66 (4.60)	4.31 (1.40)	4.40 (1.66)	4.23 (1.27)
+8	0.79 (4.68)	4.28 (1.36)	4.33 (1.66)	4.23 (1.15)
+9	1.13 (4.41)	4.25 (1.43)	4.33 (1.77)	4.18 (1.20)
+10	1.81 (4.57)	4.21 (1.39)	4.31 (1.71)	4.10 (1.17)
+11	2.14 (4.70)	4.06 (1.48)	4.15 (1.73)	3.97 (1.29)
+12	2.16 (4.83)	4.04 (1.48)	4.13 (1.65)	3.95 (1.38)
+13	2.19 (4.79)	4.05 (1.49)	4.15 (1.69)	3.95 (1.36)
+14	2.31 (4.75)	4.07 (1.52)	4.16 (1.71)	3.97 (1.41)
+15	2.50 (4.66)	4.11 (1.59)	4.18 (1.79)	4.03 (1.48)

Note Means for all countries in Sub-Saharan Africa that introduced multi-party elections between 1990 and 2012 (N = 41). "Introduction" marks the year of the first post-90 founding elections for each country. Standard deviations are provided in brackets. Freedom House scores are on a scale of 7 to 1, where 7 indicates the worst and 1 the best freedom rating. The combined Polity IV autocracy-democracy score ranges from −10 to +10, with −10 indicating a strongly autocratic and +10 a strongly democratic regime

See Table A.3.

Table A.3 Democratization in Sub-Saharan Africa per election cycle

Election	Polity IV	Freedom House	Freedom House: Political Rights	Freedom House: Civil liberties	n
1st	1.21 (4.82)	4.51 (1.31)	4.50 (1.63)	4.53 (1.14)	113
2nd	1.03 (4.93)	4.27 (1.35)	4.31 (1.65)	4.24 (1.16)	84
3rd	2.28 (5.00)	3.85 (1.50)	3.90 (1.77)	3.80 (1.29)	61
4th	2.67 (4.81)	3.78 (1.59)	3.85 (1.79)	3.71 (1.49)	52
5th	5.50 (4.26)	2.82 (1.41)	2.82 (1.67)	2.82 (1.23)	22
6th	6.44 (3.83)	2.65 (1.47)	2.40 (1.69)	2.90 (1.30)	11
7th	8.33 (1.25)	2.00 (0.41)	1.67 (0.47)	2.33 (0.47)	3
8th	8.00 (1.22)	2.00 (0.35)	1.75 (0.43)	2.25 (0.43)	4
9th	9.00 (1.00)	2.00 (0.50)	2.00 (1.00)	2.00 (0.00)	2

Note Means for all elections in Sub-Saharan Africa of the respective rank order in an uninterrupted election series. Presidential and parliamentary elections are counted as separate election series. Standard deviations are provided in brackets. Freedom House scores are on a scale of 7 to 1, where 7 indicates the worst and 1 the best freedom rating. The combined Polity IV autocracy-democracy score ranges from -10 to $+10$, with -10 indicating a strongly autocratic and $+10$ a strongly democratic regime

See Table A.4.

Table A.4 Electoral experience and democratization in Sub-Saharan Africa, as of 2012

Electoral experience	Freedom House	Polity IV
Total number of elections	−0.408** (0.141)	0.221 (0.156)
Longest election series	−0.536*** (0.112)	0.400** (0.128)
Length of current election series	−0.504*** (0.117)	0.384** (0.121)

Note All countries in Sub-Saharan Africa ($N = 48$). Total number of elections, longest election series, and length of current election series include elections that were held before 1990, if they were linked in an uninterrupted series with elections after 1990. Countries that did not hold multi-party elections between 1990 and 2012 were assigned values of "0" for these variables. $*p \leq 0.05$, $**p \leq 0.01$, $***p \leq 0.001$. Spearman Correlations, with standard errors in brackets. Freedom House scores are on a scale of 7 to 1, where 7 indicates the worst and 1 the best freedom rating. The combined Polity IV autocracy-democracy score ranges from -10 to $+10$, with -10 indicating a strongly autocratic and $+10$ a strongly democratic regime

See Table A.5.

Table A.5 Electoral competitiveness and democratization (non-founding elections)

Indicator	Corr.	N
Polity IV (post-election)	−0.531***	170
Freedom House (post-election)	0.466***	186
• Political Rights	0.474***	186
• Civil liberties	0.426***	186
Turnout (%)	0.026	169
Quality of electoral process (% acceptable)	−0.350***	156
Opposition participation (% full)	−0.489***	186

Notes Based on all non-founding direct national multi-party elections in Sub-Saharan Africa between 1990 and 2012 (N = 238). Pearson correlations with electoral dominance as dependent variable. Significance tests two-tailed. $*p \leq 0.05$, $**p \leq 0.01$, $***p \leq 0.001$. Electoral dominance is the share of votes or seats won by powerholders in first-round presidential and parliamentary elections, respectively. For other indicators, see the notes to Table 2.7

See Table A.6.

Table A.6 Violent/non-violent political mobilizations by societal groups in Sub-Saharan Africa

Year	Violent	Non-violent	Total
1990	14.49% (10)	85.51% (59)	100% (69)
1991	20.15% (27)	79.85% (107)	100% (134)
1992	28.57% (26)	71.43% (65)	100% (91)
1993	18.18% (16)	81.82% (72)	100% (88)
1994	18.18% (22)	81.82% (99)	100% (121)
1995	10.91% (12)	89.09% (98)	100% (110)
1996	18.27% (19)	81.73% (85)	100% (104)
1997	15.38% (20)	84.62% (110)	100% (130)
1998	18.18% (28)	81.82% (126)	100% (154)
1999	25.71% (36)	74.29% (104)	100% (140)
2000	17.28% (33)	82.72% (158)	100% (191)
2001	15.48% (26)	84.52% (142)	100% (168)
2002	15.70% (27)	84.30% (145)	100% (172)
2003	18.87% (30)	81.13% (129)	100% (159)
2004	23.53% (32)	76.47% (104)	100% (136)
2005	18.87% (30)	81.13% (129)	100% (159)
2006	24.00% (36)	76.00% (114)	100% (150)
2007	28.91% (37)	71.09% (91)	100% (128)
2008	20.66% (25)	79.34% (96)	100% (121)

(continued)

Table A.6 (continued)

Year	Violent	Non-violent	Total
2009	17.33% (26)	82.67% (124)	100% (150)
2010	16.81% (19)	83.19% (94)	100% (113)
2011	23.13% (34)	76.87% (113)	100% (147)
2012	22.07% (49)	77.93% (173)	100% (222)

Notes Based on all major political mobilizations by societal groups in countries in Sub-Saharan Africa with over one million inhabitants (N = 42). Numbers in brackets are absolute numbers. Violent mobilizations are riots that addressed local or national governments with grievances. Non-violent mobilizations are demonstrations and strikes with the same addressees. See the codebook of the Social Conflict in Africa Database for more details (Salehyan and Hendrix 2011). Social conflicts that mentioned the opposition as actors were excluded from this categorization.

See Table A.7.

Table A.7 Organized/spontaneous political mobilizations by societal groups in Sub-Saharan Africa

Year	Organized	Spontaneous	Total
1990	47.83% (33)	52.17% (36)	100% (69)
1991	53.73% (72)	46.27% (62)	100% (134)
1992	57.14% (52)	42.86% (39)	100% (91)
1993	60.23% (53)	39.77% (35)	100% (88)
1994	58.68% (71)	41.32% (50)	100% (121)
1995	57.27% (63)	42.73% (47)	100% (110)
1996	54.81% (57)	45.19% (47)	100% (104)
1997	56.15% (73)	43.85% (57)	100% (130)
1998	53.90% (83)	46.10% (71)	100% (154)
1999	62.14% (87)	37.86% (53)	100% (140)
2000	55.50% (106)	44.50% (85)	100% (191)
2001	57.74% (97)	42.26% (71)	100% (168)
2002	55.81% (96)	44.19% (76)	100% (172)
2003	52.83% (84)	47.17% (75)	100% (159)
2004	54.41% (74)	45.59% (62)	100% (136)
2005	47.17% (75)	52.83% (84)	100% (159)
2006	54.67% (82)	45.33% (68)	100% (150)
2007	44.53% (57)	55.47% (71)	100% (128)
2008	55.37% (67)	44.63% (54)	100% (121)
2009	57.33% (86)	42.67% (64)	100% (150)
2010	37.17% (42)	62.83% (71)	100% (113)
2011	35.37% (52)	64.63% (95)	100% (147)
2012	37.84% (84)	62.16% (138)	100% (222)

Notes Organized political mobilizations are those political mobilizations for which mobilizing organizations or coalitions could be identified. Spontaneous political mobilizations are demonstrations and riots with the same addressees where this was not possible. See the codebook of the Social Conflict in Africa Database for more details (Salehyan and Hendrix 2011). Social conflicts that mentioned the opposition as actors were excluded from this categorization.

See Table A.8.

Table A.8 Results of the Hausman test

Variable/indicator	Differences between model coefficients[a]			
	1	2	3	4
Quality of electoral process	0.57	0.72	0.65	0.65
Economic development	0.00	0.00	0.00	0.00
Electoral experience	0.15	−0.13	0.05	−0.10
Electoral type	−0.01	0.02	0.02	0.00
Electoral rule	−0.38	−0.42	−0.54	−0.42
Intensity of social conflict	−0.06			
Electoral contestation by opposition	0.25	0.28	0.39	0.31
Political mobilization by opposition		−0.01	−0.09	−0.04
Political mobilization by societal groups		0.10		
• Pro-democratic mobilization			0.53	
• Socio-economic mobilization			−0.15	
• Organized mobilization				0.02
• Spontaneous mobilization				0.24
Political mobilization by ruling elites		0.11	0.13	0.08
Social conflict between societal groups		0.25	0.35	0.21
p (Hausman test)	0.991	0.969	0.698	0.975

Notes [a]Result of the subtraction of coefficients estimated by a random-effects model from coefficients estimated by a fixed-effects model

See Table A.9.

Table A.9 Descriptive statistics for study and control variables

Variable	Indicator	Min.	Max.	Mean	Std. Dev.	N
Electoral dominance	Share of seats (parliamentary) or votes (first-round presidential) won by powerholders	5.31	100.00	63.01	22.48	255
Quality of the electoral process	Composite indicator of election quality, from 0 (low) to 1 (high)	0.00	1.00	0.50	0.31	261
Economic development	GDP per capita/PPP (in constant 2005 intern. dollars) in year prior	74	15,912	1288.29	2597.08	278
Electoral experience	Rank number of current election in series	1	8	2.25	1.35	284

(continued)

Table A.9 (continued)

Variable	Indicator	Min.	Max.	Mean	Std. Dev.	N
Electoral framework	Election type (parliamentary = 1, presidential = 2)	1	2	1.48	0.50	284
	Electoral rule (PR = 1, plurality = 2)	1	2	1.38	0.49	284
Intensity of social conflict	Political mobilizations by all actors, 18–6 months prior	0	87	6.86	11.28	238
Mobilization threat	Major opposition parties, electoral participation	0	2	1.66	0.64	284
	Political mobilization by oppositional elites	0	8	0.32	1.03	238
	Political mobilization by societal groups	0	43	3.87	6.05	238
	• Pro-democratic	0	14	1.55	2.82	238
	• Socio-economic	0	29	2.32	3.97	238
	• Organized	0	23	2.02	3.49	238
	• Spontaneous	0	25	1.85	3.38	238
	Political mobilization by ruling elites	0	17	0.68	1.64	238
	Social conflict between societal groups	0	39	1.94	4.84	238

Notes Study population consists of all authoritarian elections in Sub-Saharan Africa between 1990 and 2012 (N = 284)

Reference

Salehyan I, Cullen SH (2011) Social Conflict in Africa Database: codebook and coding procedures. Robert S. Strauss Center for International Security and Law, Austin, Texas

Printed by Printforce, the Netherlands